EARLY AMERICAN
WOMEN CRITICS

Early American Women Critics demonstrates that performances of various kinds – religious, political, and cultural – enabled women to enter the human rights debates that roiled the American colonies and young republic. Black and white women staked their claims on American citizenship through disparate performances of spirit possession, patriotism, and poetic and theatrical production. They protected themselves within various shields that allowed them to speak openly while keeping the individual basis of their identities invisible. Cima shows that between the First and Second Great Religious Awakenings (1730s–1830s), women from West Africa, Europe, and various corners of the American colonies self-consciously adopted performance strategies that enabled them to critique American culture and establish their own diverse and contradictory claims on the body politic. This book restores the primacy of religious performances – Christian, Yoruban, Bantu, and Muslim – to the study of early American cultural and political histories, revealing that religion and race are inseparable.

Gay Gibson Cima, Professor of English and Director of the Humanities and Human Rights Initiative at Georgetown University, has published widely on feminist performance and critical race theory. Her work appears in anthologies such as *The Sage Handbook of Performance Studies* and *Women and Playwriting in Nineteenth-Century Britain* as well as in journals such as *Theatre Journal, Theater*, and *Theatre Survey*. She is the author of *Performing Women: Female Characters, Male Playwrights, and the Modern Stage*. The American Society for Theatre Research has recognized her work on women critics through the Kahan Prize and a Senior Research Fellowship.

EARLY AMERICAN WOMEN CRITICS:

Performance, Religion, Race

GAY GIBSON CIMA

CAMBRIDGE
UNIVERSITY PRESS

CAMBRIDGE UNIVERSITY PRESS
Cambridge, New York, Melbourne, Madrid, Cape Town, Singapore, São Paulo

Cambridge University Press
The Edinburgh Building, Cambridge CB2 2RU, UK

Published in the United States of America by Cambridge University Press, New York

www.cambridge.org
Information on this title: www.cambridge.org/9780521847339

First published 2006

Printed in the United Kingdom at the University Press, Cambridge

A catalogue record for this publication is available from the British Library

ISBN-13 978-0-521-84733-9 hardback
ISBN-10 0-521-84733-8 hardback

To Ronald J. Cima,
Gibson Alessandro Cima,
Anna Francesca Cima,
Geraldine Smith Gibson,
and the memory of Richard M. Gibson

Contents

Acknowledgments

I carved this book out of a much larger project, and I am truly grateful to all those who have helped me along the way. I am particularly indebted to the anonymous Cambridge University Press readers who took the time to read the earliest draft of the manuscript; their reports were invaluable. My Georgetown University friends and colleagues have shaped my work in ways that have been life-giving and inspiring: without Valerie Babb and Kim Hall's insights, I would not have begun working on this book, and without Angelyn Mitchell, Lucy Maddox, and Michael Ragussis's guidance, I would not have finished it. I want to express heartfelt thanks to my research assistant, Kathryn Sciarretta, a Georgetown University graduate (2001), whose intelligence, research talents, attention to detail, and assistance in gathering primary materials was invaluable from 1998 to 2000. I am indebted to the members of Georgetown's Critical Race Theory Forum for providing me with an interdisciplinary context in which to imagine revisions. From the first, my colleagues in the American Society for Theatre Research and the Association for Theatre in Higher Education offered constructive comments on my work, and I am particularly grateful to the encouragement and feedback that Tracy C. Davis, Shannon Jackson, Ellen Donkin, and Harry Elam have consistently offered. I am equally grateful to Marylynn Salmon for reading and responding to an early version of chapter 1.

It is a pleasure to acknowledge Travis Wesley and Thelma Todd, Reference Librarians in the Newspaper Division of the Library of Congress, for their expert assistance over a number of years, and to thank Georgia Higley, Head of the Newspaper Division, for her generous help in more recent months. Jeffrey M. Flannery and the staff of the Manuscript Reading Room in the Library of Congress – Patrick M. Kerwin, Ernest J. Emrich, Joseph D. Jackson, and Bruce R. Kirby – have been equally forthcoming with their time and talents, and I would like to recognize their crucial and ongoing assistance. Elizabeth Walsh, Head of Reader Services at the Folger

Shakespeare Library, helped me locate eighteenth-century Southern newspapers, and Amy Quesenbery, Librarian of the South Carolina Room at the Charleston County Public Library in Charleston, South Carolina, identified documents relevant to Elizabeth Timothy. Suzanne L. Flynt, Curator, and Shirley Majewski, Library Assistant, at the Pocumtuck Valley Memorial Association Library in Deerfield, Massachusetts, kindly helped me locate archival material relevant to Lucy Terry Prince. Some of the preliminary soundings for this manuscript were taken at the Schomburg Center for Research in Black Culture in The New York Public Library and at the Moorland-Spingarn Center at Howard University, and I am happy to thank Diana Lachatanere, Curator, and the staff of the Manuscripts, Archives, and Rare Books Division at the Schomburg Center, and Joellen El Bashir, Curator of the Manuscript Division at the Moorland-Spingarn Center, and her staff, for their kind assistance. Henry Louis Gates, Jr., Rosemary Zagarri, and Karen M. Poremski graciously replied to my detailed email inquiries about Wheatley, Warren, and Rowson.

Rosemary Fry Plakas, American History Specialist in the Rare Book and Special Collections Division of the Library of Congress, graciously helped me locate the cover art for this book. Don A. Sanford, Historian Emeritus, and the Reverend Mike Burns of the Seventh Day Baptist Historical Society, were also extraordinarily generous with their time and resources, and I thank them particularly for the color version of the image. Michael Showalter, Museum Educator of the Ephrata Cloister, Joël Sartorius, Reference Librarian in the Rare Book Department of The Free Library of Philadelphia, and Maja Keech, Reference Specialist in the Prints and Photographs Division of the Library of Congress, also kindly assisted me, along with Jan Stryz of Michigan State University; R. A. Friedman, Rights and Reproductions Coordinator in the Historical Society of Pennsylvania; Valerie-Anne Lutz, Head of Manuscripts Processing and Library Registrar at the American Philosophical Society; and Jocelyn K. Wilk, Assistant Director of the University Archives & Columbiana Library at Columbia University.

It gives me special pleasure to recognize and thank the talented staff of Georgetown University's Lauinger Library, especially Jill Hollingsworth, Reference Librarian; Jeffrey Popovich, Circulation and Reserves Coordinator; and Joan Cheverie, Director of the Government Documents and Microforms Department.

Although female theatre critics make only a cameo appearance in these pages, they prompted my initial curiosity about women's entrances into cultural, political, and religious debates: Brooks McNamara and Maryann

Chach kindly gave me a tour of the Shubert Archives years ago, and I happened to pull from the shelf a sheaf of script evaluations written by women working for the Shubert Theatre. I thank Brooks and Maryann for the tour which sparked my interest in writing this book.

I would like to thank Don Wilmeth, Editor of the Cambridge Studies in American Theatre and Drama series, for encouraging me in the early stages of my work. An early version of sections of chapter 2 appeared in *Theatre Journal*, under the generative auspices of Susan Bennett's editorship and David Roman's co-editorship. I am very grateful to the American Society for Theatre Research for the Senior Research Fellowship that supported my research in the summer of 2001, and to Georgetown University for a Senior Research Fellowship in the fall of 2000 as well as several Summer Research Grants.

Victoria Cooper, Commissioning Editor of Drama and Music at Cambridge University Press, shepherded my manuscript through the review and publication process with graciousness and patience. I appreciate all the time and attention she has given my work. I also wish to thank Rebecca Jones, Assistant Editor of Drama and Music at Cambridge, for her continuing and kindly assistance. Elizabeth Davey, Production Editor, and Audrey Cotterell, Copy-Editor, at Cambridge University Press, have been most helpful to me.

As a graduate student many years ago, I worked with extraordinary teachers whose guidance continues to shape my work: the late Maxine Trauernicht of the University of Nebraska as well as Frank Galati, Leland Roloff, and the late Wallace Bacon, Robert Breen, and Lilla Heston of Northwestern University taught me to imagine the performance of non-dramatic and dramatic texts as acts of criticism. Marvin Carlson and the late Bert O. States, then of Cornell University, taught me to read performance history, theory, and criticism in tandem. I count myself fortunate to enjoy their abiding presence, and am very pleased that my students and colleagues have continued the education they launched.

I am blessed with family and friends whose presence makes life joyful and scholarship an act of sharing. I thank Rich and Judy, my brother and sister-in-law, and all of my friends for helping me celebrate each step toward the completion of this project.

Finally, I am ever grateful to my husband and our son and daughter for their love, their hopefulness, and their confidence in my work. Ron has supported me in so many ways large and small that he deserves a separate book of praise. He is, quite simply, my beloved partner in all things, including this book. Gib gave me a synonym for "surrogate," and in that gift offered me a means of encapsulating my theory about women critics. My conversations with him always open up exciting new ways of thinking about performance. Anna first taught me about the evils of theodicy, and her insights prompted me to consider more closely the relationship between religious and political debates. She is a wizard woman. My mother and father gave me an invaluable legacy – a curiosity about life and hope for the future – and I wish they could know how very grateful I am.

Introduction

On 4 July 1740, women originally from Angola, Gambia, Senegal, West India, the Netherlands, France, Spain, England, Ireland, Scotland, and various corners of the American colonies rushed into the streets of Charles Town, South Carolina. They panted, wept, laughed, and fell on the ground shuddering and groaning, only to rise, shout, and commence "damning all others round about them." In 1772 a prominent Whig playwright excoriated her Governor, King George III's representative in the Massachusetts Colony, characterizing him in scene after scene as "Rapatio"; her play was performed in patriots' parlors across the colony and published in major newspapers. The following year in Boston, as prostitutes began to troll the docks and a diverse, transatlantic community of Christians surfaced, a young West African slave girl published poems and recited them in her mistress's home on the main thoroughfare, warning local Harvard boys to shun the "transient sweetness" of sin and reminding King George that his smile could "set his subjects free." In the 1790s a Boston minister's wife produced a play which excused married women's flirtations (and her own), even after the publication of a vicious, serialized parody of her as a woman guilty not only of adultery but also of the violent domestic abuse of her husband. In her collected works, she renamed one of her plays *Virtue Triumphant.* At the opening of the nineteenth century, an unlicensed African American preacher heeded God's command to call upon the wealthiest man in her hometown and reduce him, his family, and their guests to tears by acquainting them with "all things that ever they did." Thus launching a successful career as an itinerant, she traveled throughout the Eastern and Southern United States and England, rousing "a great shout of victory."[1]

Where, how, and why did these women stage their disparate acts of criticism? This book addresses that question by investigating their sites and methods of access as well as the criticism itself. From the 1740s to the 1830s, thousands of early American women acted as "Criticks": either in person or in print, they passed public judgments on religious, political, and cultural issues, thereby shaping and contesting incipient notions of race, religion, American-ness, and gender. They shaped critical practices and discourses, gaining the respect of selected local spectators and readers. Initially amateurs, they often built a framework for professional opportunities and financial remuneration. Some critics supported themselves through their cultural criticism. Gathering these women together under the rubric "critic" creates a broad-based genealogy that illuminates their strategies for claiming a place in the early American body politic. It allows a consideration of women's diverse critical practices in relation to one another, thereby clarifying the discrete moves of any one critic or group of critics, the distinctive advantages and disadvantages of any one strategy, and the varied ways in which early American culture responded to women's initiatives. Women critics devised clever pathways into the public sphere, adjusting to fluid local conditions and institutions. Religion, partisan politics, and the arts offered them opportunities to gain access to public debates and create new ideas about "American identity."

Since criticism was regarded as a European male prerogative, these early American women critics frequently cloaked their critiques as revelation, autobiography, or fiction: they engaged in religious exhortation, printed a spiritual autobiography, sang a ballad, published a poem, staged a play. By avoiding genre-based distinctions foreign to the period or unimportant to the writers and speakers themselves, I grant these women status as serious-minded cultural commentators, even as I hold them responsible as arbiters of early American culture. I follow the lead of Americanists, African Americanists and performance theorists in allowing a diverse range of texts to act as criticism. As William C. Spengemann argues, "the boundaries we now draw between fiction and 'non-fiction' ... did not exist in most of the periods [Americanists] study" (*Mirror*, 23). To understand early American women's cultural criticism, we must recognize it on its own terms, blurring distinctions between practice and critical theory, fiction and non-fiction. African American scholars have long advocated this approach to black culture. Valerie Smith and Deborah McDowell, for example, "allow literary history, oratory, and even autobiography to function as theory," and Geneviève Fabre and Robert O'Meally "have resisted the conventional wisdom of viewing orality and literacy as opposite cultural modalities." In like fashion, performance scholars routinely regard theatrical practice as a critical act. This book works at the intersection of these conversations, illuminating the ways in which women critics from various "climes" issued their criticism and shaped early America.[2]

I take seriously the ways in which women's live performances were intertwined with religious, political, and cultural rhetoric and, conversely, the ways in which their writing was performative or self-consciously theatrical. They did not perceive performance and writing as opposites, but rather as linked systems whose operations were inextricable. Written publications were routinely regarded as performances or productions, and sermon performances, for instance, were viewed as criticism, subject to legal action. As a theatre and performance historian, I regard all performances as "scripted" through prior behavioral models, but also, paradoxically, as irreproducible. Performances resist, undercut, reshape and create new gestural patterns and modes of interaction, even as they keep cultural traditions alive. I have paid careful attention to the public record, but I have also interpreted the gaps and shadowy traces of women's interventions and unexpected performances, particularly of race. Daily performances of religious, political, and cultural affiliation were intertwined with racial discourse, as critics solidified traditional ideas of race, tried to articulate notions of race based on common denominators other than geography or pseudo-science, or tried to dispense with race altogether.

In each successive chapter of this book I investigate early American women critics' *sites of access:* the religious, political, and cultural avenues through which they gained access to the public sphere or through which they redefined private space as public. I examine the critics' *methods of access*, demonstrating that their central performance strategy was to create *host bodies* through which to issue their critiques. I analyze the various gestural or rhetorical host bodies they created to shield themselves from censure as they spoke, whether in person or in print. By borrowing gestures and rhetoric from the mainstream and re-contextualizing them, by exchanging behaviors or rhetorical figures at the margins, or by fabricating surrogates out of their bodied imaginings and discursive fancies, women critics created provisional surrogate bodies through which they could safely issue their critiques. Finally, I consider the commentaries that they delivered as *performing critics* in marketplaces, streets, parlors, ferries, literary salons, churches, theatres, and schoolrooms, and devote equal attention to their work as *performance critics* publishing in newspapers, broadsides, journals, commonplace books, subscription volumes, play scripts, novels, textbooks, catechisms, and spiritual autobiographies. I illuminate the ways in which early American women critics entered the public sphere by performing within religious, political, and cultural host bodies that enabled them both to shape and to critique notions of race, American-ness, and gender.

These bodies provided women with particularly useful pathways into civic conversations. They offered various ways of claiming American-ness while articulating a sense of identity separate from dominant formulations. A host body is a spectral body, a generic body in movement, an abstraction which nonetheless serves as a life-like bodily shield. A host body may be donned in print through a set of rhetorical moves, or in person through a set of gestural and oral patterns. Because of its non-material status, the host body provides the woman critic with a certain safety. It acts as a prophylactic against censorship or censure. Sometimes it is even regarded as a sacred, inviolate body. Because host bodies emerge from the cauldron of locally defined, constantly shifting claims on the abstract "personhood" of citizenship, they are politically efficacious. Host bodies claim citizenship by aligning with and simultaneously resisting acceptable "American" bodily practices. The host body may take a variety of shapes. Critics may invent host bodies, or they may adopt hosts that others have initiated, sculpting them to their own needs.

Women's abstract host bodies – the body of the "evangelical" engaged in a conversion experience; the body of the "possessed" practicing African spirit possession; the pseudonymous or anonymous body; the body of a "rational" or "activist" Christian; of a literate and politically engaged "Afric"; of a "patriot"; a Quaker "Friend"; a "cultured American" critic – are readily apparent in the performance practices and discursive moves of African, African American, European, and European American women critics from the early eighteenth through the early nineteenth centuries.

Women critics created these ingenious host bodies to deflect attention from and to redefine their material bodies as they wedged their way into public debates, in person and in print. From every corner of the globe, women fashioned hosts out of competing religious, political, and cultural performances and discourses, simultaneously encoding and contesting inchoate notions of race and gender. They borrowed a productive gesture here, a useful word there, and re-contextualized them or imagined them in new combinations. They used self-conscious performance within these host bodies as means of manipulating the performativity of an increasingly racialized American womanhood, claiming respectability and intelligence as they repositioned themselves in terms of religious affiliation, political commitments, or artistic goals. Sometimes they hid behind anonymous or pseudonymous bodies, and sometimes they created bodies that earned validation through Christian activism, Whig politics, or the drive toward American letters. Often these bodies were aligned with race or a developing sense of nationhood, but not always in the customary geographic or biological ways. When necessary, critics could don multiple host bodies, appealing simultaneously to disparate viewers or readers.

Women adopted diverse bodies, borrowing from a variety of discourses and behavioral systems. They created hosts in every sense of that term. They accepted the consecrated host body of Christ or of the spirits of their African ancestors, ordaining themselves as cultural critics. They attached themselves parasitically and pseudonymously to male or politically partisan bodies. They borrowed transplanted cultural practices through host bodies. They adopted the social mask of the host, transforming their homes into political arenas and their schools into training grounds for woman orators. And they established themselves as hosts for a networking web of information-sharing, becoming colonial, national, transnational, and diasporic cultural critics. In this sense, the host body granted them a collective body, a way of imagining relationality alongside of or outside of nationhood. It offered a way of being in one "body" despite their geographic dispersion. Host bodies enabled women critics to acknowledge their own individually embodied experiences even as they created new, socially acceptable bodies through which to enter and affect religious, political, and cultural movements.

With good fortune, a woman critic's host body was taken up by like-minded others, who helped wedge it into the sphere of public respectability. Hosts were often variously interpreted by the critic's culture, variously marked in Manichean terms of "blackness" or "whiteness," within fiercely contested debates. Often a host body granted a critic authority with one audience and not another. The nature of that authority depended upon a critic's ability to manipulate both the diachronic process of bodies replacing one another over time and the synchronic process of an exchange of gestures or rhetorical moves developing cross-culturally at any given moment in time. Critics fabricated host bodies out of gestural bits and rhetorical gambits they invented or learned from adjacent cultures, in addition to keeping alive and reinventing behaviors and discourses that preceded them.

Within theatre studies, Joseph Roach has been particularly interested in developing a theory of bodily substitutions, but the process that I am articulating in this book differs from his concept of "surrogation" in several important ways. In *Cities of the Dead*, Roach defines diachronic replacement, the process through which new material bodies replace those that have vacated a particular social space, as "surrogacy." He is especially interested in embodied performance: "into the cavities created by loss through death or other forms of departure," he suggests, "survivors attempt to fit satisfactory alternates." To illuminate the hybrid performances of the "circum-Atlantic" world of the slave trade, Roach builds his concept of surrogation, in part, on René Girard's studies of the relationship between violence and the sacred. Girard was primarily concerned with the ways in which a community holds violence at bay by locating – through religious rituals – a surrogate victim, a fringe figure who can be violently erased and replaced by a substitute, an effigy. This process of locating a "monstrous double" restores the social equilibrium.[3] I find these theories rich and illuminating; they eloquently describe many of the performances of early American culture. But I think that the concept of the surrogate requires amplification. It requires a more acute attention to gender performances and to the ad hoc ways in which critics – who are not quite a part of the community and yet who refuse to become sacrificial victims – perform through "host" bodies. I am interested in the middle ground between center and margins, material and immaterial. I hope, then, to extend Roach's theory of surrogation and to remind performance scholars of Girard's lead in placing religious performances at the core of thinking critically about race, culture, and politics.

The phenomenon I am exploring in this book differs from displacement concepts of surrogation in crucial ways. I am interested in the ways in which women critics attempted to find a zone in between embodiment and abstraction, a bodily space within which they could safely speak or write, while protecting their material bodies and creating new hermeneutic pathways for perceiving those bodies. I am calling this space the "host body." Host bodies resist materialization. They move toward the abstract rather than the fleshy, toward efficacy rather than effigy. They protect the bearer's flesh. They may be collectively occupied. They may be passed down from one generation to another, but they may also be invented on the spot, a self-construction of an individual critic. Host bodies also are enmeshed in a synchronic process of exchange. Like Roach, I investigate the ways in which cultural groups exchange and merge practices, creating hybrid performances. This synchronic process of exchange is routinely a part of the creation of host bodies: women critics borrowed from one another's cultures in ways conscious and unconscious, adopting the gestural patterns and notions of the "body" that seemed useful at the moment. A consideration of these host bodies enables scholars to recognize the ways in which material and abstract bodies connect, the ways in which performance and writing participate in overlapping systems.

Another customary approach to thinking about what might be called a host body has been to focus upon the abstract body of the citizen. Feminists, critical race theorists, and Americanists have disclosed the ways in which Enlightenment notions of the abstract body of the citizen functioned to build nationhood in the late eighteenth century. By taking part in the politicized public arena, each potential citizen in the emerging American republic took on a new body, suppressing his or her own material body in the abstract, bodiless personhood of citizenship. In return, the community promised the person protection. White male privilege was embedded in this generic, bodiless citizen, however, because the concept of personhood legitimated an implicit standard of propertied white male embodiment. The white, propertied male body, then, was the person's route to legitimacy, but only white males might appear to be disembodied and universal while occupying that body. Only white male property-owners were truly American citizens.

What is missing from this narrative of access to American-ness, I contend, is a consideration of the ways in which particular abstract religious, political, and cultural host bodies that preceded the national body are also implicit in the abstract body of the citizen. The notion of the American citizen in the colonial, revolutionary, and republican periods is inextricably tied to a highly contested Christianity, partisan politics, and American literary and dramatic efforts. Especially during the pre-national period, performance and proffers of religious liberation complicate issues of visibility, invisibility, and access. The Christian host body, I argue, haunted eighteenth-century notions of citizenship, despite American rhetoric of the separation of church and state. This Christian host body was variously imagined through different denominational lenses. The New Light Anglicans and Congregationalists argued with the Old Lights within their congregations about the nature of the Christian body and its relationship to performing whiteness and blackness. The Methodists, Baptists, and African Methodist Episcopalians disputed mainstream notions of the relationship between the Christian body and abstract notions of citizenship. In what Paul Gilroy calls "radical Methodism," for instance, African Americans found a useful host body (Gilroy, *Against Race*, 118). Religious performances, I contend, have allowed for more crucial substitutions than have been previously recognized.

The abstract body of the American citizen was also haunted by various, divisive ideas about its political affiliation, as Whigs and Tories or Anti-Federalists and Federalists tried to claim citizenship as theirs only. This partisan dispute is particularly evident at the end of the eighteenth century. In addition, the "cultured American" body was also implicit in the abstract body of the citizen, because there was a pressing need to articulate and materialize a unifying notion of American-ness through literature and the arts. This cultured body, however, was fluidly shaped and inhabited by women of disparate national and diasporic affiliations: women from Gambia as well as women from England and the shores of Massachusetts created cultured host bodies, with widely different notions of what that body signified. These additional, hotly contested avenues of access to the abstract body of the citizen – these religious, partisan, and cultural host bodies – aided women critics. So, while Lauren Berlant, among many others, has contended that "American women and African-Americans have never had the privilege to suppress the body," in fact religionists, political propagandists, and literary and theatrical adventurers in the eighteenth and early nineteenth centuries often did just that. They adopted host bodies to suppress their material bodies and claim abstract citizenship, in social and gradually in legal terms, paradoxically and fluidly redefining the relationship between their material bodies and American-ness in the process.[4]

A consideration of strategies for gaining access to the public sphere and claiming the abstract body of the citizen has often circulated within performance studies in debates concerning "strategic anonymity." The most complex articulation of this strategy may be found in Peggy Phelan's pivotal study *Unmarked*, which calls for contemporary feminist critics to practice "an *active* vanishing, a deliberate and conscious refusal to take the pay-off of visibility." Remaining "unmarked" seems a useful tactic to avoid the pitfalls of identity politics, to value that which cannot be seen or named, and to mute the effects of privilege. Phelan adds the caveat that "for the moment, active disappearance usually requires at least some recognition of what and who is not there to be effective. (In short, this has largely been a possibility for white middle- and upper-class women.)" Phelan sees this caveat as a *momentary* concern, but this book demonstrates that the white upper- and middle-class exclusivity that can be exercised through strategic anonymity is an *ongoing* and problematic performance practice: historically, anonymity and pseudonymity have often enabled European American women to escape gender constraints while implicitly claiming "whiteness," reinforcing racial boundaries and racism.[5]

Early American women's strategies for gaining access to public debates depended upon specific, local contexts. Both visibility and invisibility proved useful, and they were not always readily distinct from one another: identities sometimes depended upon invisible entities such as the "spirit," but were also linked to visible practices, such as conversion "fits." Furthermore, sometimes readers and viewers willfully ignored a critic's "actual" identity in preference to a pseudonymous identity that served a useful purpose.

Many European and European American performing critics tried to claim American-ness by appearing as members of an evangelical or cultured "race" in street revivals, churches, literary salons, and theatres. Others entered the public sphere as performance critics. While a few performance critics, shielded by influential patrons or by their record of successful prior publication, signed their own names to their work, most adopted strategic anonymity or pseudonymity to protect their class status and perform white privilege. They appeared as male citizens or as generic feminine amateurs until they felt safe to appear under their own names and profit from their work. This strategy of claiming the whiteness of the abstract citizen through anonymity and pseudonymity enhanced their financial gain even as it complicated their ability to own their intellectual property and establish ties with other critics.

African and African American women, on the other hand, could not readily claim the abstract American body through anonymity. It was difficult for black women to publish anonymously until the anti-slavery and black press emerged. In addition, they benefited from a visible demonstration of their intelligence and humanity, so they developed other footholds on eighteenth-century ideas of colonial and national citizenship. They typically published under their own names as performance critics or appeared in person as performing critics. They often shielded themselves within a Christian host body, disguising their critiques as revelation. By the early nineteenth century, they managed to publish their spiritual autobiographies. Through literate "Afric" host bodies, they revalued blackness and revised American-ness. They also critiqued and claimed privilege by performing within "cultured American" host bodies, visibly demonstrating their cultural literacy and artistic or moral equality – or superiority – as Americans, as citizens of an African diaspora, and as citizens of a Christian realm they were determined to call into being.

This book revises the history of early American women and performance by confounding the customary boundaries between the performances of religion, politics, and culture. Each chapter focuses upon how women critics from various nations developed particular, localized performances that granted them access to public debates in the American colonies and the emerging nation. Their performances trouble the grand narratives of American performance history, the balkanization of religious history, the genre distinctions of the literary world, and the division between the literary and performative. The first chapter, "Colonial women critics: performing religion, race, possession, and pornography," examines colonial women's entrance into the public sphere through disparate performances of spirit possession that resembled, to the eyes of many beholders, sexual acts. It focuses upon a Southern widow's editorial coverage of the religious revival known as the First Great Awakening (1725–65), which is often viewed as a Northern phenomenon, but which swept through Charles Town, South Carolina, in the 1740s when Elizabeth Timotheé (*c.* 1700–57) governed the only newspaper in the colony, the major news venue in the South. Through the anglicized host body of her son, Timothy disseminated critiques of the ways in which the colony's tax-supported Anglican church (like its northern counterpart, the Congregational church) linked the performance of whiteness to certain *visible* "signs of salvation" – wealth, good health, good fortune. Her columns reveal that revivalists donned evangelical host bodies to redefine whiteness as *invisible* salvation and respectability, open to all. The converted not only damned the religious and political elite in Charleston and the Northern colonies, but also claimed that conversion on American soil was sufficient for salvation. English soil no longer anchored access to salvation, political or cultural standing; this opened the way for revolt.

In the mid eighteenth century, women of virtually every demographic sector staged their religious exhortations in Charleston's streets and in the marketplace, which – to the distress of the town council – was controlled by African and African American slave women working on the task system. Licensed to earn their own profit after their mandatory ten hours' worth of daily labor, slave women parlayed their African trading skills and their knowledge of local South Carolina markets into economic, religious, and cultural agency. Some practiced African spirit possession, disguised as Christian conversion, in full view of their owners, who were dependent upon them for the very food on their tables. Some converted directly to Christianity. Protected by their ancestral or evangelical host bodies, these market critics called out slaveholders as black and sinful. Through their performing criticism, they unified diverse tribal and

Muslim practices into a politically efficacious African-ness, simultaneously staking a claim on the abstract American body.

Chapter 2, "Revolutionary women critics: performing rational Christianity, patriotism, and race," moves north, to the rural frontiers, the seacoasts, and the cities of New England and the mid-Atlantic colonies, particularly Vermont, Massachusetts, and Pennsylvania. There women critics created efficacious host bodies for their criticism as Enlightenment notions of reason, natural rights discourse, and the arts revised performances of Christianity and built toward Revolution. From the 1740s through the 1780s, many African and African American critics shielded themselves by performing within rational Christian host bodies as commentators, balladeers, courtroom defendants, and poets. They sidestepped the dangers of Enlightenment discourse by linking these reasonable, religious bodies, grounded in creative and independent readings of the Bible, to the "Afric" host bodies of literate artists or Biblical figures. They helped shape and critique the new republic even as they imagined a relationality beyond the divide of slave and citizen. "Alice" (fl. 1700s), a ferrier in Pennsylvania, and Lucy Terry Prince (Luce Bijah, *c.* 1725–1821), the author of an early ballad, established themselves as local legends, unifying fellow townspeople even as they revised local histories. Phillis Wheatley Peters (*c.* 1753–84) acted as a performance critic as well as a performing critic, publishing her poems as well as reciting them. All of these critics tried to keep the basis of identity invisible, to deflect attention from their material bodies even as they fleshed out their claims on American-ness. Wheatley transformed the seeming disability of her visibly policed identity into an advantage at crucial moments, however, capitalizing on her literary Afric as well as her rational Christian host body to claim both intelligence and patriotic citizenship.

During this Revolutionary period, European American critics often donned anonymous and pseudonymous patriotic or cultured American bodies to act as performance critics. They tried to perform whiteness within partisan politics and transatlantic literary circles. Mercy Otis Warren (1728–1814), for example, posed as a "Columbian patriot" to engage in Whig politics and define American masculinity. From her home near Boston, she dashed off theatrical satires and critiqued British tyranny through political commentaries, verse dramas, and poems. In nearby Pennsylvania, other women critics assumed cultured American bodies, trying to align womanhood with American letters and arts: Quaker women invented a host of individual feminine pseudonyms so that they could exchange poetic critiques in hand-crafted commonplace books, while a smaller group of European American women donned feminine pseudonyms to publish their theatrical commentaries in public newspapers. Theatre critics went so far as to defend women's right to pleasure. Unlike their evangelical predecessors, Revolutionary women critics concentrated upon crafting rational, even heroic bodies, rather than abject or possessed bodies.

The third chapter, titled "Republican women critics: performing Christian activism, American culture, and race," tracks women critics' strategies for entering public discourse during the early years of the new Republic (particularly the 1790s) and the Second Great Awakening (the 1820s and 1830s). The opening of newly politicized American theatres and the independent black church movement mark these two periods and anchor the chapter. Women critics found hosts within the theatre and emerging Christian denominations, as well as within the burgeoning newspapers and journals of the new nation. They struggled to articulate a culture that might be declared peculiarly American and they devised a Christianity linked to activism. Through their host bodies, they pursued artistic or moral equality – and superiority. European American women continued to enter the public sphere through religious discourse and American letters. Judith Sargent Murray (1751–1820), for example, initiated her career through an anonymous primmer for the new Unitarian denomination, while Susanna Haswell Rowson (1762–1824) relied initially upon the host body of an English duchess. Murray revised Christian notions of salvation to argue that under a rational God, all were invisibly saved, even without a conversion experience, record of denominational affiliation, or a habit of church-going. She severely undermined this early religious liberalism, however, by aligning American culture with federalism. This chapter offers revealing archival evidence regarding her efforts to juggle masculine and feminine pseudonymous bodies to protect her respectability and pays particular attention to Murray's and Rowson's plays. In the section on Rowson's *Slaves in Algiers* (1794) – which depicts Anglo-American Christians "enslaved" by African Muslims – I reprint and analyze a heretofore lost prologue to *Slaves*, written by Rowson herself in 1794. Rowson, unlike Murray, signed her own name to her work, gaining thereby a certain freedom. She expanded Murray's concept of the cultured American body by training elite young women in oratory and by experimenting with notions of invisibility and identity in the theatre. The stage, paradoxically, enabled Rowson to be simultaneously visible and invisible: she was present to her audiences, but only through dramatic characters that she scripted and portrayed onstage.

As this third chapter goes on to demonstrate, African American women critics at the turn of the nineteenth century entered civic conversations primarily through literary societies or through religious activism. The spiritual leaders of the Second Great Awakening redefined sin and salvation. Following in the wake of the Revolution's celebration of colonists' free will to determine their fate, ministers began to argue that individuals, like the republic itself, could and should forge their own pathways. Men and women were not "sinners in the hands of an angry God" so much as individuals capable of moral action.[6] At a time when racial discourse was gradually moving from the Biblical monogenetic model, in which race was understood to be the visible result of differences in environment, to a polygenetic model, in which race was viewed as an invisible, biological fact separating the races from one another at birth, many African American women critics tried to use Christianity to thwart an emerging polygenesis. They identified whiteness with invisible Christian respectability rather than a visibly marked Anglo-American race, and they linked blackness with sinfulness rather than racial or national others. Conversion became a call to activism, and as early as 1807, African American evangelicals Jarena Lee (1783–?) and Zilpha Elaw (c. 1790–?) answered that call. The third chapter examines how they donned Christian activist bodies in parlors, sanctuaries, and open meadows, launching itinerant ministries and preaching to ad hoc, integrated congregations about an inclusive, anti-racist Christian America. They also galvanized black congregations. They merged evangelical rhetoric and practices with natural rights discourse, hiding their resistance in the language of republicanism. They spoke, for example, of their "unusual life and liberty."[7] They saw themselves as possessing superior moral insight. A luminous whiteness shielded them, while the unconverted of all races languished in darkness. This revised whiteness echoes African images of white as the color of the ancestors, the dead. Itinerants performed religion as race and nation, turning to the Bible to sanctify their host bodies and create a "regenerated Constitution."[8] Although their published theories about womanhood were conservative, in practice they abrogated and revised these theories. They tackled racial and class discrimination and helped build the African Methodist Episcopal Church, a center for political action as well as religious interpretation.

Early American women critics produced an eclectic, hybrid legacy. Through their diverse host bodies, they performed critiques in person and in print. They registered their judgments and articulated their visions, wider than the path toward nationhood, across the colonies and the

United States. Their body of criticism – bold, clever, and fluid – reveals their fierce determination to expose the limits as well as the possibilities of performing religion, race, politics, and culture.

NOTES

1 For an account of female exhorters "damning all others round about them," see Garden, "Take Heed," 19. For a glimpse of "Rapatio" as a character in *The Adulateur*, a play by Mercy Otis Warren, see *Plays*, 26. Within her *Poems on Various Subjects, Religious and Moral*, Phillis Wheatley warned boys about "transient sweetness" (in "To the University of Cambridge, in New-England") and addressed King George about "setting his subjects free" (in "To the King's Most Excellent Majesty"): see *Collected*, 15–17. Judith Sargent Murray excused herself in *The Traveler Returned* and retitled *The Medium* as *Virtue Triumphant* (see Murray's *Gleaner*); Robert Treat Paine, Jr. savagely parodied Murray and her husband (see Paine, Jr., "For the Federal Orrery" and "Nineholes' Drawing Room"). Itinerant preacher Zilpha Elaw tells of reducing the wealthiest white family in her hometown to tears (Elaw, *Memoirs*, 92). For an account of Elaw's preaching with fellow preacher Jarena Lee, see Lee, *Religious*, 51, 88.

2 Smith, *Not*, xviii; Fabre and O'Meally, *History*, 9. While I am keenly aware of the dangers of focusing on only African, African American, European, and European American critics to the exclusion of women marked by other racialized and ethnic labels – Native American women, for instance, during the historical period I am investigating – I am also very conscious of the fact that there is a historical *particularity* to the positioning of these overlapping groups of women critics in the United States, a particularity that I hope may be usefully addressed in a single study, despite the risks. A word on terminology: I regard "race" as a performance and as a social phenomenon that shapes experience. Carole Boyce Davies, noting the dangers attending any racial label, uses the term "black" (Davies, *Black*, 5–14). I am using the terms "African American," "African," and "black" as well as "European American," "European," and "white," not just because I am writing at a moment when there is disagreement about which words are most useful politically, but also because I want to recognize critics' performances of nationalities and traditions while also acknowledging that in the eighteenth century the term "African American" or "European American" signified a specific claim: a claim on citizenship as the new nation emerged. These labels also potentially work against linking perceived skin tone to concepts of racialized identity. Obviously, the terms are deeply vexed, particularly in light of the impossible fiction of race and the interracial sexual contact, forced and unforced, that characterizes colonial and US history. To make myself comprehensible, I have to rely on vexed terminology. Like Davies, I am aware that racial terms represent a misnaming and the "striving of the dispossessed for full

representation"; I use these terms "provisionally," aware that they contain "an original misnaming" and must be "subject to new analyses, new questions and new understandings" (Davies, *Black*, 5).

3 Roach, *Cities*, 2. See Girard, *Violence*.

4 Here, and in my discussion of the abstract citizen, I am drawing particularly on Lauren Berlant's formulation ("National," 113). See also Berlant's *Queen*, Karen Sanchez-Eppler, Carolyn Sorisio, Saidiya Hartman, and Pauline Schoelesser.

5 It is necessary, I think, to distinguish between the viewer or reader and the critic: the viewer or reader may, I think, always productively concentrate on the invisible or unmarked, "inhabit[ing] the blank without forcing the other to fill it" (Phelan, *Unmarked*, my italics, 19, 33). However, the critic may or may not productively refuse "the payoff of visibility." This is a crucial distinction, precisely because race, as well as class and gender, are implicated in any concept of anonymity. In a different but closely related tradition of "active disappearance," Catherine Gallagher explains that the eighteenth-century British literary marketplace "is often the setting for what might be called the authors' vanishing acts. It is a place where the writers appear mainly through their frequently quite spectacular displacements and disappearances in literary and economic exchanges." Gallagher perceives this as an integral part of the commoditization process at that historical moment, linking "the rhetoric of authorship with one of dispossession . . . the presentation of authorship as the effect of the writer's inability to *own* the text remains constant and is explicitly linked to the author's gender" (Gallagher, *Nobody's*, xviii, xx). British women's vanishing acts functioned somewhat differently than American ones, however, partly because of the fact that in the United States there was no copyright law until 1790 and the marketplace developed later than in England.

6 Edwards, "Sinners."

7 Lee, *Religious Experience*, 23. While I agree with Catherine Brekus (*Strangers*) that female preacher's *writings* often take a conservative stance on gender, I think their *performances* belie that stance, and I see in African American women's preaching a repeated emphasis upon natural rights discourse.

8 Elaw, *Memoirs*, 51.

WORKS CITED

Berlant, Lauren Gail. *The Queen of America Goes to Washington City: Essays on Sex and Citizenship*. Durham, N.C.: Duke University Press, 1997.

"National Brands/National Body: Imitation of Life." *Comparative American Identities: Race, Sex, and Nationality in the Modern Text*. Ed. Hortense J. Spillers. New York: Routledge, 1991: 110–40.

Brekus, Catherine A. *Strangers & Pilgrims: Female Preaching in America, 1740–1845*. Chapel Hill: University of North Carolina Press, 1998.

Davies, Carole Boyce. *Black Women, Writing, and Identity: Migrations of the Subject*. London; New York: Routledge, 1994.

Edwards, Jonathan. "Sinners in the Hands of an Angry God: A Sermon Preached at Enfield, July 8th 1741." Boston: S. Kneeland and T. Green, 1741. Early American Imprints. First series, no. 4713.

Elaw, Zilpha. *Memoirs of the Life, Religious Experience, Ministerial Travels and Labours of Mrs. Zilpha Elaw, An American Female of Colour; Together with Some Account of the Great Religious Revivals in America [Written by Herself].* London: Published by the Authoress, 1846. Rpt. in *Sisters of the Spirit: Three Black Women's Autobiographies of the Nineteenth Century.* Ed. William L. Andrews. Bloomington: Indiana University Press, 1986.

Fabre, Geneviève, and Robert O'Meally, eds. *History & Memory in African-American Culture.* Oxford: Oxford University Press, 1994.

Gallagher, Catherine. *Nobody's Story: The Vanishing Acts of Women Writers in the Marketplace, 1670–1820.* Berkeley: University of California Press, 1994.

Garden, Alexander. "Take Heed How Ye Hear." Sermon delivered 13 July 1740. New York: J. Peter Zenger, 1742. Early American Imprints (EAI), First Series; no. 4959, 4801.

Gilroy, Paul. *Against Race: Imagining Political Culture beyond the Color Line.* Cambridge, Mass.: The Belknap Press of Harvard University Press, 2000.

Girard, René. *Violence and the Sacred.* Trans. Patrick Gregory. Baltimore: Johns Hopkins University Press, 1981.

Hartman, Saidiya V. *Scenes of Subjection: Terror, Slavery, and Self-making in Nineteenth-Century America.* New York: Oxford University Press, 1997.

Lee, Jarena. *Religious Experience and Journal of Mrs. Jarena Lee, Giving an Account of Her Call to Preach the Gospel, Revised and Corrected from the Original Manuscript, Written by Herself.* Philadelphia: Printed and Published for the Author, 1849. Rpt. in *Spiritual Narratives.* Ed. Sue E. Houchins. New York: Oxford University Press, 1988.

McDowell, Deborah E. *"The Changing Same": Black Women's Literature, Criticism, and Theory.* Bloomington, Ind.: Indiana University Press, 1995.

[Murray, Judith Sargent.] Constantia. *The Gleaner.* 1798. Ed. Nina Baym. Schenectady, N.Y. Union College Press, 1992.

Paine, Jr., Robert Treat. "For the Federal Orrery," by "Ned Gingerly, Wiswal-Den, Cambridge," "Extracts from a new play, called, 'The tables turned: or, a bug with a guinea,'" *Federal Orrery* 26 March 1795: 1, 46: 2.

"Ninehole's Drawing Room," *Federal Orrery,* 30 March 1795: 1,47: 1.

Phelan, Peggy. *Unmarked: The Politics of Performance.* London; New York: Routledge, 1993.

Roach, Joseph. *Cities of the Dead: Circum-Atlantic Perfomance.* New York: Columbia University Press, 1996.

Sánchez-Eppler, Karen. *Touching Liberty: Abolition, Feminism, and the Politics of the Body.* Berkeley: University of California Press, 1993.

Schloesser, Pauline. *The Fair Sex: White Women and Racial Patriarchy in the Early American Republic.* New York: New York University Press, 2002.

Smith, Valerie. *Not Just Race, Not Just Gender: Black Feminist Readings.* New York: Routledge, 1998.

Sorisio, Carolyn. *Fleshing Out America: Race, Gender, and the Politics of the Body in American Literature,* 1833–1879. Ahens: University of Georgia Press, 2002.

Spengemann, William C. *A Mirror for Americanists: Reflections on the Idea of American Literature.* Hanover and London: University Press of New England, 1989.

Warren, Mercy Otis. *The Plays and Poems.* Ed. Benjamin Franklin V. Delmar. N.Y.: Scholars' Facsimiles and Reprints, 1980.

Wheatley, Phillis. *The Collected Works.* Ed. John C. Shields. New York; Oxford: Oxford University Press, 1988.

CHAPTER I

Colonial Women Critics: Performing Religion, Race, Possession, and Pornography

[The Reverend] has scared half the People, especially Women and Children, almost out of their Wits ... he has made an amazing Alteration, and *all Faces gather Blackness* ... after his last Sermon there was an amazing universal Groan.

> Postscript, *The South-Carolina Gazette,* 18 June 1741: 2, my italics

The Wheels of a heated Imagination set thus a going, God only knows where they will stop, whether in *Bedlam,* or *Rome,* or *no Christianity,* or *no Religion at all.*

> Anglican Commissary Alexander Garden, "Take Heed How Ye Hear," 1740 sermon

The First Great Awakening began with a crisis of belief. As colonists fell away from Puritan churches, they lost confidence in civic institutions in general. They no longer perceived church boards or town councils as representative, so they began to question their Old Light ministers and lay leaders. Since laymen in "established" or state-supported churches held high political offices as well, this religious questioning held political ramifications. The New Light ministers of the Great Awakening, rebelling against the governing Old Light Congregationalists, Presbyterians, and Anglicans, started preaching Biblical narratives of liberation in addition to old Puritan stories of obedience and damnation. New Lights also re-imagined the nature of identity. Old Lights had argued that identity was visibly marked on one's body and that wealth was a mark of God's grace. They had valued book learning and confirmation on English soil. New Lights replaced this ideology. They viewed identity as invisible, as an inner grace and simplicity. The key to this invisible identity, for New Lights, was salvation through an ecstatic conversion experience. Suddenly religion depended upon feelings and divine inspiration rather than reason and Biblical scholarship, which enabled untutored women to claim authority more easily. Revivalist preachers denounced not only the ruling classes and political leaders but also those unfeeling ministers who failed to empathize with their congregants, and women critics amplified those denunciations in rowdy street conversions. New Light Christian doctrine suddenly, and unwittingly, offered women critics acceptable models of resistance and opportunities to create new and diverse narratives of identity. European, European American, and free African American women gathered in churches and in town squares to don host bodies and perform their salvation as well as their critiques of American culture. African and African American slave women, some of whom had already been introduced to Christianity through the European colonization of Africa or through sporadic and desultory colonial attempts to Christianize slaves, discovered that they could either convert to New Light Christianity or use it as a ruse to perform traditional African spirit possession on public streets: through them, the ancestors could call out the sins of the colonies. Various African deities – the *Inkices* of the Bantu (from Angola) and the *Orishas* of the Yoruba (from Benin and current-day Nigeria) – oversaw these traditional African possession rituals. African Muslims from Senegal and Gambia witnessed the spectacle, linking the possession fits to *bori* possession cults or to evil spirits (*jinn*) in Islam. The general effect of the Great Awakening was disruptive and electrifying, even though it was not always meant to be. Newspaper editors, including female editors, eagerly covered the story of women's conversions and impromptu street-preaching, thereby binding the colonies together in a networking web linking religion, politics, and culture with race in new and conflicting ways.

This chapter investigates the performance criticism published by Elizabeth Timotheé (*c.* 1700–57), editor of the sole newspaper in South Carolina during the height of the Great Awakening, to illuminate how Timotheé managed to enter the public sphere and moderate public debates and how the female exhorters glimpsed in her columns critiqued colonial culture. These exhorters gained access to new critical powers as they donned host bodies of various kinds. They engaged in politicized religious practices which stood in for and reshaped concepts of race, American-ness, and gender, with liberal as well as conservative effects.

For some African and African American women, conversions were a matter of observation rather than participation: mere background noise, a diversion from numbing work, a source of amusement or disgust. For others, the Awakening offered opportunities for invention and resistance. It offered a chance to practice tribally defined spirit possessions, which superficially resembled Christian conversion performances. Bantu and Yoruban women could suddenly engage in spirit possession publicly and with impunity. Through these performances they spoke publicly in the voices of ancestors or gods and negotiated across tribal boundaries to create, out of disparate Angolan, Gambian, Senegalese, Yoruban, and West Indian performance practices and languages, a unifying "African-ness." Through these religious performances, they formulated their own idea of an African "race," valuing "blackness" as a tie to the ancestors and gods and reinterpreting "whiteness." They accomplished this goal before the articulation of late eighteenth-century pseudo-scientific typologies that linked African-ness with negative attributes such as docility and indolence. They forged their own notion of race. Spirit possession enabled participants to critique, through indirection, the unmentionable sin of slavery, and to proclaim spiritual freedom explicitly and earthly freedom implicitly. Many Africans and African Americans performed religion as politics as well as race: they planned slave revolts under the "hush arbor" cover of nighttime gatherings, inspired by the presence of Maroon or escaped slave settlements in the nearby wilderness.[1] For a different group of Africans and African Americans, conversions were not a ruse or a chance to practice African spirit possession. They were, instead, an opportunity to perform equality through a newly embraced Christian performance that re-imagined the convert's body as inviolate and impervious to threat. For these converts to Christianity, performing religion meant claiming a Christian body that secured the idea that all humankind descended from the same two individuals, the same evangelical "race."

For some European and European American women, conversions tendered a different kind of possession: a sadomasochistic minstrelsy. In an attempt to find a "feeling" body, these converts imagined their way into "black" bodies that paradoxically suffered torture and experienced ecstatic pleasure at the same time. Through this curiously pornographic theatrical performance, working-class and middle-class white women proclaimed themselves the primary group oppressed by colonial rule, even as they claimed self-righteousness for themselves alone. They also shaped a notion of the black body that had positive and negative effects: the "black" body they used as a host was not only sentient but also emotionalized. Through their conversion fits and pretend martyrdom, these European and European American women performed in the fashion of a realistic actor, "as if" they were inside the abject bodies of the enslaved, displacing the slaves' quite real agony with their own imaginary version. Some believed that their misery was the "awful spectacle" that proved the magnitude of the Almighty, that they were "Sinners in the

Hands of an Angry God."[2] They performed religion as a negotiation with race in order to wedge their way into public discourse. Even though they donned black host bodies during their conversions, these critics wished to claim white privilege: through their performance as the most sinful of the sinners, they claimed to become the whitest of the white. Some performed conversion to exorcise their complicity in slavery: they declared their sinfulness and started anew without having to name their slave-owning as a sin. Some were exhibitionists who enjoyed displaying what for all practical purposes looked like a simulation of sexual bondage or ecstasy. They performed religion as sexual politics. Most, however, launched a political critique of the class-bound, patriarchal government tied to the Anglicans in the South and Old Light Congregationalists and Presbyterians in the North. Working-class critics, in particular, looked to the Awakening for this social mobility. They tried to elevate their social code of plain speech, plain garments, and plain prayer over the competing elegance of Anglican rhetoric, dress, and ritual. They championed evangelical gatherings over theatrical productions, assemblies, and balls. They performed piety and abjection on their way toward whiteness and merchant-class political power.

For a very few European and European American evangelicals, however, the Awakening provided a quite different opportunity: a chance to build what would later be called cross-racial ties. Some of these religionists preached anti-slavery, while others simply acknowledged slaves' right to literacy. These critics, according to local authorities, assisted African and African American-led anti-slavery efforts, performing religion as liberal politics and landing themselves in jail.

"Possessed" by the spirit in interracial gatherings, women as well as men railed on street corners, in houses transformed into multi-room meeting places, and at unofficial marketplaces run solely by African and African American women. They foregrounded their host bodies and called out a litany of cultural and individual sins. These acts of possession forced a tangle of changes, both liberal and conservative, in domestic arrangements, pedagogical practices, and courtroom procedures.[3] Revival services in Charles Town, South Carolina – initially held in St. Philip's Anglican Church and then moved to Josiah Smith's Independent Congregationalist Church – spilled into adjacent lawns and streets as revivalists began to exhort independently of church-sponsored gatherings. Female exhorters of all nationalities troubled issues of representation and authority: who was authorized to speak for whom within the colonies? By performing on "the Ecclesiastical Stage," they unsettled structures of governance. Officially, most of the South was Anglican, but revivalists aligned themselves with a dissident Anglican, Reverend George White-field (1714–70), the star itinerant performer of the Great Awakening, who offered a New Light, potentially democratic alternative to earthly as well as heaven-bound life.[4]

At a time when the line between performance onstage and performance in print was blurred, Whitefield, despite his abhorrence of theatre, was routinely described in terms of theatricality. Commentators analyzed his explosive performance style and his "audience's" (rather than his "con-gregation's") empathetic bodily and emotional response to it. His fol-lowers spoke of his "productions," while detractors denounced him as a "Stage Declaimer," a "Strolling Player," and a "Mock Preacher." His followers were dismissed as low-class stock characters and ethnic types: as Sir John Falstaff or the Irish bumbler "AT-ALL in the play."[5] On English stages, political satires were being replaced by comic operas, pantomimes, and sentimental comedies, but in the American colonies, theatrical political critiques were flowering – in evangelical gatherings led by Whitefield.[6] Conversion performances were so much more uninhibited than other kinds of theatrical activity that they held center stage for a long time, replacing incipient efforts at staging drama. Whitefield both evoked and sublimated the sexual tension generated by his performances. He presented himself as representative of dispossessed American colonists, linking revivalists across boundaries of national origin. Almost all of Elizabeth Timotheé's correspondents commented on the public bodily presence of the evangelists and their democratic "possessed" host body. Since Timotheé published commentaries on Northern as well as Southern conversions, she created a common, highly contested colonial host body, on which women critics made various claims.

A widow, Timotheé established herself as a performance critic by Anglicizing her name and adopting another kind of host body. She posed as her underage son, "Mr. Peter Timothy," to edit *The South-Carolina Gazette* during the initial rush of the Awakening. Although her name does not appear on the ship's register (as her husband's and children's names do), Timothy probably sailed from Rotterdam to Philadelphia on 21 September 1731, with her French Huguenot husband (Louis/Lewis) and their four children ranging from one to six years old. Louis immediately found work with Benjamin Franklin, who helped him purchase the year-old *South-Carolina Gazette* in 1734. The Timotheés flourished in King Charles' Town by performing "Englishness" under Anglicized names, but in December 1738, a fatal accident took Lewis's life. Elizabeth suddenly assumed the editorship of the major newspaper in the Southern colonies, the only newspaper in the South Carolina colony, from 1738 through 1746.[7]

Colonial editors typically published an eclectic mix of foreign and local news, paid advertising, brief essays, poems, and excerpts from other papers. At times of political unrest, however, they often remained neutral by concentrating on foreign news and local advertisements. Timothy – herself a member of the state-established Anglican Church roiled by the debates of the Great Awakening – did not follow this safe route. Instead, she risked providing full coverage of the contradictory voices within the Awakening. She reported on the revival's sweep across New England and the middle colonies into the South, focusing particularly on Whitefield and his converts. Whitefield preached in her parish church, St. Philip's Anglican Church, during his first visit to America. His visit launched a protracted and acrimonious public debate with the local Anglican Commissary, Alexander Garden (*c.* 1685–1756), who eventually launched ecclesiastical court proceedings against Whitefield.

Like most editors, Timothy typically did not write original columns, but for seven years she decided which cultural performances to cover, which critics to print, how long to sustain the public debates she generated, and how to frame the participants. She demanded that all participants identify themselves to her, so she was the only person who knew, for certain, the identity of the combatants. While most of her personal papers are lost, her editorial policies reveal a critic self-possessed enough to foster a contentious religious and political debate with serious ramifications concerning race and class. While she supported class mobility and helped usher European immigrants into a Christianized whiteness, she blanched at anti-racism and anti-slavery. In the host body of the propertied English male "Peter Timothy" (rather than as an immigrant Dutchwoman widowed by a Frenchman), she wielded considerable power as a cultural critic.

In contrast, Whitefield's female converts gained access to the public sphere through conversions which placed their womanly bodies in full view. They tried to protect themselves from censure by imagining their way into possessed host bodies, validating an identity based on *invisible* salvation. In this way, they created an inhabitable public body capable of licensed cultural critique. The licensing agencies themselves – dissident Anglicanism in the South and New Light Presbyterianism and Congregationalism in the North, as well as the emerging Methodist and Baptist denominations – were marginal but supportive. While Timothy was assumed to be a white male (and that fiction was upheld even among those who interacted with her in person), there was a protracted debate over how evangelical bodies would be marked in racial terms: were female converts "white" or "black"? The answer depended upon the participant or viewer.

During Whitefield's appearances in Charles Town, slaves, free African Americans, lower-class Europeans and European Americans, upper-class European American women, and youth, in particular, gained access to public platforms for the first time. Their exhortations were "cultural performances," repeated group behaviors that reinforced but also reshaped traditions.[8] In the 1740s, Charles Town housed diverse traditions, languages, and cultures. It differed considerably from the original 1670 English settlement of planters and their Barbadian slaves, ringed by Native Americans and uneasily hugging the coast. The population of Charles Town proper was only 6,800, but just outside the city limits 20,000 Africans and African Americans lived and worked, with some escaping to found Maroon settlements.[9] The non-native population in the American colonies had doubled between 1700 and 1730 (from 250,000 to 500,000), and Charles Town itself had mushroomed. In addition to English colonists, it housed Dutch, German, Scots-Irish, Scottish, Welsh, and French Huguenot immigrants as well as freemen and slaves. There were Christians, Jews, and nonbelievers. About seventy free African Americans, whose religious practices remain undocumented, lived in or near Charles Town, some on the frontier west of town. Aside from second- and third-generation West Indians, the slaves were primarily from Angola, on the southwestern coast of Africa. Slaves also arrived from the west coast of Africa: from Gambia, in particular, as well as Senegal, Sierra Leone, the Ivory and Gold Coasts, and Benin – not to mention the Central African regions further inland. These slaves spoke many different languages and practiced diverse religions. Only a handful of the West Indians had been converted to Anglicanism.[10] Most newly disembarking Africans observed traditional tribal religions that shared certain common aspects, such as belief in a primary God supported by many lesser deities. Tribal religions typically also honored some version of spirit possession.[11] Many Africans who practiced tribal religions had been exposed to Christianity through the European colonization of Africa: Angolans, for example, had encountered Portuguese Catholicism as early as the fifteenth century. Many had already joined tribal practices to Christianity, linking minor deities, for instance, to Catholic saints. Some Africans, such as the West African Bundu, practiced Islam.

Prompted by Whitefield and the more radical John Wesley (1707–91), these diverse colonists debated whether salvation, and therefore identity, was visible, as Anglicans claimed, or invisible, as radical revivalists from disparate "climes" believed. If grace and identity were invisible, as Wesley contended, the old Puritan notion of the visibly elect had to be scrapped and colonial American identity had to be re-imagined. Wesley argued that the idea of the predestination of the visibly elect "inspire[d] contempt or coldness towards those whom we suppose outcast from God."[12] This coldness, he came to believe, sustained slavery. African, African American, European, and European American women critics carved out various routes of access into the debates sparked by Whitefield and Wesley as they established, through host bodies, revised ideas about the (in)visibility of race, American-ness, and gender.

SITES OF ACCESS

Most European and European American women exhorters in Charles Town gained access to public debates by attending Whitefield's revival services in churches and town squares. However, Elizabeth Timothy and many African and African American women exhorters spoke out at their workplaces. They capitalized on their "knowledge of accompts" to enter into public debates.

"Being born & bred in Holland, where the Knowledge of Accompts makes a Part of Female Education," Timothy was well prepared for her editorial post. In fact, Ben Franklin, co-owner of the *Gazette*, reported that although Louis had been "ignorant in Matters of Account," Elizabeth assiduously updated records and accounted "with the greatest Regularity & Exactitude," eventually buying out her partner and establishing her son as owner. Franklin cited Timothy to justify math education for American women.[13]

Despite colonial women's low literacy rates, Timothy's editorship was not unique. European American women often assumed editorial roles or managed printing shops after the death of a male relative. Timothy tried to make her four-page weekly "entertaining and correct," covering the revival as well as political meetings, military exercises, educational presentations, and theatrical productions.[14] The primary need, however, was for information about trade. A majority of South Carolina's inhabitants were slaves whose knowledge of rice and indigo growing seasons had transformed Charles Town into the largest and wealthiest city in the South, a port trading directly with European markets. Forty percent of all

African slaves in the colonies arrived by way of Charles Town. South Carolina was far from stable economically, however: during the war over Austrian succession and subsequent King George's war against France (1744–48), rice prices fell sharply and smallpox and fever epidemics struck. Slave resistance continued despite increasing surveillance. In 1739, slaves had launched the Stono Rebellion, one of the largest slave revolts of the eighteenth century, just outside of Charles Town. Elizabeth Timothy did not intend to be an inflammatory editor at this juncture. She was an Anglican and an unapologetic slaveholder. In fact, she had publicly countenanced her husband's grotesque mistreatment of London, one of their African slaves, who had tried twice to run away: the second runaway notice had, shockingly, described London as wearing an "iron head-piece." It is clear that Timothy did not wish to foment religious revolution or alter slavery or indentured servitude. However, as a widowed Dutch immigrant with many children, she wished to elevate her financial and social status – and she benefited economically from local class unrest against the English and Old Light Anglican power base.[15]

Like Timothy, many African slave women in Charles Town possessed a "knowledge of accompts." Educated in West and South African agricultural and trading skills, they edged their way into public markets and debates. In South Carolina at this time, slavery still operated primarily on the task system: slaves were responsible for work that would take most laborers ten hours to complete. As long as they completed the tasks their masters assigned them, they could exercise judgment about how to use the rest of their time. They were generally granted part of Saturday or Sunday to earn money to feed and clothe their families. Many of Charles Town's slave women took advantage of this loophole, putting their knowledge of markets to impressive use. They set up a wildly popular unofficial marketplace in Charles Town. As early as 1720, officials proscribed trading with "Negroes, or other Servants, & Slaves," a sure sign that much trading was taking place. In fact, by 1739 African and African American slave women controlled the distribution of Charles Town's food supply. Their grip on the food chain was so strong that authorities tried, unsuccessfully, to set up an official counter-marketplace for trading goods and information. In 1747 an exasperated local official presented a petition complaining that these women critics lived "free from the government of their masters." An unenforceable 1751 act banned slaves from selling rice or Indian corn.[16] Market-women critics condemned the slave system by earning significant profits, and as they undermined the economic and governance structures of the city, they talked their way through the day, commenting on the local scene to everyone who had to purchase groceries. Some of them participated in the Awakening.

To acknowledge that many of the African and African American women working in the Charles Town market were better off financially than a number of Europeans and European Americans in Charles Town is not to ignore their slave status, but to suggest that through their performances as evangelical market critics, they complicate the ways in which we might imagine African and African American women's participation in colonial culture in general, and the Great Awakening in particular. As these market women practiced African spirit possession or as they experienced Christian conversion in the streets, they unnerved authorities, precisely because of their knowledge and partial control of trade. As owners of their own market stalls, they redefined their status as commodities for sale (not to mention as fetishes for white male fantasies), even as they performed their spiritual success, either as their own ancestors or as the beneficiaries of Christian salvation. They deployed religion as race, to perform a diasporic connection, to unify African tribes as nation, to claim "American-ness" as their own. And they simultaneously created communities through which they could stage resistance to pre-nationalist discourses.

These women critics had to devise a means through which to gain access to the civic conversation. To speak without censure, they created host bodies that either made them invisible or contested spectators' attempts to read their visible, material bodies as their identities. The women's methods of access were diverse and ingenious.[17]

METHODS OF ACCESS

By occupying, in print, the "pseudonymous body" of her male heir, Elizabeth Timothy made herself invisible even as she achieved hypervisibility as a major arbiter of civic conversation in the South. She protected her respectability and simultaneously acknowledged her underage son Peter as her host, the eventual owner of the family business. Pseudonyms protected the laws of primogeniture, collapsing the mother's identity into the eldest son's: Timothy routinely received and replied to letters addressed to "Mr. Editor." Since printing shops were gathering places, local customers knew Elizabeth operated the business, but her masculine pseudonym enabled them to maintain the public fiction that a man governed.

Timothy's multiple performances – in print as Peter Timothy and in person as the Anglicized Mrs. Timothy (shadowed by the immigrant "Mrs. Timotheé") – complicated her identity. Her customers heard her speak Dutch, French, and Dutch-accented English, but as they read the *Gazette*, they heard an English gentleman, Peter Timothy ghosted by other accents. To *Gazette* readers unaware of the shop, Elizabeth Timothy was simply invisible; "Peter Timothy" eclipsed her entirely. This status as a parasitic or invisible critic within a pseudonymous host body raised questions about the performativity of identity: if Mrs. Timothy performed the work typically completed by a man, why could she not claim that work directly? What gendered performance codes prohibited her appearance in print, and how did her appearance in her shop complicate them? If locals knew she edited the paper, why bother with the mask of her thirteen-year-old son's body? Timothy's work suggested that women should be able to appear in public, in an embodied fashion, to voice their views. As her columns reveal, however, female converts also had to borrow host bodies to issue their cultural commentaries.

European and European American converts borrowed "black" host bodies during their conversion experiences, simultaneously making visible and displacing the unspeakable: slavery in the body politic. Slavery was central to the performance of colonial identity. Haunting the vivid cultural memory of Charles Town's residents were glimpses – imagined, witnessed, or experienced – of the torture of Africans in the Middle Passage, the defiant rebellion of runaway slaves, and the ecstatic enactments of African spirit possession. At the moment of Christian conversion, when European believers were wracked by physical convulsions, wrenched by pain and ecstasy as they faced the fires of hell, they carried these imaginings or memories of tortured, fleeing and redeemed "black" bodies with them. They echoed the movements they imagined or glimpsed. Conversions, then, were more than a simple admittance of individual sin. Because the guilt thus exorcized could be felt but remain unnamed, conversions were particularly useful to a European populace grappling with the unnamable sins of slavery.

Slavery was not the only cultural practice that Timothy's readers were trying to justify, mitigate, terminate, or escape. Also haunting Anglicans in the South and Congregationalists in the North was the practice of communion. Anglican and Congregationalist communion was a legally sanctioned, privately enacted and seemingly unimpassioned ritual validating the salvation of the *visibly* "elect," whose wealth supposedly proclaimed their grace. This communion linked visible wealth to

Christian and colonial identity. Wesley's evangelism contested this notion of visible salvation and identity, instead positing identity as performative and salvation as invisible and "free" rather than predestined.

Evangelical conversion performances during the Great Awakening echoed seventeenth-century Scots-Irish Presbyterian practices as well as African possession rituals. The typical seventeenth-century Scots-Irish Presbyterian conversion occurred at a multi-day revival involving thousands. The physical symptoms and emotional responses resembled those reported during the colonial Awakening. Westerkamp identifies these Scots-Irish communal possession rituals as resistant, tied to a critique of English individualism as well as a championing of a Scottish national discourse. She also demonstrates that these seventeenth-century rituals developed from a battle between the laity and the clergy and translated into a welcoming attitude toward Whitefield's ministrations in the colonies, especially in the mid-Atlantic Presbyterian circles where Scots-Irish immigrants settled before Whitefield's first visit. Scots-Irish conversions usually were characterized by enervation, however, while African conversions energized participants, as many colonial conversions did.[18]

The Awakening, which suddenly valued the *invisible* within converts, helped colonists negotiate between their ghostly memories about slavery and salvation. As Jacques Le Goff explains, memories are "the raw material of history," whose often unconscious workings change over time.[19] Under construction was the very nature of memory, salvation, slavery, and therefore American identity. Was salvation something that could be seen on the "elect," or something that was invisible within the "evangelical" or "possessed" body? How was it performed, and what, if anything, made it American? How did slavery and "race" connect to salvation and American-ness?

Charles Town critics addressed these questions in disparate ways. Many lower- and middle-class whites who participated in the Awakening sought to identify themselves as "free" in relation to two opposing groups of "slaves": the Anglicans (deemed to be "enslaved" by their lack of passion), and the Africans and African Americans (most of whom who were actually enslaved). These marginalized whites were dissatisfied with Anglican authorities and eager to claim feeling, empathetic bodies as their own. They demanded that the church and state accept them as full participants and they established their own communities to re-interpret the Bible. By 1745, these lower-class whites had become so unruly that Timothy had to print "An Act for the better regulating and governing of white servants."[20]

Conversions were the means through which these working-class and merchant-class others hoped to negotiate their way into whiteness. They auditioned as surrogates not just for the enslaved and free blacks in their midst, but also for the white elite. From the margins, working whites tried to revise respectability and privilege. They tried to replace mainstream Anglican customs, claiming grace and whiteness for themselves. They simultaneously displaced slaves and free blacks, by arguing that they were the ones most mistreated by the dominant culture. And, indeed, the upper-class viewed this group as "black." Anglo-American town fathers believed that "all Faces gather[ed] Blackness" during the evangelical conversions of the working and middle classes. They routinely linked evangelicals with "swarthy" indentured servants as well as the foreign French and Spanish. As in the early modern period in England, the American colonial "trope of blackness had a broad arsenal of effects . . . meaning that it [was] applied not only to dark-skinned Africans but to . . . groups that needed to be marked as 'other.'"[21]

For many Africans and colonial-born blacks, the Awakening served a quite different function. It served as a means of remembering rather than forgetting. Through the Awakening, blacks enacted, center stage, the invisible: through conversions they secretly embodied tribal loyalties, alliances, and ancestor spirits. They rebelled against colonial laws and social codes and established a political base. South Carolina slaves were Angolans, Senegambians ("Guineans"), and Barbadians, who sustained, created, and transformed "African" traditions, sometimes through Christian conversion, to disguise their political intents. Conversions offered a cover through which they could speak of being "free" and publicly proclaim all (white) men and women sinful. They could label false Christians, including slave-owners, as damned souls, and usher true Christians – slaves and free blacks – into American-ness and African-ness. They could identify a few white allies. They could create an African diasporic community and a "Christian upper class" that claimed dominance through moral force. They could legitimately rebel against Anglican authorities.

Building within their primary language groups, Bantu, Wolof, and Sudanic, South Carolina's slaves fashioned a common African culture, devising performance practices that would unite Angolans, Gambians, Senegalese, and West Indians. Senegambian Wolofs were excellent translators, forging communications across linguistic and cultural divides. The isolated Africans on the coastal islands of South Carolina developed the Gullah language and culture out of diverse African practices and

American borrowings.²² Africans on the mainland developed syncretic performances or assimilated. It helped that the Christian cross resembled ancient cruciforms of African cosmologies such as that of the BaKongo (Congolese and Angolans), whose crossroads symbol signified the poles of birth, maturity, death, and rebirth. While Christians linked whiteness with Christ and salvation, many Africans linked whiteness with the ancestors and with spiritual leadership: for the BaKongo, for instance, the world of the ancestors was *mpemba*, "the land of all things white," and for the Sande, spiritual leaders were always clad in white. Muslim Africans also found certain vaguely familiar practices in the colonies. As Holloway explains, the Malinke and Arab-descended Fulani, among other ethnic groups from the Senegambian region, practiced their own Muslim possession ceremonies. Sub-Saharan Hausa Muslims practiced spirit possession through the *bori* cult, which in some quarters was associated with womanly power and lesbianism: single adult women and other marginalized people served as the host bodies for spirits who possessed them and issued cultural criticisms through them. Lovejoy contends that Muslims, including those in South Carolina, only pretended to convert to Christianity, but Gomez explains that "African-born Muslims related Yahwah to Allah and Jesus to Muhammed."²³

These disparate African cultures fostered multiple theologies, one strand of which became a "Black Theology of Liberation" that functioned through possession rituals. These rituals sometimes merged Christian and African practices. Raboteau contends that (African-inflected) Christian conversions assisted slave critics by positing "the total acceptance and affirmation of self by God." Possession psychologically freed a new self to emerge from an old, enslaved self by striking the latter dead: this was, Earl argues, "a spiritual source of double consciousness in the mind of the slave." The new self emerged a whole, embodied, sacred questioner, connected to a community, and ready to act as a moral agent. Instead of internalizing the message "I belong to my master" or "I am my master's body," slaves could, through conversions, reclaim their own bodies by saying "I am my body" – and not simply body, but body, heart, mind, and soul.²⁴

For a handful of radical blacks and whites, the Awakening offered yet another function. It squashed the Puritan concept of the *visibly* "elect," positing that there were no individuals whose wealth and social status established them as visibly saved. All individuals were equally sinful, equally "black," and, if they experienced conversion, they were equally able to represent one another in Christian oneness. These revivalists argued that identity was tied to the *invisible*, manifesting itself internally and fleetingly in a group performance of salvation. They found their leader not in Whitefield, who upheld the doctrine of the elect, but in John Wesley, who believed in "free grace." These radicals shifted the colonial performance code from one in which visible saints ran the church and the government to one in which the invisibly saved evangelical "race," composed of all nationalities, strove to re-imagine or overthrow existing systems of political and social regulation. They envisioned a world in which conversions linked Christian bodies. These bodies were "othered" by the larger culture, marked as "black" and moved into hierarchies as the evangelical movement solidified, but within the earliest, incipient and emerging communities of the newly possessed, in moments here and there, a new concept of American colonial identity emerged: a colony in which all were equally capable of salvation and therefore, logically, equally human and equally citizens.

Evangelical and African diasporic street exhorters acted as performing critics, visible to their audiences as they issued their critiques, while Elizabeth Timothy functioned as a performance critic, invisible to readers as she published her columns behind her male pseudonym. Together, they initiated a civic conversation that undermined Anglican church–state notions of the visibly elect. They posited the idea that identity, in fact, was not only invisible but also performative. Identity was not about the nature of one's birth or how wealth marked one's body. Identity was something a person *performed*.

PERFORMING CRITICISM/PERFORMANCE CRITICISM

South Carolinians viewed themselves as having a common biological ancestor: the Bible supported this notion of "monogenesis." In 1735, however, taxonomist Carl von Linne began a project that eventually dismantled monogenesis. He started classifying homo sapiens into various "types." By 1758 he had differentiated four groups whose purported characteristics were caused merely by environmental conditions: Europeans ("fair, gentle, acute, inventive, governed by laws"), Americans ("copper-coloured, obstinate, content, free, regulated by customs"), Asiatics ("sooty, severe, haughty, covetous, governed by opinions") and Africans ("black, crafty, indolent, negligent, governed by caprice").[25] This pre-national typology set the stage for the gradual emergence of race as a marker of identity, vaguely linked to a real or imaginary place of origin. It made possible the eventual construction of Europeans and European

Americans as a separate white race aligned against black Africans, Asians, and Native Americans – even as Angolans, Gambians, and others formulated their own concepts of African-ness. Linne's typology also served as a backdrop for the fierce public debates about evangelical conversions: at stake in debates over the Great Awakening was the question of what the performance of "blackness" and "whiteness" meant – not only in religious terms, but also in terms of the conversation taxonomists were initiating about race and place of origin, not to mention class.

Evangelicals prompted colonists to argue about who was performing whiteness and who was performing blackness. There was fierce disagreement about how these performances signified, which made the performativity of nationality or race quite apparent. Performativity in this context "must be understood not as a singular or deliberate 'act,' but, rather, as the reiterative and citational practice by which discourse produces the effects that it names."[26] In other words, religionists did not consciously don blackness or whiteness. Instead, rhetorical formulations of religion and race tangled in competing and contradictory ways as they were variously cited in performative practices during the Great Awakening. Participants in the evangelical debate cited blackness and whiteness for different purposes and with different effects. By foregrounding the performative nature of Christianity, its presence as a site of contestation, evangelicals momentarily destabilized its primary dualism: the meaning of blackness and whiteness was under negotiation, not only as a religious but also as a racial and place-of-origin designation.

Old Light Anglicans, like their Northern Congregationalist and Presbyterian counterparts, tried to hold onto the performance of whiteness launched during the Puritan Awakening. Valerie Babb has demonstrated how late seventeenth-century religionists linked English whiteness and wealth to Christian concepts of salvation: Puritan ministers like Cotton Mather (1663–1728) joined "the promise of mobility and self-mastery to being white," to protect their emerging middle-class status. During the Great Awakening, tradition-bound Anglicans and Congregationalists joined this whiteness to English baptism and French fashion, balls, and concerts. To perform Christianity, in their view, was to perform civilization. Christianity, as Kim Hall explains, "has long provided the Western world with a symbolic order in which good, purity, and Christianity itself are associated with light and whiteness, while evil, sexuality, and difference are linked with darkness." Old Lights performed this definition of whiteness by marking the evangelicals – along with foreigners, indentured servants, slaves, women, and others – as dangerous, pornographic, different, and "black." Anglican Commissary Alexander Garden worried about where this *"enthusiastick* Race," "this *Methodist Race"* would "terminate," imagining not just slave revolts but also "mixed-race" children.[27]

Anglicans viewed evangelical gatherings as obscene political displays that fostered insurrection in the dark. One of Timothy's outraged *Gazette* correspondents feared converts who gathered *"Cabals* of *Negro's"* about them, "without public Authority, at unseasonable Times, and to the Disturbance of a Neighborhood." He was outraged that converts filled blacks' heads with *"Cant-Phrases, Trances, Dreams, Visions, and Revelations,* and something still *worse,* and which Prudence forbids to name." This critic is titillated as well as outraged by the illicit nighttime interracial gatherings: is the "something still *worse"* a slave uprising or an image of interracial liasons? Interracial relationships were not uncommon; officials had even tried to abolish them in a 1717 law. In 1737 a visitor commented upon their "preponderance," noting that the English married "black" as well as "Indian" women, and that some became Anglican converts.[28]

Threatened by the concept of racially mixed and resistant congregations unified as one body in Christ, Anglo-American colonial leaders depicted evangelicals as a conglomeration of discrete, sexually charged, and obscene bodily parts overlapping with one another and gathering blackness. They viewed exhorters as performing pornographic abjection. They were transfixed by their peep into a world of interracial interaction. One colonist described how a leading evangelical preacher scared townspeople, "especially Women and Children, almost out of their Wits," and "made an amazing Alteration," so that "all Faces gather Blackness." Some converts "were so stung, that they made such Cries and Groans" that the preacher was drowned out and they had to be carried out of the assembly. And after the final prayer, "there was an amazing universal Groan."[29] Charles Town's upper-class Anglicans were appalled by the idea of release from visible bodily boundaries, revolted and fascinated by the "amazing universal Groan[s]" that ended the most erotically charged conversion experiences. They sought not just a white colony, but an upper-class English and Anglican one – the imperatives of race, class, religion, and colonization were intertwined – and they required visible, secure, controllable boundaries.[30] Nonetheless, they found intertwined and ecstatic black bodies "amazing" and voyeuristically satisfying. David Garrick, the renowned actor who "in a sense *represented* ['British middle-class'] culture," allegedly confided that "he would give a hundred guineas to be able to pronounce 'O!' as Whitefield did," an intriguing desire in light of the repeated references to the "groans" of the evangelicals during their conversion fits.[31] Was Garrick jealous of Whitefield's curiously wider berth in the expression of passion, including sexual passion?

While Old Lights cast evangelicals as black and bestial, many New Light followers of Whitefield simply inverted the trope: they associated the refined remoteness of the traditionalists with sinful, unfeeling blackness. They claimed whiteness for themselves: purity represented by plain dress, church-going, and daily worship. Often working- or middle-class, these exhorters argued that through their invisible change of heart, accessed through an ecstatic conversion, they replaced the wealthy descendants of the original English settlers as the better Christians. It was invisible salvation and not visible wealth that proved their claim on whiteness. These revivalists marked both Old Light Anglicans and diasporic Africans as black. Slavery, in their view, was God's just punishment for the race of Ham. Slaves were black with sin; unfeeling Anglicans were black with sin, but evangelists through conversion became pure and white.

A few radical Methodists embraced John Wesley's competing notion that there were simply no elect. Everyone performed blackness, for everyone was sinful. Through Christian conversion, however, everyone merged into a single body of believers with uniform access to free grace and Christian whiteness. As early as 1738 a few radical evangelists such as Reverend Anthony Gavin began to preach anti-slavery as well as New Light salvation around Charles Town. These evangelists hoped that slave conversions would lead to emancipation, as in England.[32] They were less worried about interracial relations, including the interracial marriages in Charles Town. The Governor and Council, in fact, had given their blessing to at least one interracial marriage in 1731: they had allowed a "mulatto carpenter" named Gideon Gibson to enter South Carolina with his European American wife; the Gibson who became a prominent Regulator may have been their son (Weir, *Colonial*, 199). Interracial connections were not unusual, and slave resistance was strong: the Spanish had been fomenting slave resistance against the English for some time. At the urging of Catholic missionaries, slaves had been fleeing to Spanish Florida since 1720, and by 1738 the Spanish had issued a royal edict freeing all slaves and protecting them from their former masters within a special fort just outside St. Augustine, Florida. This knowledge further fueled resistance within English colonies such as South Carolina.

In 1739 several slave uprisings erupted in South Carolina. Slaves in St. John's Parish in Berkeley County revolted. Then, on 8 September 1739, slave leaders learned that Spain -- whose missionaries freed slaves -- had declared war on England. At daybreak on 9 September 1739, at the Stono River south of Charles Town, an Angolan leader named Jemmy launched the Stono Rebellion, one of the most widely publicized slave revolts of the early eighteenth century. The Stono Rebellion solidified the local Angolan, Gambian, and West Indian performance of "African-ness," as rebels linked blackness to their own notions of freedom and grace. Around twenty blacks met Jemmy by the river in St. Paul's Parish, some twenty miles south of Charles Town. Brandishing signs announcing their "Liberty" and chanting that claim as they walked, they gathered fellow insurgents. They commandeered weapons and ammunition, fighting off and killing white storekeepers and plantation owners and burning houses as they fled. Kindly slave-owners were spared. Almost a hundred slaves joined the insurrection, most facing capture or death as they fled toward Spanish-owned Florida. Twenty-one Europeans and forty-four Africans and African Americans died.[33]

A well-known white surveyor and planter named Hugh Bryan, along with a small group of fellow planters, began to preach liberation to slaves south of Charles Town within a year of the Stono Rebellion, just after Timothy began her coverage of Whitefield's sermons. From 4 July to 20 July 1740, as Timothy reported, Whitefield preached twice a day in Charles Town, with "such Flame and Power" that hundreds converted; in one evening he collected over four hundred pounds.[34] Inspired by Whitefield's preaching, Hugh Bryan's brother Jonathan opened a school for African Americans in 1740, despite opposition from the South Carolina Assembly. In 1742, rumors began to circulate that the Bryans were practicing Wesleyan-style anti-slavery activity. The brothers were trying to convince fellow Anglican planters to join them in hiring a teacher and expanding their school. Most refused, and the Assembly quickly ruled that slaves could only be taught within private families.

Disaffected with Anglican religious and civil authority, the Bryans and a few fellow planters reacted by leaving the church entirely and establishing their own interracial Independent Presbyterian Church, with their "Negro School" teacher doubling as preacher. This act of interracial public rebellion could not stand. By March 1742, authorities had confiscated Bryan's journal, containing "sundry enthusiastick Prophecies of the Destruction of *Charles-Town*, and the Deliverance of the Negroes from their Servitude." They charged "that by the Influence of the said

Hugh Bryan, great Bodies of Negroes have assembled together, on Pretence of religious Worship, contrary to law, and destructive to the Peace and Safety of the Inhabitants of this Province." Performing religious convictions was a racial, political act: Bryan, his brother Jonathan, William Gilbert, Robert Ogle, and all who had been "propagating the aforesaid Notions, or assembling of Negroes, and preaching to them at private Houses without Authority" were brought before Chief Justice Benjamin Whitaker and a Grand Jury on 7 March 1742. In simultaneous actions, a foreman pleaded for a court house, a better jail, and, most importantly, for "*an Act to ascertain the Manner and Form of electing Members to represent the inhabitants of this Province in the Commons House of Assembly*, the Qualifications therein mentioned being (as we apprehend) too small, and may be of ill Consequence." Authorities moved swiftly against these evangelical planters and their families performing blackness alongside "Negroes." They insured that radical evangelists would not serve on the Assembly, though it is far from clear that the Bryans advocated immediate emancipation, let alone revolution.[35] To the political and religious authorities, what J. L. Austin would call "the speech act" of preaching liberation – of teaching slaves to declare "I am free" – was an *act* of rebellion because it materialized an individual and collective body capable of revolt.

A year later, in 1743, Anglican Commissary Garden decided that he had better lead the interracial movement toward black literacy himself and redirect it toward obedience rather than revolt. He initiated a fund drive to build a school for Charles Town's "Negroes and Indians." He planned to purchase slaves, teach them to read the Bible, and employ them as schoolmasters to teach "all such Negro or Indian Children as may be born in the said Colonies," without any charge to their masters. He focused on Ephesians 6:5: "Slaves be obedient to your masters." The students of the new school (which lasted until 1764 despite later laws banning it), however, interpreted the Bible for themselves. By 1746 the school had graduated twenty-eight children and enrolled fifty-five more, along with fifteen adult night students. Itinerancy, liberation rhetoric, and black literacy set the stage for a more radical interpretation of the scriptures, and by 1780, the Annual Methodist Conference passed a directive that all "traveling preachers" ought to set their slaves free and that "slavery is contrary to the laws of God, man, and nature."[36]

Interracial schools popped up in unlikely places. After eight thousand Philadelphians gathered to hear Whitefield in the spring of 1740, a former dance master there, having been convinced of the sinfulness of his profession, established an interracial school. In less than a month he had "no less than 53 Black Scholars." Initially he was arraigned in violation of the law forbidding teaching black children how to read, but after his revivalist defense, he was "order'd by the Foreman of the Grand Jury to continue his School without Interruption."[37] As the Awakening spread, and as "Negros and Indians" became visible as a part of the body politic, a few were granted limited access to literacy, at the cost of a new attempt at control.

Laws emerged across the South as officials attempted to staunch radical notions of how to perform blackness. In 1744, for example, Virginia arrested laymen who gathered to read Whitefield's sermons aloud instead of attending their parish church, and by 1747 the colony had instituted a law against itinerant preachers. Itinerancy had been banned in colonies such as Connecticut as early as 1742, but it continued throughout the colonies nonetheless. Itinerants circulated through the colonies, providing a much more efficient means of mass communication than newspapers, political or religious tracts. They established the route to be taken some years later by professional actors.[38] Some itinerants continued to preach anti-slavery.

If white colonists' conversion performances are viewed as appropriations of African spirit possession – as performances of blackness – they may be said to function as precursors to the minstrel shows that gained popularity a century later. Lower-class and middle-class Europeans forged a sense of community with each other, simultaneously articulating their cross-racial desires and fears, by imagining and borrowing performance practices from African spiritualism. This blackface disclosed some Europeans' identification with Africans and African Americans at the same time that it revealed their unease with and displacement of all they considered black. During the Great Awakening, the justification for this process of "love and theft" was "pure salvation" instead of "pure fun."[39] There are many important historical differences, of course, between the two cultural performances, of conversion and minstrelsy, not the least of which is that Africans, African Americans, Europeans, and European Americans converted together in the earliest street revivals. For a few, this momentarily promised hope for a joint future without slavery.

Yet another performance of blackness emerged: Africans and African Americans forged alliances across disparate tribal lines by performing a unifying "blackness" or "African-ness" through African spirit possession as well as revolts. Since conversions visually resembled West African spirit possession, African and West Indian women such as Charles Town's market critics suddenly had a safe way to engage in their own religious practice of spirit possession, under cover but in full view of their fellow townspeople. Spirit possession meant a distinguished visit from a god or an ancestor with a crucial and a positive message, and the ancestors ferried requests to God, so their presence was reassuring. Spirit possession shared certain characteristics across West African, sub-Saharan, and Caribbean cultures: it typically began with dancing and rhythmic chants and drumming, involved a period of "overbreathing" or deprivation followed by a short collapse, then moved to a stage of accelerated activity, marked by "a fine tremor of head and limbs; sometimes grosser, convulsive jerks," and, finally, sleep or a sleep-like state. The possessed might fall into a "fit" or leap into the air. In his defense of the idea that African spirit possession affected American conversion performances, Raboteau explained that while drumming was typically forbidden, "hand-clapping, foot-tapping, rhythmic preaching, hyperventilation, antiphonal (call and response) singing, and dancing are styles of behavior associated with possession both in Africa and in this country."[40] Since African drumming served the purpose of communication and also signified an African basis for possession rituals, it was quickly banned.

Herskovits and Raboteau both argue that African ecstatic behavior influenced American conversions. As late as the Second Great Awakening, for instance, slaves shaved their heads during conversions, reflecting Yoruban and Dahomean-influenced rituals. Water cults in Nigeria and Dahomey may have inspired Baptist rituals of immersion. African American Christian conversion narratives often mention nighttime woods and a "little man," evoking African notions of nighttime spirits and the West African trickster who not only tests man but also acts as a mediator between man and God.[41]

African customs were also echoed in the revivalist format of incorporating songs and multiple, overlapping speakers into the religious observance. The African tradition of call and response was translated into a participatory service in which multiple voices interacted. Significantly, "in the black charismatic spiritual tradition, women do not allow the preacher the last word": their bodies and voices intervene, interrupt, and interpret.[42] An itinerant preacher from Long Island, for example, organized a service in which

one would make a short Prayer, then another gave a Word of Exhortation; Then one would propose a Psalm, than another a Prayer, then another a word of Exhortation, and so on, without any certain Order or Method, to that in one

Meeting of 2 or 3 Hours, there would be it may be 20 or 30 distinct Exercises carried on by 5 or 10 distinct Persons; some standing to the Pulpit, some in the Body of Seats, some in the Pews and some up Gallery; and oftentimes several of them would speak together; so that, some praying, some exhorting & terrifying, some singing, some screaming, some crying, some laughing and some scolding, made the most amazing Confusion that ever was heard.

An Anglican observer in Charles Town perceived such interracial call and response services as madness: "There were about the Town singing Processions of Hundreds, the Voices with *no* Uniformity or set Rules, but every one delivering the *Tell* he was particularly inspired with, join'd with all the mad Gestures and Actions that *Franticks* show."[43]

Many Africans and African Americans in the South, like "black Yankees," perceived the Christian message to be that "slavery and the slave trade were the great sins of the white man and his pagan African allies," and God was about to punish those sins and benefit African Americans in the process. Gradually Christian practices were incorporated into West African and Caribbean practices, and African customs transposed into Christian ones, over a period of many years.[44] As Africanist scholar Cheikh Anta Diop illustrated in his groundbreaking work in the 1970s, Christianity, Judaism, and Islam are all rooted in African traditions: in ancient Egypt 25 December was celebrated as the birthday of the sun God Ra; the term "Christ" emerged in the fourth century from a similar Egyptian expression referring to Osiris, the Redeemer who died and rose again to save humans; and the trinity and virgin birth have precursors in African religious philosophy. Emmanuel K. Twesigye points out that Moses, one of the crucial figures in revivalist sermons, was born in Africa, raised at the Egyptian royal court, educated in the Egyptian Religion of the Mysteries, and married to the "daughter of a Kushite/African priest who further educated him and counseled him on his role as both prophet and priest."[45] The performance of Christianity and of African spirit possession was more closely linked than most colonists realized, both in the past and in their present.

African and African American slave women who operated the most popular fruit and vegetable market in Charles Town used evangelism to cover their re-appropriation of African traditions. For them, conversions meant publicly owning African performance traditions, in full sight of those whites trying to appropriate them. Conversions meant they could call out, in code, the evils of the culture. To some West Africans, it also meant that their souls could visit Africa, as in their dreams. African religions tended to view God as a "Protector of the poor" who passed judgment on the sinful in a world that merged the secular with the sacred and balanced self and society. The Bible, too, promised that the poor would inherit the *earth*, not just a heavenly reward. African religions, like Christianity, spoke of death and immortality, though African death was a step toward ancestor status, toward immortality fashioned through one's progeny, family, rituals, and accomplishments.[46]

Inter-colonial communication among enslaved and free blacks grew as a result of outdoor, nighttime religious gatherings. African Americans created a separate inter-colonial identity through what became the independent black evangelical movement in the later eighteenth century. Anti-slavery revolts followed, and it took time for authorities to retaliate through government regulations and church hierarchies.[47] Having found an inhabitable public body, African Americans built their own institutions and tried to hold whites accountable for theirs. By the Revolutionary period, black preachers such as George Liele, Sampson Bryan, Lott Cary, and Andrew Bryan built black congregations, generating black teachers, and validating the need for black assemblies. And shortly thereafter, despite serious opposition, female preachers joined the ranks of female market exhorters who critiqued the elite.

As the Great Awakening emerged, Southerners re-classified slaves. When human beings were for sale, they were still called slaves, and were still visually equated with horses by pictorial illustrations of similar size and placement. However, when slaves were offered for re-sale, or reported as runaways, the men and children were routinely called "Negroes," while women and girls sixteen years old and up were called "Wenches," with qualifiers ranging from "Angola" to "Mustee" to "Yellow." At that time, indentured servants who ran away, as well as French and Spanish laborers, were equally likely to be described as of a "swarthy" or "black" complexion.[48] "Race" and nationality, like "race" and religion, were loosely linked, as non-English colonists as well as slaves and evangelicals were deemed "black."

By 1745, after the Revival was well established, however, slaves suddenly appeared in the pages of the *South-Carolina Gazette* as "Negro Women" and "Negro Men" instead of being labeled more equivocally.[49] In other words, possession enabled Angolans, Senegalese, Gambians, and their fellow Africans to claim status as equals on the basis of gender designation. In the newly redeployed racial coinage, the same gendered terms that applied to whites applied to blacks. Humanity followed the performance of evangelical Christianity and possession, and depended upon the intersection of race with gender. The moment blacks were labeled the same as whites in terms of gender, however, they were re-marked as unequal in terms of race: they were, with a new uniformity, labeled "Negro." This "ritual misnaming" was an effort to erase newly created African nationality and cross-tribal loyalties.[50] It also conflated free black with slave status and combated the notion of a morally upper-class Christian race.

Public conversions served multiple and often contradictory functions, fulfilling a desire to establish intra-racial, inter-colonial, and – for a very few – interracial, connections, but also feeding the conflicting, dominant desire to continue to link race with skin color as a means of governing those connections. Race intersected with religion and politics within a nexus of performativity that also articulated gender. And this gender performance was linked to industry or intelligence.

When African and African American women market critics partici-pated in evangelical gatherings, their exhortations echoed with the power that they possessed as intelligent and industrious businesswomen. Just as audiences who have seen actors in numerous productions remember aspects of their earlier performances and incorporate them into their understanding of the scene at hand, those who listened to market women exhort heard more than simply their excoriations of sinful colonial cul-ture. They heard the haunting echoes of the women's voices calling out the prices of produce, controlling the domestic economy in ways that baffled and enraged local authorities. As these market critics were surely aware, their layered voices critiqued their status as objects of auction block rituals, lawfully for sale.[51]

European American critics were expected to embody virtue more than intelligence or industry. The first published rationale for admitting colonial women to the world of the press, in fact, was "to promote Virtue and real Goodness": the editors of the *New England Courant* announced in their 25 June–2 July 1722, issue that, with that as their goal, they had "lately admitted two of the *Fair* Sex into our Society."[52] "Fair" in this context signified not just female, but also white, well-bred, and virtuous.

To shift the focus onto their reasoning power and business acumen, some European American women began to experiment with feminine instead of masculine pseudonyms, so that their appearances in print were not attributed to male intelligence (as Elizabeth Timothy's clearly were). For example, Elizabeth Magawley sent a letter to the *American Weekly Mercury* in 1730/31 under the pen name "Generosa." She argued that there were, in fact, "Women of Sense" in the colonies. She undermined traditional notions of ladylike virtue by pointing out that "the Word Ladies is an ambiguous Term, to which no single Idea can be affix'd." A couple of years later, in 1733, New York widows published a petition protesting their second-class status despite their industry. They, too, claimed their gender as well as their prerogatives as Americans: "most of us are she Merchants, and as we in some measure contribute to the Support of Government, we ought to be Intituled [entitled] to some of the Sweets of it."[53] These performance critics represented women as industrious, tax-paying Americans.

The Awakening forcefully raised this issue of American-ness: who could claim to be "American"?[54] Female exhorters of every nationality claimed American-ness through their conversion performances, and Whitefield and Wesley, curiously, assisted them. Whitefield lived simultaneously at the center and at the margins of English and American culture. The son of an English innkeeper, he worked his way through Oxford University as a servant to wealthier students. He joined John Wesley off campus to preach to the impoverished and imprisoned, thereby earning the derision of fellow Oxford students, who had already tagged Wesley and his other colleagues as the "Holy Club." Ordained an Anglican minister, Whitefield was soon driven from British pulpits for his extreme views. He followed Wesley, launching missionary excursions to the colonies. From 1735 to 1738 John and his brother Charles Wesley conducted missionary work in Georgia, establishing a ready, often working-class, audience for Whitefield, who shortly thereafter set up an orphanage there. Whitefield made seven trips in all to the colonies. He arrived for his second tour of the colonies in 1740, a year after Timothy took over the *Gazette*. He quickly established himself through a religious rhetoric of liberation that prompted, willy-nilly, a more democratic notion of America. And he helped devise a rhetoric of damnation that enabled colonists to negotiate their way through or past slavery for decades to come.

Theatre critics have often viewed church-related activity as the enemy of the drama, noting that religious fundamentalists have routinely closed down theatres. The itinerant preachers of America's Great Awakening, however, assumed starring roles in a colonial drama that delayed the development of professional theatre in America for decades – not so much by arguing against it, but by standing in for it. This religious theatre was central to colonial cohesion, granting colonists a seemingly common performance through which to articulate American-ness as well as a way to form alternative communities. Evangelical conversions and

African tribal and Muslim spirit possessions galvanized the body politic, providing a cultural performance that all could see, enact, or reject. Performances of possession linked colonists as Americans. Actual theatrical performances in Charles Town were few and far between, but Timothy worked hard to grant Whitefield, arguably the most brilliant actor of the day, ample coverage.[55] Her advance coverage of his visits established a consumer appetite for religious conversion even before he arrived.

In 1706 South Carolina had begun the process of establishing the Anglican Church as the representative church of the colony. It never became the majority choice, however, as many found it unfulfilling and some among the upper ranks, often Deistic in their leanings, deemed it a formal obligation rather than a source of spiritual enrichment. Nonetheless, all of Charles Town's citizens paid taxes to support the church, whether or not they belonged, and laws protected Anglican clergy from "disparagement" so that their authority would remain intact. Jealous of the ministers' power, the Anglican vestry, comprised primarily of wealthy planters and small landholders, refused to set up any of the institutional safeguards standard in other denominations. For example, they did not install an Anglican bishop in the American colonies, reserving for themselves the power to hire priests, often on year-to-year contracts so that the priests' allegiance to the lay vestry would outweigh their obedience to the Bishop of London and his representative in the new world, Commissary Garden. As a result, Anglican church-goers could only be confirmed in England, by an English bishop. And only those so confirmed were allowed to take communion in the colonies.[56] Only white aristocratic bodies confirmed on English soil were understood by Anglicans to be visibly representative of the full power of true salvation, and they were, in turn, ensconced as representative Americans in colonial government. Unlike New England, South Carolina had no rule preventing church officials from doubling as government officials. Partially as a result of this refusal to share power, the Anglican Church failed to ingratiate itself with the local population in Charles Town.

Dissenters already included Huguenots, Baptists, and Quakers, as well as the Presbyterians who had been encouraged to settle in the Carolinas at the end of the seventeenth century to guarantee the colony's defense against the French and Spanish Catholics to the South. Non-Anglicans were required to apply for a charter before building a church, and to hold their religious meetings in private, but they were allowed to vote and hold civic office. Few slaves had converted in the seventeenth century, but already civil authorities perceived those initial conversions as a threat. Virginia passed a law in 1662 dictating that transforming African slaves into Christians "in no way altered their social standing." By 1708, when blacks began to outnumber whites in South Carolina, many plantation owners opposed ministers on the issue of converting slaves. Nine separate South Carolina ministers reported to the Bishop of London in 1724 that it was difficult to convert slaves because "their Masters will not consent to Have them Instructed."[57]

However, the new evangelical religion did not depend upon instruction: the conversion experience replaced catechism, which meant that those denied English print literacy had a new and easier access to respectability and "knowledge" of Christ. And they could find salvation *on American soil.* In South Carolina, converts' claim on salvation was peculiarly representative of American-ness, poised as it was against official Anglican rites on English soil. The Reverend Anthony Gavin baptized "almost as many blacks as whites" on his 1738 sweep through the country around Charles Town, preaching anti-slavery as well as liberation theology. When Whitefield arrived in Charles Town, then, even though he himself did not preach anti-slavery, evangelism was associated in the local public mind with anti-slavery as well as American-ness.[58]

Because Whitefield's services were ecumenical, congregants from different church denominations prayed together, often in outdoor street services, because the crowds could not be accommodated indoors. Suddenly, and for the first time, rites that were not strictly Anglican were allowed a public outdoor forum in Charles Town. Meetings were often held at night, increasing their instability and subversive potential. Whitefield himself faced possible impeachment for failing to use the traditional Book of Common Prayer.

Those who read or listened to others read Elizabeth Timothy's *Gazette* found useful information about evangelical Calvinism. While predecessors believed that Christians atoned specifically for *Adam's* original sin, Whitefield held that *all* individuals were full of original sin, so that suddenly it became legitimate to name the wealthy Anglican plantation owners, the church and civic elite, as sinful.[59] Additionally, if all were equally sinful, all equally able to convert, then any one American body, logically, could represent another or the group as a whole.

However obliquely, this acknowledgment of universal sinfulness and representative power contributed to the beginnings of revised notions of political representation in America, as is evident in one of the first Whitefield reviews that Timothy published. Harvard-educated Josiah

Smith reported that he was especially pleased to hear Whitefield's doctrine of *universal* original sin. Smith expressed surprise that anyone would
want to undermine this doctrine, since "a public Representation of
Persons, is the general Principle upon which the World now acts, in all
national Affairs, and from whence alone the Justice of them, in my
Opinion must emerge." Any one sinner could represent another in
America, Smith reasoned. Whitefield, however, stopped short of dismantling the idea of the elect. It was John Wesley who attacked that
doctrine. He struck at the heart of Anglicanism and Congregationalism,
which had rested on the authority of an agreed-upon leader and the idea
that the church certified that leader as a *"visible saint"*: since civic and
religious leaders were thus singled out by God, obeying them was obeying
God.[60] If there were no visible saints, if everyone had access to God's
"free grace" through conversion on American soil, as Wesley contended,
then community leaders could be disobeyed.

Charles Brockwell, an Anglican dispatched to Salem, Massachusetts, by
the Society for the Propagation of the Gospel in Foreign Parts, abhorred
the success of what became known as "enthusiastic" preaching, precisely
because it granted congregants a sense of their own bodies as representative entities. Brockwell was especially alarmed that members of the
community, including the dispossessed and disenfranchised, began to
preach on their own. American colonists began, in fact, to represent
themselves onstage, in unaccountable ways, to claim their own base of
knowledge, independent of the mother country's appointed representatives: "Men, Women, Children, Servants, & Nigros [*sic*] are now become
(as they phrase it) Exhorters. Their behaviour is indeed as shocking, as
uncomon [*sic*], their groans, cries, screams, & agonies . . . some leaping,
some laughing, some singing, some clapping one another upon the back."
Anxious about this process of mutual self-representation, Brockwell
reported that their meetings often were "acted in the Night & often
continued to the noon of the next day." Children, white women and
blacks – French, Spanish, Native Americans, Irish, Welsh, Africans and
African Americans – discovered that they could, in fact, *represent themselves* as Americans on the revival stage. Whitefield appealed directly to
congregants, linking fearless self-righteousness with ideas of America, as is
evident from the repeated second-person address in his sermons: "What
then should you fear? You are made the righteousness of God . . . you
may be called 'The Lord our righteousness.' Of what then should you be
afraid? What shall separate you henceforward from the love of Christ?"[61]
By granting each individual colonist the righteousness that was normally

reserved for upper-class Anglican parishioners, and by placing that individual citizen's spiritual needs before the needs of the parish, Whitefield redefined virtue for American colonists and named them all representatives of God and the body politic.

Righteousness, however, in Whitefield's world could mean owning people, including the saved. Christian self-righteousness without a commitment to anti-slavery and anti-racism held the peculiar American institution of chattel slavery firmly in place, even as it undercut Anglican and Congregationalist rule. Except for the anti-slavery activists, this was an unholy club. It was, however, one of the few clubs open to women seeking to redefine respectability.

Respectability was the key to the successful performance of citizenship. Female editors were viewed as respectable because they appeared pseudonymously and worked out of familial need. In addition, work spheres were not yet rigidly defined by gender codes. Evangelical critics tried to claim respectability in a different way. They forged ethical standards of judgment based not on the Anglican footholds – reason and education, family and class – but rather on devoutness and sobriety, traits open to all. As Mathews explains, "*Respectable* came to mean 'pious' or 'moral,' rather than 'capable of eliciting respect by reason of social rank'; and *vulgar* came to mean 'impious' or 'immoral,' rather than indicating commonness or 'low social rank.'" Working and middle-class revivalists redefined virtuous gender performance: converting in the streets and exhorting in church were moral and righteous (read "white"), while theatre-going, dancing at balls, and attending assemblies were immoral and frivolous (read "black"): "Busy *Marthas*" attended a "House of Prayer, instead of a Tavern or Play-House."[62]

Public codes of performance shifted during the Awakening. Disobedience became a valid performance choice: ministers attacked one another publicly in Timothy's *Gazette*, so parishioners felt they could speak up, too. On 16 March 1740, Garden labeled Whitefield a Pharisee for preaching against fellow clergymen, which prompted Whitefield to reply that he would "break their slavish bands, and cast their chains away." Garden countered (from the pulpit of St. Philip's on 13 July 1740) that Whitefield was guilty of "disobedience" and "Disturbance of the Church's Peace," and Whitefield retaliated by forcing Garden to recuse himself from the bench. When Whitefield castigated religious and civil authorities in this manner in front of thousands – and Franklin estimated that he could preach to thirty thousand at once – each marginalized group within his audience imagined respectably throwing off its own particular oppressor.[63] Africans and African Americans envisioned the end of slavery, indentured servants release from their contracts, European and European American women and children escape from their dependence on their husbands and fathers, the lower classes – particularly young men – their economic freedom, and religious dissenters their freedom from the established church. For one brief cultural moment, as the Boston minister Thomas Prince explained, "they are almost together, both Whites and Blacks, both Old and Young, both Prophane and Moral, awakened."[64]

After converting, white and free black women critics could respectably, "in all innocence but with innate political shrewdness, cite Biblical passages and ministerial aphorisms to contradict or mitigate male authority." A certain "E. R.," emboldened by the Awakening, sent "Mr. Timothy" a poem critiquing courtship rituals, demanding "equal Laws" and "More Freedom." Timothy reprinted a satire which critiqued the relationship between heterosexual white women's reproductive capacity and colonization: it warned white men that if they continued to shun mating rituals within the white community, the "Security" of the colony would be jeopardized. The anxiety was not just about the number of offspring, but about their racial demarcation. If white men refused to take responsibility for the supposed "purity" of the race – if they continued to rape (or marry) black women and increase the number of "mulattoes" listed in the *Gazette* runaway ads, instead of marrying and impregnating white women – the colony itself would purportedly pay a price.[65]

Respectable upper-crust Anglicans and Congregationalists abhorred the practice of "encouraging WOMEN, yea, GIRLS to speak in the assemblies for religious worship," claiming that public speaking stripped women of virtue: "It is a shame: for WOMEN to speak in the church ... FEMALE EXHORTERS are condemned by the apostle" St. Paul.[66] They feared that evangelicals would eclipse Anglicanism and eliminate their tax base. Even more chilling was the notion that traditionalists' own spiritual status had become suspect. If they did not respond empathetically to the revival, perhaps they were not "saved," after all.

Upper-class men attacked lower- and middle-class women's attempts to shift the gender code and link feminine virtue to frugality. If their wives could not perform wastefulness, how could elite males distinguish themselves as elite? "Philanthropos," for example, complained that Whitefield transformed women "into great Sluts ... sending them to worship before the Deity in Garb they ought to be asham'd to pay a common visit in to their Fellow Mortals."[67]

Anxiety about fluid boundaries and altered rules of public performance fueled the backlash against revivalists. Instead of staying within their strictly bounded workplaces, people strayed to Whitefield's sermons. Instead of spending their money on goods and services within the colony, they contributed to the Reverend's charitable funds. And finally, instead of obeying authorities and remaining strictly within customary social boundaries, respectable people began to experiment with new social and bodily behaviors. While converts celebrated the respite offered by the revival, authorities voiced apprehension about their lack of productivity. Impressionable Harvard students and young unmarried Southern women shunned work and flocked to evangelical meetings as if to rock concerts: "neither Cold nor Rain, nor Snow, cou'd keep the Red-Riding-Hoods at Home by Night or by Day," and "not one Stroke of Work was done for _three Weeks_ by Man, Woman, or Child" during more than one revival.[68] It became respectable for pregnant women to participate in public gatherings: "a big-bellied Woman from an hind Seat straddled into the Pulpit to assist ... extending her Arms every Way, and not a Muscle of her Body but in Action." The very notion of such a woman usurping a public platform to speak outraged this listener, even though it was not uncommon for pregnant actresses to perform in the theatre, where their speeches were scripted in advance. Many were outraged by Whitefield's encouraging "the feeling Sisters" to "employ their Tongues" and sense their own fleshliness.[69]

New Light preachers lashed out against the flesh, but they simultaneously validated passionately embodied feelings through an "enthusiastic" preaching style, a bodily performance that was often sexualized. They spoke not at a distance from their bodies from a set script, but, as an actor might phrase it, from a bodily center, extemporaneously. They re-mapped the acceptable public performance of the body in the American colonies, granting women critics a more direct access, not only to their own bodies but also to others'. Evangelicals freely touched one another, shaking and holding hands, praying arm in arm, sometimes greeting each other with a ritual kiss. These performance practices were routinely viewed as immoral and even pornographic. Performing religion was tied to sexual politics. Boston's William Douglass worried that the Awakening had promoted "Wantonness between the Sexes" and Southern itinerant Charles Wood-mason charged that evangelical "Love Feasts" and "Kisses of Charity" led to "Lasciviousness or Wantonness, Adultery or Fornication."[70]

In fact, the diverse crowds that clustered around revivalist preachers sometimes resembled enthusiasts at a rock concert in terms of their shared excitement and bodily closeness. One believer escaped from the rowdy crush of congregants at an outdoor service by "finding a Way thro' under the Stage." A Boston critic, writing about the bodily closeness of the religionists, worked himself into frenzy: in his account, the markers governing race, class, gender, and age threaten to evaporate:

Multitudes of all Sexes and Ages are bro't under Conviction and *real Distraction* ... Men and Women, Boys and Girls, Whites and Blacks strole about ... crying, howling, barking, screaming, laughing ... two Teachers being set form one pray'd in one Room, the other in another, a Shoemaker in the third and a Girl in the fourth. – God knows what these Things will come to![71]

The reference to "all Sexes" betrays a submerged homophobia as well as an anxiety about uncontrolled and perhaps uncontrollable women and girls, and the references to teachers and the shoemaker signals an apprehension about class distinctions and authority. By the end of the passage, the observer sneaks a look at evangelists' exhorting in separate rooms as if peeping at prostitutes in a brothel.

Revival conversions simultaneously enacted and attempted to corral emotional and sexualized contact between European and African men and women. Many Europeans believed in a potent African sexuality, and by "projecting upon Africans their own internal disorder and then bringing blacks under discipline" through Christian rituals, they thought they could discipline their own sexuality as well.[72] Obviously, however, the black–white power imbalance and the number of mixed-race colonists forced some tortured projections on the part of whites: conversion allowed those elite whites who were guilty of raping slaves to project their own sinfulness onto lower- and middle-class whites commingling with blacks in revival meetings.

In various ways, early street conversions granted women a new sense of their bodies and their sexuality. Spurred on by young itinerant preachers, young women embraced the sexualized romance of becoming a bride to Christ, sometimes developing a devotion to a particular itinerant preacher. Women who had suffered abuse could announce that they were "defiled" and "full of Wounds, Bruises, and putrifying Sores," and then imagine their bodies anew, reclaiming them as chaste and untouched by any but Christ himself.[73] Free black and slave women gained a sense of their bodies through performing as if within their ancestors' bodies. Slave converts claimed a body that could never be owned: only their ancestors, or Christ, could possess them.

Efforts to control women's bodies, especially within courtship and reproductive rituals, were, of course, customary at the time, and contributed to women's desire for independent access to their own bodies and sexuality. Within conversions, European American women found a new avenue of bodily exploration. They played at sexual initiator, voyeur, pliant victim, outspoken critic. Whitefield framed one sermon especially for young Anglo women, telling them that Christ sought them as spouses and was "exceeding desirous of their beauty." Their marriage with Christ, he explained, entailed mutual choice, affective union, and obligation – an improvement over many earthly marriages. However, Whitefield told these women that they had to perform abjectness before Christ could free them: "you are deformed, defiled, enslaved, poor, miserable and wretched, very despicable and loathsome, by reason of sin." Christ's proposal could transform "slavery" into "liberty" if only they performed their bondage to sin. These women routinely spoke of being "ravished" by God's love as Whitefield preached. Others could look on, voyeuristically titillated by their pornographic display. As if narrating the progress of the conversion fits, from panting to jerking and shouting, Whitefield called out: "Your souls pant and long for him ... Christ doth lay hold on you; and by faith, you do lay hold on him; and thus the match is made." Bashfulness in this context was a sin: "Be not coy," Whitefield admonished, repeatedly asking the girls, "Do you desire one that is great ... Do you desire one that is rich ... wise ... potent ... good ... beautiful? ... one that can love you?" Whitefield informed the girls that Christ tells each spouse, "Thou hast ravished my heart." At the girls' death, Whitefield promised, "the nuptials between you shall be solemnized."[74] This theatre of the passions depended upon Whitefield as a provocateur, safely ensconced in spiritual power, leading Anglo women to a deeply ambivalent performance linking sin, bondage, sex, and salvation. Religion, "race," and pornography were inextricably linked. Men, too, imagined themselves as married to Christ: for instance, in the 1760s one male convert professed

to feel Ardent Desire After nearness ... to be Encirkled in those Blessed Arms of Everlasting love ... I do here, upon the bended knees of my soul ... Joyn my Self in Marriage Covenant to him ... I Do take thee for my head & husband for all times & Conditions, to love, to honour, & to Obey thee before all Others.[75]

For African and African American women, particularly slave women, the Awakening's focus on embodied emotion carried different meanings. Perhaps free black women also enjoyed the sensual experience of conversion, especially if they were participating within an intra-racial setting that valued a positive performance of blackness. Within African traditions, the secular and sacred, body and spirit, were merged rather than separated. Possession tendered African and African American women critics an opportunity to merge the everyday and the hallowed. Slaves may have valued conversions as a licensed means to repossess their bodies. For them, "the practice of loving one's body and consecrating it to the spirit [was] *in itself* a radical practice."[76]

Conservatives viewed these physical manifestations of conversion – the sudden release of all pent-up social reserve – as inhuman, bestial, sexual, and unclean, particularly when interracial interaction was involved. They dismissed exhorters as animalistic, low-class pretenders who transformed their bodies into grotesque shapes: they were a "Tribe of Lay-Animals," "crying out *stink*, shewing putrified *Sores*" and discharging "at our Tables as well as in the Pulpit Such Nastiness ... such spiritualizing of carnal Things." They were "an insolent brazen Crew of Raggamuffan Pole Cats."[77] The Awakening flung marginalized bodies onto the public stage. The lesions on that body, detractors argued, were the fault of those who suffered from them: they were "sores," not wounds. Revivalists – the previously unseen and ignored, the bodies that did not matter – were suddenly visible to the elite, and they appeared grotesque indeed. They were figured as a jumbled mass of disarticulated arms and legs, the bodies of women and men, all nations entangled. But the newly converted and the possessed, at least momentarily, recognized shared wounds inflicted by the unfeeling Anglican and Congregationalist elite. And they ran away from their abusers.

Before Whitefield's revivals, Timothy typically carried only one or two notices of runaways weekly, but after his visit anywhere from eight to thirteen runaway slaves might be listed weekly, and slaves were not the only ones to flee.[78] The revival, obviously, was only one of a myriad of factors contributing to the increase in runaways, but it was an important one, because it offered an ideology of freedom that might be shaped to various ends. One of Timothy's slaves, "Pierro," escaped after the first revival, prompting the editor to offer a reward and remind readers of the new fugitive slave law, which punished those harboring fleeing slaves. This dual emphasis is echoed in other contemporaneous notices, and eventually a new pictograph appears in Timothy's columns: the figure of a *fleeing* slave. One such pictograph shows the runaway's brand, warning that "whoever harbours the said Boy, may depend upon being severely prosecuted."[79] Radical evangelists were warned not to harbor fellow Christians of any "clime."

Slaves were not the only runaways. Wives, servants, and sailors also fled. Some followed itinerants or themselves preached. Of Whitefield, Deborah Sherman, for instance, wrote:

let the hard hearted Wretches say what they will, we will go to hear you preach, we will follow you, we will come to all your Lectures, have as many as you will, the more the better; and for my own Part, I would go with you with all my Heart to *Georgia*, and I know a great many more would do so too.[80]

Sherman exposed her infatuation with Whitefield, but also her relief at being able to articulate a rebellion against those who cajoled her "to keep at home." The repetition of "we [women] will go," not only signaled but actually helped her perform a gender consciousness and defiance of family strictures.

The reinstatement of the boundaries between men and women and between blacks and whites was accomplished in Charles Town through a variety of means, including various "Negro Acts." Perhaps one of the most curious and effective means of reinstating boundaries was a theatrical exhibit staged by Mr. Joel Potatfelt. On 30 May 1743, Timothy published a *Gazette* ad titled "TO BE SHEWN." For five shillings each, residents could pass through Mr. Potatfelt's home during certain appointed hours to view a living tableau which, for them, had the effect of a pornographic display: "a WHITE Negro Girl, of Negro Parents, she is as white as any *European*, has a lively Blush in her Countenance, grey Eyes, continuously trembling, and Hair frizzed as the Wool of a white lamb."[81] Even though she was visibly "white," she was still, the ad invited readers to conclude, inescapably a "Negro." Her "lively Blush" may have signaled her ostensible "whiteness," but it also marked her abject status, and her "trembling" eyes – or body – signified that Europeans need not fear her, not as a "Negro" or as a girl approaching womanhood. They could take voyeuristic pleasure in this exhibit. This "Negro Girl" muted the exhortations of the African and African American women in the Charles Town market and gestured toward European control over the fluid performances of blackness and whiteness. Charles Town's gentry could not control these performances nearly that easily, however. When female exhorters spoke out in revival gatherings, they, like Elizabeth Timothy, inadvertently prompted a renegotiation of social performances of various kinds. Their performing criticism constituted a complex street theatre, part guerrilla warfare and part obedience training.

As the next generation of women critics emerged, poetry readings and theatrical presentations began to replace religious performances as the primary entertainment and spiritual food, especially for the privileged classes. The new temples of art and salon-type parlor performances prescribed a very different kind of virtue and intelligence for Americans in general and women in particular. By the 1770s, a national discourse emerged, subsuming the Christian rhetoric of invisible salvation within a concept of the abstract American citizen. Enlightenment notions of the "rational body" revamped the performance of religion and affected its relationship with the performance of politics and race. The successors of the Great Awakening would have to revise their strategies for gaining admission to public debates.

NOTES

1 In the colonies, the two strands of political resistance that Paul Gilroy identifies in *Small Acts* – the politics of fulfillment (which challenges dominant structures to fulfill the promise of their rhetoric, mainly through verbal or textual means) and the politics of transfiguration (which operates under the radar screen to *perform* a utopian politics) – overlap (133–35). They are difficult to disentangle because words and gestures are inextricably intertwined and because any given performance serves multiple goals: an intra-racial performance that is under the radar screen may articulate a transformative interpretive community and simultaneously stage a challenge to dominant powers. For instance, many of the Angolan, Gambian, Senegalese, and West Indian critics who engaged in spirit possession engaged in a forbidden and utopian exchange of their disparate religious practices, transfiguring their social relationships with each other at the very moment that they appeared to onlookers to be evangelical Christians demanding "liberty." They created an Afric host body even as they were understood to be claiming a place as "citizens of Zion." Their host bodies, furthermore, constituted a political force, not a claim to an authentic, natural, stable, and racialized self. They established what Glissant calls a poetics of relation, a rhizomatic connection that speaks multilingually.

2 Edwards, "Sinners." Jonathan Edwards (1703–58), Yale graduate and minister in Northampton, Massachusetts, starting in 1729, was a leader of the Awakening in New England. Evangelical culture was rooted in "the Puritan emphasis upon the spiritual journey of the individual, and the deeply emotional, sometimes passionate, always personal, connection with God" (Westerkamp, *Women*, 87); Africans and the Scots-Irish added a communal emphasis to spirit possession.

3 McLoughlin, *Revivals*, viii. For overviews of the Awakening, see Bonomi, Lambert, Clark. See Westerkamp's *Triumph* for an overview of the British movement. Historians usually contend that the Great Awakening either loosened social and political strictures and provided new symbologies (Stout,

Nash, Heimert and Miller) or continued the conservative policies of earlier efforts to purge religion (Heyrman, and Butler, "Enthusiasm"), but I am arguing that the performative dimension of the Awakening meant that both radical and ultra-conservative effects emerged, simultaneously. Once staged, either in print or in person, a performance is viewed variously and acted upon in unpredictable and contradictory ways.

Regarding slave religion: my study, like many others, "seeks not to deny the opiate quality of much slave religion but to offer the suggestion that there were significant, identifiable black responses to religion which often stormed beyond submissiveness to defiance" (Harding, "Religion," 110). I acknowledge that slave masters often justified torture in the name of Christianity, and find studies such as Dwight N. Hopkins' *Down, Up, and Over* convincing in their scathing portraits of the uses of Christianity. I also agree with Maulana Karenga that conversions were often based on "culturally chauvinist assumptions" such as the notion that God created slavery so that whites could save blacks' souls (Karenga, "Black," 285; Earl, *Dark*, 5). I view as sound Peter H. Wood's conclusion that there was genuine disagreement among slaves regarding conversion ("Jesus," 1–7). Furthermore, I understand that resistance emerged in many guises: Albert J. Raboteau, Richard Brent Turner, Sylviane A. Diouf, and Paul E. Lovejoy, for example, have written tellingly of African Muslim resistance in the colonies, Ronald A. T. Judy, Allan D. Austin, and Terry L. Alford have illuminated African Arabic slave narratives, and Anthony B. Pinn has researched the African humanist tradition (Pinn, "African Americans"). It is also crucial to acknowledge that some Africans were exposed to Christianity in Africa, through seventeenth-century Portuguese missionaries and through contact with Christianized slaves that returned to Africa from Europe in the late eighteenth century (Raboteau, *Slave*, 6). In this chapter, then, I am not denying forces other than Christianity, nor am I denying the nefarious uses to which Christianity was put, but focusing upon one of many performative possibilities of resistance to those uses. This resistance was a part of a complex subjectivity incorporating what Lewis Gordon calls "a meaningful, multifaceted way of being" that involved necessary contradictions, with both conservative and radical effects (qtd. Pinn, *Terror*, 158). As Raboteau explains, even when the itinerant preaching and street conversions were superceded by hierarchical multi-racial Christian church congregations, "it was difficult to control [blacks'] efforts toward autonomy, particularly when the churches stressed an inner, personal, experimental approach to religion and thus encouraged individualism" (Raboteau, "Rule," 56).

4 The Anglican Church was "established" in the Chesapeake, Carolinas, and Georgia, and dominant in Virginia and Maryland (Westerkamp, *Women*, 76). In the North, the Congregational Church was "established": Connecticut's Congregational Church was finally disestablished in 1818; the Massachusetts legislature separated church and state in 1833 (Brekus, *Strangers*, 125).

5 Postscript, *Gazette* 12–19 September 1741: 1–2. [First] postscript to *Gazette* 25 June 1741: 1–2. For reviews of Whitefield's sermons, often in dialogue, epistolary, or sermon form, as "performances" see, for example, *Gazette* 31 May–7 June 1740: 2; 18 February 1745: 1.

6 Davis treats colonial religious dialogues as dramatic fare ("Plays," 222–34).

7 For information on the Timothy family's arrival in Philadelphia, see Linn and Egle, *Pennsylvania Archives*, 28–32. "Louis Timotheé" disembarked from the Ship Britannia of London and appeared at the Courthouse of Philadelphia on 21 September 1731. Between 8 September 1735, and 16 December 1736, "Lewis Timothy" purchased Land Plats for 801 acres on the Pon Pon and Santee Rivers: Series S213184, vol. 0003, page 00143, items 1, 2; Series S213019, vol. 0043, page 00200, item 1; Series S213019, vol. 0041, page 00072, item 0; Series S213184, vol. 0003, page 00519, item 02, South Carolina Department of Archives & History, Columbia, South Carolina.

8 Singer coined this term (*Traditional*, xiii). Carlson gives a useful overview of its emergence within performance studies in *Performance*, 16–17. See also Turner, *From Ritual*.

9 Norton, *People*, 71, 74; compared with Boston's 16,000, Philadelphia's 13,000, and New York's 11,000 (Bumsted and van de Wetering, *What*, 9; Weir, *Colonial*, 145). Wood considers the implications of this newly arrived *Black Majority* in South Carolina, the only colony so situated: in 1740 there were 39,155 slaves in South Carolina, 2,447 in Charles Town (Wood, *Black*, 153 n. 68).

10 See Wood, *Black*, 333–41, Appendix C, and 160–61, on slave arrivals in Charles Town from 1735 to 1740: 70 percent were from Angola, about 6 percent from Gambia, and 1 percent from the West Indies. The rest were captured in undisclosed regions in Western and Central Africa. Men outnumbered women, two to one. About 1 percent or 68 people were free blacks in 1740 (Wood, *Black*, 103, 157). Gomez provides a map of the West African slave trade ("Muslims," 676). Littlefield and Philips both argue that Senegambian slaves were accorded more respect and responsibility than other Africans: Littlefield attributes it to their knowledge of rice cultivation, Philips to their Islamic roots (Littlefield, *Rice*; Philips, "African," 236). Many enslaved Muslims were literate, well-traveled merchants who segregated themselves from other slaves, often in positions requiring administrative ability. Samuel Thomas, an Anglican missionary, started converting slaves in 1702, and St. Andrew's Parish laywomen followed suit in 1711 (Raboteau, *Slave*, 116; Dalcho, *Historical*, 336–37). Anglican missionaries, however, countenanced atrocities against slaves, to ingratiate themselves with slaveholders; some owned slaves (Wood, *Black*, 136–37).

11 Matory, for example, lists multiple Yoruban spirit possession rituals, associated with the deities Oyo, Shango, and Oshun ("Rival," 509). Oya is the wife of Shango, the god of thunder and lightning, and is associated not only with fertility but also with the wind that fans Shango's fire, destroying homes, trees, and crops.

12 See Wesley, *Free*. Wesley published an early indictment of slavery, largely borrowed from American Quaker Anthony Benezet's "Some Historical Accounts of Guinea" (1771): see Wesley, *Thoughts*.

13 See Lemay and Zall's edition of Benjamin Franklin's *Autobiography* (96). As a "poor afflicted Widow" with "six small Children and another hourly expected" during the first month of her editorship, Timothy succeeded partly by expanding her inventory. Initially she printed only English Bibles, Anglican Common Prayer Books, "primmers," hornbooks, and Poor Richard's Almanack, but within two years her inventory required twenty-five lines of print, including "Plays of Several Sorts" (*Gazette*, 4 January 1739: 4; 30 July–6 August 1741: 4). When her son assumed the editorship in May 1746, she opened a bookstore. When he died in 1781, his widow Ann Donavan Timothy edited the *Gazette* until her own death ten years later.

14 Almost half of New England's white women were literate, and despite lower literacy rates in the South, widows and single women there ran businesses, too. By 1820 thirty-two American women had worked as publishers (Mott, *American*, 25).

15 See Wood, *Black*, 247 on London's attempts at escape. In 1757 Elizabeth Timothy died, leaving three houses and a tract of land. Her attitude toward her eight slaves is also evident in her will: she bequeathed "to my said daughter Mary Elizabeth two Negro Woman Slaves named Molly and Flora to her and her heirs for ever ... to my daughter Catherine ... my Negro Slaves Dianah with her two Children Doll and Hagar" as well as "my Negro Slaves Named Abraham, Amsterdam and Judith." She regarded "her" slaves and their children as the property of her family, forever, and yet simultaneously used the language of the Awakening to humanize, homogenize, and mark them. Though they were property, they were gendered (and therefore humanized) as "women." However, wherever they were from and however long they had been in the colonies, they were all homogenized as "Negro" – they were marked racially rather than by nation of origin. Elizabeth Timothy's Will, written 2 April 1757, probated 6 May 1757, is on file at the Charles Town County Public Library, South Carolina Room, Charles Town, South Carolina. Her burial is noted in the St. Philip's Episcopal Church Burial Register (page 288 in the microfilmed original): see Smith and Salley, *Register*, 283. Peter Timothy's wife Ann signed a Release of Dower to Elizabeth Timothy, dated 15 August 1757 (Charles Town County Public Library, South Carolina Room, Charles Town, South Carolina), and according to the South Carolina Department of Archives and History (Columbia, South Carolina) Alphabetical Index, Elizabeth Timothy was also conveyed two pieces of property (Public Register Conveyances 1719–76 record series, 007 001). There are no further Timothy papers or *Gazette* ledgers.

16 On the 1720 law, see Wood, *Black*, 210; on women critics living "free from the government of their masters," see Hine and Thompson, *Shining*, 46–48. On the task system and market proscriptions, see Wood, *Black*, 138–39 and

210–11: gradually Anglican missionaries convinced planters to feed and clothe slaves and claim all of their time.

17   In the North, African American women created host bodies through Election Day and Pinkster celebrations. Women's singing and dancing literally incorporated African and African American culture and critiqued as well as appropriated white culture. On Election Day, blacks chose governors, kings, and judges entrusted with trying disputes, West African style. They donned masters' clothes to mock whiteness, and whites observed them, fueling a "train of racial burlesque and counterburlesque that surely helped inspire blackface miming" (Lott, *Love*, 47). Festivities incorporated African music and ring dancing: participants moved counterclockwise in a circle to enter the spirit world of the ancestors. No US queen was elected, despite West Indian, Cuban, and Brazilian precedents, and typically men led the ring dance, but women did dance, sing, and clap (Piersen, *Black*, 126). Women also celebrated Pinkster, Dutch for Pentecost, a Christian holiday traditionally observed seven weeks after Easter. Associated with the rites of spring, Pinkster was especially popular in the Dutch-influenced areas of New York and New Jersey, where slaves were granted an unusual reprieve from work. As on Election Day, Pinkster celebrants engaged in role reversals, parades, singing, and dancing. Albany, New York, blacks, for example, took over Capitol Hill and renamed it Pinkster Hill for a week. A white observer noted the "Congo" dances, "King Charley," mock-generals in "British costumes" and wielding autocratic power (Gutman, *Black*, 333). Charley led flower-bedecked participants from the master's house to the burial ground, performing not only the trajectory of many a slave's life but also a reinterpretation of that trajectory in terms of surplus African arts, politics, and self-governance. As a 1770 eyewitness explains, couples danced as Charley's "vocal sounds were readily taken up and as oft repeated by the female portion of the spectators not otherwise engaged in the exercises of the scene, accompanied by the beating of time with their ungloved hands"; tellingly, the black women were every hue from "Ebon black to lily fair" (qtd. Stuckey, "African," 172–73). African praise songs at Pinkster enabled blacks to communicate among themselves, since very few colonists studied African languages (Stuckey, "African," 169). Over a thousand blacks, women as well as men, enslaved and free, danced on what was then "a general burying ground" in Washington Square within New York City, "'divided into numerous little squads, dancing and singing, "each in their own tongue," after the customs of their several nations in Africa'" (Gutman, *Black*, 332). Through these celebrations Northern African Americans maintained diverse ties to Africa and performed a common African American identity. Pinkster and Election Day revelries subsided as white anxieties increased, bans were put into effect, and as Northern free and freed blacks became citizens in the early nineteenth century (Buckley, "Paratheatricals," 430–31).

18 See Westerkamp, *Triumph*. Westerkamp also notes Dutch sources for conversion fits, particularly through Theodorus Jacobus Frelinghuysen, the Dutch minister in Raritan, New Jersey (*Women*, 86).

19 Le Goff, *History*, xi.

20 *Gazette* 18 February 1745: 2.

21 Postscript *Gazette* 18 June 1741: 2. See also, for example, 4–11 November 1739: 4; 2–9 October 1740: 3; 30 July–6 August 1741: 4; 16–23 August 1742: 1. Hall, *Things*, 7.

22 Raboteau outlines the debate between Melville J. Herskovits (pro) and E. Franklin Frazier (con) regarding whether or not African religions survived in the New World. See Raboteau, *Slave*, 48–92. See Pierson, *Black*, 149 on a "Christian upper-class." See Turner, *Africanisms*, on the Gullah language. The Gullah developed secret societies which linked notions of citizenship with membership in Gullah-led praise houses (Creel, "Gullah," 79). They held onto such West African customs as the "ring shout," a counterclockwise circular dance that often followed the conversion of a new member. In the ring shout, participants form a circle, stamping or "shuffling their feet and shaking their hands while bystanders outside the ring clap, sing, and gesticulate" (Creel, "Gullah," 80; see also Stuckey, "African").

23 See Lovejoy, *Slavery*. Arabic-speaking Muslims lived in many areas of West Africa: in the royal courts of coastal Waalo, Cayor, and Jolof; in Futa Toro along the Senegal River; in Bundu; in parts of Sierra Leone; in Oyo; and along the Niger River. On the BaKongo, see Creel, "Gullah," 80–82; on Sande, see Thompson, "Kongo," 153; Holloway, *Africanisms*, 5, 13; see also Fisher and Fisher, *Slavery*, 47. On the *bori* cult, see Montana, "Ahmed," 176, 190–91; Lovejoy, "Slavery," 6, 14, 20; Gomez, "Muslims," 707.

24 See Hayes, *And Still*, 8 on liberation theology. Raboteau, *Fire*, 157; Earl, *Dark*, 7, 174.

25 von Linne, *Systema*, 20–22.

26 Butler, *Bodies*, 2.

27 Babb, *Whiteness*, 23; Hall, *Things*, 69; Garden, Preface to "Take," 26–28.

28 *Gazette* 17–24 April 1742: 1. Wood, *Black*, 98–99, 234. By June 1742 the officials' anxiety about the revolutionary power of interracial anti-slavery evangelism extended to a fear of Native Americans and the French, against whom England had declared war. Reports arrived from Annapolis that the Native Americans in Somerset and Dorchester Counties planned "to massacre all the white People, and proceed to Philadelphia, and there to be join'd by their *swarthy* Brethren the French, and Northern Indians" (*Gazette* 16–23 August 1742: 1, my italics). Charles Town learned on 20 June 1744 that the British had declared war against the French and the "Indians."

29 Postscript, *Gazette* 18 June 1741: 2, my italics. Gilbert Tennent, a Scots-Irish Presbyterian minister, was one of the four sons of Reverend William Tennent (1673–1746), a religious refugee from Ireland who established the influential Log College seminary in Neshaminy, Pennsylvania, to educate young men for the Presbyterian ministry (1726–46). Princeton University, among other

institutions of higher learning, sprang from the Log College. Gilbert Tennent toured with Whitefield and visited Charles Town in April 1741.

30 I am especially indebted to Valerie Babb and Kim Hall for their insights into how this process of representation works.

31 Donkin, *Getting*, 26; Bumsted and van de Wetering, *What*, 75.

32 Bonomi, *Under*, 119; Raboteau, *Fire* 18–19.

33 On Stono, see Weir, *Colonial*, 193, Norton, *People*, 93. Most of the field slaves in South Carolina were Bantu-speaking Angolans like Jemmy; the relatively "homogeneous culture" of the different tribal groups who spoke some form of Bantu meant that they could communicate relatively easily – in fact, Holloway argues that the Bantu affected African American culture most deeply (*Africanisms*, xiii, 6–8). Scholars have thought that the restrictive "Negro Acts" were not enforced until after the Stono Rebellion, but Timothy's coverage proves that they were, in fact, established before then and may have contributed to the revolt (*Gazette*, 5–12 April 1739: 2). See also 1–8 January 1741: 4. Laws cannot fully curtail performance traditions once they have been launched, however. In terms of education, for example, blacks who knew how to read before reading was banned did not discontinue reading or teaching others to read, nor did wealthy whites necessarily follow the laws. A wealthy European American teenager, Eliza Lucas Pinckney (*c.* 1722–93), for example, taught two African American girls how to read and write while she ran her family's Charles Town plantation from 1739 to 1743, with the hope that they would, in turn, educate others (Harris, *American*, 111).

34 *Gazette* 18–25 July 1740: 3.

35 Cornelius, "*When*," 22; *Gazette* 20–27 March 1742: 1; *Gazette* 20–27 March 1742: 1. Indeed, while Jonathan Bryan gave his personal servant Andrew Bryan (*c.* 1716–1812) permission to preach in one of his barns in the mid 1770s, he did not free him, even on his deathbed. Andrew purchased his freedom from Bryan's son in 1790, two years after Jonathan's death (Thomas, *First*, 6–7). Baptised by the famous black Baptist George Liele (1752–1825) in 1782, Andrew Bryan founded the first black Baptist church in Georgia, perhaps the first Baptist Church in the colonies, in Savannah in December 1777.

36 *Gazette* 11 April 1743: 4; Pennington, *Thomas*, 29–30; Purifoy, "Methodist," 19.

37 *Gazette* 18–25 July 1740: 2.

38 McLoughlin, *Revivals*, 90–91. Many of the itinerants were Yale and Harvard-trained men who had to pretend they had no formal training in order to emulate Whitefield's new style of preaching, but others had no credentials at all (Stout, *New*, 200).

39 In this paragraph I am indebted to Lott, *Love*, 6–8.

40 Simpson, *Black*, 131–32; Parrinder, *West*, 78; Raboteau, *Slave*, 65. Maultsby includes "Protestant psalms, hymns, and spiritual songs" in her list of compositions altered by Africans in the New World ("Africanisms," 198).

41 Raboteau, *Fire*, 155.

42 Anderson, "Calling," 119. Eventually this multiplicity of voices was transformed into a lay leader's reading of "the psalms line by line for the congregation to follow," restoring some of the set structures of Anglican and Congregational church services, but that custom took years to develop and was not uniformly applied (Piersen, *Black*, 66). Marks qtd. Raboteau, *Fire*, 150.

43 Postscript, *Gazette* 9 January 1742: 1; *Gazette* 14–21 June 1742: 5.

44 Piersen, *Black*, 149. Over a hundred years later, for instance, a black female exhorter in Virginia still combined African spirit possession with the Christian faith, and "with many extravagant gestures, cried out that she was 'young King Jesus'" (Piersen, *Black*, 71).

45 Diop, *African*; Karenga, "Black," 279–80; Twesigye, "African," 26.

46 Hopkins, "Slave," 4–5; Karenga, "Black," 274.

47 By 1815 white Methodists began to protest that black leaders were not properly disciplining their brethren. In 1817 Black Charles Townians – 4,300 strong from one church alone – seceded and joined the African Methodist Episcopal Church. (During the American Revolution, the Anglican Church had been disestablished and the Protestant Episcopal Church organized in its place.) By 1822 black freedman Denmark Vesey, a member of this new church, and thirty-four others were hanged on charges of plotting to seize Charles Town. The church was forced to disband, members admonished to return to mixed-race congregations. Efforts surfaced to make black literacy illegal. Reportedly "Vesey quoted Bible passages on the deliverance of the Children of Israel from Egypt, invited slaves to challenge white preachers about key Bible verses, and incited violence by reading 'from the Bible where God commanded, that all should be cut off, both men, women, and children'" (Cornelius *"When,"* 30). "George Liele," *African American Biographical Database*, Bell & Howell (1998–2000), 30 August 2000 <http://141.161.93.5/wm/aabd>: *The Negro in American History*, p. 17, 63, 66; "Stono," *African American Biographical Database*, Bell & Howell (1998–2000), 30 August 2000<http://141.161.93.5/wm/aabd>: *Negro Builders and Heroes*, p.41; "Jonathan Bryan," *African American Biographical Database*, Bell & Howell (1998–2000), 30 August 2000<http://141.161.93.5/wm/aabd>: *The First Colored Baptist Church*, pp. 21–22.

48 See *Gazette* 4–11 November 1739: 4; 30 July–6 August 1741: 4; 2–9 October 1740: 3; 16–23 August 1742: 1. See also Davis, *Who*.

49 For instance, the 30 July–6 August 1741 *Gazette* lists "A big belly'd run away Negro Woman" (4), and the 18 February 1745 two "Negro Men" and a "Negro Woman" (4). "Negro," of course, was the word for "black" in Spanish and Portugese, and had been in and out of circulation for some time.

50 Bassard, *Spiritual*, 11.

51 See Carlson, *Haunted*. Spillers explains that slavery "elaborated 'home' and 'market-place' as a useless distinction" (Spillers, "Changing," 28).

52 Bleyer, *Main*, 56.

53 Qtd. Harris, *Women*, 138, 252.

54 See Spengelman, *Mirror* for a definition of New World American-ness that recognizes the disparate languages, cultures, and histories of those living in the landmass called America.

55 See Wilmeth and Curley, "Timeline," for a theatrical timeline (Wilmeth and Bigsby, *Cambridge*, 20–109). By the late seventeenth century, students at Harvard and William & Mary engaged in dramatics, but the first professional performances recorded in Charles Town were those of British actor Anthony Aston in 1703. By 24 January 1735, Henry Holt, a London dancer and performer, had gathered a company in Charles Town. For two years Holt produced plays, first at Charles Town's Court Room and then, starting in February 1736, at the newly built Queen Street Theatre. The fare was standard British: Addison's *Cato*, Otway's *The Orphan*, Lillo's *The London Merchant*, Farquhar's *The Recruiting Officer*. Perhaps Holt fled Charleston's smallpox epidemics in 1738 and 1739, or perhaps his rocky partnership with Charles Shepherd drove him away. By 1740 Reverend Whitefield's visits had made theatre unnecessary as well as unwelcome. See Johnson and Burling, *Colonial*, 48, 112–23.

56 Bonomi, *Under*, 89.

57 Mathews, *Religion*, 10; Bonomi, *Under*, 120. As of 1700, there were approximately 4,000 white residents in South Carolina: "some 500 were Huguenots, 1300 Presbyterians, 400 Baptists, and 100 Quakers, while another 1700 adhered to the Church of England" (Bonomi, *Under*, 32). Between 25 and 33 percent of all adult Americans "attended worship or claimed formal church membership" at this time, but as many as two-thirds of New Englanders joined a church (Butler, "Coercion," 18). Between 1740 and 1743 over 40,000 colonists converted to evangelical Protestantism (McLoughlin, *Revivals*, 45). Before the Great Awakening, most plantation owners refused missionaries the time to catechize slaves. Sometimes planters made exceptions for their house slaves, many of whom regarded Christian ministers as enemies who tried to cut their ties to their ancestors and families. The ministers, for their part, often regarded ancient African religious practices as barbarism.

58 Bonomi, *Under*, 119. Also see Ruttenberg, "George." By the 1780s the Methodists, Presbyterians, and Baptists had joined the Quakers in publicly condemning slavery.

59 As one commentator explained, "Adam was the Representative of his Posterity" (*Gazette* 26 June–1 July 1740: 1).

60 *Gazette* 5–12 January 1740: 2; Miller qtd. in Rutman, *Great*, 142, 160.

61 Qtd. Lovejoy, *Religious*, 65–66; qtd. McLoughlin, *Revivals*, 61–62.

62 Mathews, *Religion*, 35. Irish preacher Samuel Finley, January 1741, qtd. Heimert and Miller, *Great*, 153–54. In a typical year there might be three to six balls. Assemblies were a new elite custom, launched in the late 1730s (Garden, "Take," 18). While Garden regarded the balls as "innocent," to Whitefield they were immoral.

63 Garden, "Take," 5; Lovejoy, *Religious*, 37.

64 Qtd. Bumsted and van de Wetering, *What*, 127.

65 Mathews, *Religion*, 105; *Gazette* 15 August 1743: 3; *Gazette* 11 April 1743: 1.

66 Reverend Charles Chauncy (1705–87) qtd. Bonomi, *Under*, 123–24.

67 (First) Postscript, *Gazette* 25 June 1741: 1–2.

68 Postscript, *Gazette* 18 June 1740: 1. All citations in this paragraph, unless otherwise noted, are from this same source.

69 *Gazette* 9–16 October 1740: 1–2.

70 Bumsted, and van de Wetering, *What*, 144–45. By the 1750s a Massachusetts group associated itself with Antinomianism, or the belief that their direct communion with God meant they were not subject to man's laws: women could leave legal husbands and claim spiritual ones, even having children with their newly adopted spiritual husbands.

71 Heimert and Miller, *Great*, 130; "Bostonian," Postscript, *Gazette* 18 June 1741: 1.

72 Mathews, *Religion*, 71.

73 Qtd. Brekus, *Strangers*, 40. Brekus reads the passages quoted in this paragraph as evidence that the women suffered from "a greater sense of original sin than men," but I regard the passages as proof of the women's desire to perform their sense of violation in an imperfect world.

74 Whitefield, "Christ."

75 Diary of Benjamin Lyon, 26 December 1763 and 23 July 1765, qtd. Juster, *Disorderly*, 63 and Westerkamp, *Women*, 89.

76 Anderson, "Calling," 128.

77 *Gazette* 25 May 1745: 2.

78 See, for example, *Gazette* 30 July–6 August 1741: 4, and 18 February 1745: 4.

79 *Gazette* 7–14 June 1740: 3; *Gazette* 13 February 1744: 3.

80 *Gazette* 18 March 1745: 1. Runaways notices were often briefer, and posted by those abandoned. See, for example, *Gazette* 9–16 October 1740: 2; *Gazette* 1 April 1745: 4; *Gazette* 11–18 June 1741: 4.

81 *Gazette* 30 May 1743: 3.

WORKS CITED

Alford, Terry L. *Prince Among Slaves: The True Story of an African Prince Sold into Slavery in the American South*. Reprint. Oxford: Oxford University Press, 1986.

Anderson, Telia U. "'Calling on the Spirit': The Performativity of Black Women's Faith in the Baptist Church Spiritual Traditions and Its Radical Possibilities for Resistance." *African American Performance and Theater History: A Critical Reader*. Ed. Harry J. Elam, Jr. and David Krasner. Oxford: Oxford University Press, 2001: 114–31.

Austin, Allan D. *African Muslims in Antebellum America: A Sourcebook*. New York and London: Garland Publishing, 1984.

Austin, J. L. *How to Do Things with Words*. Oxford: Clarendon Press, 1962.

Babb, Valerie. *Whiteness Visible: the Meaning of Whiteness in American Literature and Culture.* New York: New York University Press, 1998.

Bassard, Katherine Clay. *Spiritual Interrogations: Culture, Gender, and Community in Early African American Women's Writing.* Princeton: Princeton University Press, 1999.

Bleyer, Willard Grosvenor. *Main Currents in the History of American Journalism.* Boston: Houghton Mifflin, 1927.

Bonomi, Patricia U. *Under the Cope of Heaven: Religion, Society, and Politics in Colonial America.* Oxford: Oxford University Press, 1986.

Buckley, Peter G. "Paratheatricals and Popular Stage Entertainment." *The Cambridge History of American Theatre.* Ed. Don B. Wilmeth and Christopher Bigsby. Vol. 1. Cambridge; New York: Cambridge University Press, 1998: 424–81.

Bumsted, J. M., and van de Wetering, John E. *What Must I Do To Be Saved?.* Hinsdale, Ill.: Dryden Press, 1976.

Butler, Jon. "Coercion, Miracle, Reason: Rethinking the American Religious Experience in the Revolutionary Age." *Religion in a Revolutionary Age.* Ed. Ronald Hoffman and Peter J. Albert. Charlottesville: University Press of Virginia, 1994: 1–30.

"Enthusiasm Described and Decried: The Great Awakening as Interpretive Fiction." Journal of American History. 69 (1982–83): 305–25.

Butler, Judith. *Bodies That Matter: On the Discursive Limits of "Sex."* New York: Routledge, 1993.

Carlson, Marvin. *The Haunted Stage: The Theatre as Memory Machine.* Ann Arbor: University of Michigan Press, 2003.

Performance: A Critical Introduction. London; New York: Routledge, 1996.

Clark, Stephen R. L. *God's World and the Great Awakening.* Oxford: Clarendon Press, 1991.

Cornelius, Janet Duitsman. *"When I Can Read My Title Clear": Literacy, Slavery, and Religion in the Antebellum South.* Columbia: University of South Carolina Press, 1991.

Creel, Margaret Washington. "Gullah Attitudes Toward Life and Death." *Africanisms in American Culture.* Ed. Joseph E. Holloway. Bloomington: Indiana University Press, 1990: 69–97.

Dalcho, Frederick. *An Historical Account of the Protestant Episcopal Church in South-Carolina.* Charles Town: E. Thayer, 1820.

Davis, F. James. *Who Is Black?: One Nation's Definition.* University Park: Pennsylvania State University Press, 2001.

Davis, Peter A. "The Plays and Playwrights: Plays and Playwrights to 1800." *History of American Theatre.* Ed. Don B. Wilmeth and Christopher Bigsby. Vol. 1. Cambridge; New York: Cambridge University Press, 1998: 216–49.

Diop, Cheikh Anta. *The African Origin of Civilization: Myth or Reality.* Trans. Mercer Cook. New York: L. Hill, 1974.

Diouf, Sylviane A. *Servants of Allah: African Muslims Enslaved in the Americas.* New York: New York University Press, 1988.

Donkin, Ellen. *Getting into the Act: Women Playwrights in London, 1776–1829*. London: Routledge, 1995.

Earl, Jr., Riggins R. *Dark Symbols, Obscure Signs: God, Self, and Community in the Slave Mind*. Maryknoll, N.Y.: Orbis Books, 1993.

Edwards, Jonathan. "Sinners in the Hands of an Angry God: A Sermon Preached at Enfield, July 8th 1741." Boston: S. Kneeland and T. Green, 1741. Early American Imprints. First Series, no. 4713.

Fisher, Allan G. B. and Humphrey J. Fisher. *Slavery and Muslim Society in Africa: The Insitution in Saharan and Sudanic Africa and the Trans-Saharan Trade*. Garden City, N.Y.: Doubleday & Company, 1971.

Garden, Alexander. "Take Heed How Ye Hear." New York: J. Peter Zenger, 1742. Early American Imprints. First Series, nos. 4959, 4801.

Gilroy, Paul. *Small Acts: Thoughts on the Politics of Black Culture*. London: Serpent's Tail, 1993.

Glissant, Edouard. *Poetics of Relation*. Trans. Betsy Wing. Ann Arbor: University of Michigan Press, 1997.

Gomez, Michael A. "Muslims in Early America." *The Journal of Southern History*. 60.4 (Nov. 1994): 671–710.

Gutman, Herbert G. *The Black Family in Slavery and Freedom, 1750–1925*. New York: Vintage Books, 1977.

Hall, Kim. *Things of Darkness: Economies of Race and Gender in Early Modern England*. Ithaca, N.Y.: Cornell University Press, 1995.

Harding, Vincent. "Religion and Resistance among Antebellum Slaves, 1800–1860." *African-American Religion: Interpretive Essays in History and Culture*. Ed. Timothy E. Fulop and Albert J. Raboteau. New York: Routledge, 1997: 108–30.

Harris, Sharon M., ed. *American Women Writers to 1800*. New York: Oxford University Press, 1996.

Hayes, Diana L. *And Still We Rise: An Introduction to Black Liberation Theology*. New York: Paulist Press, 1996.

Heimert, Alan, and Perry Miller. *The Great Awakening: Documents Illustrating the Crisis and Its Consequences*. Indianapolis: Bobbs-Merrill, 1967.

Herskovits, Melville J. *The Myth of the Negro Past*. Boston: Beacon Press, 1958.

Heyrman, Christine Leigh. *Commerce and Culture: The Maritime Communities of Colonial Massachusetts, 1690–1750*. New York: Norton, 1984.

Hine, Darlene Clark, and Kathleen Thompson. *A Shining Thread of Hope: The History of Black Women in America*. New York: Broadway Books, 1998.

Holloway, Joseph E., ed. *Africanisms in American Culture*. Bloomington: Indiana University Press, 1990.

Hopkins, Dwight N. *Down, Up, and Over: Slave Religion and Black Theology*. Minneapolis: Fortress Press, 2000.

"Slave Theology in the 'Invisible Institution.'" *Cut Loose Your Stammering Tongue: Black Theology in the Slave Narratives*. Ed. Dwight N. Hopkins and George C. L. Cummings. Louisville: Westminster John Knox Press, 2003: 1–32.

Johnson, Odai, and William J. Burling. *The Colonial American Stage, 1665–1774: A Documentary Calendar.* Madison, Wis.: Farleigh Dickinson University Press, 2001.

Judy, Ronald A. T. *(Dis)Forming the American Canon: African-Arabic Slave Narratives and the Vernacular.* Minneapolis: University of Minnesota Press, 1993.

Juster, Susan. *Disorderly Women: Sexual Politics and Evangelicalism in Revolutionary New England.* Ithaca: N.Y.: Cornell University Press, 1994.

Karenga, Maulana. "Black Religion." *African American Religious Studies: An Interdisciplinary Anthology.* Ed. Gayraud Wilmore. Durham, N.C.: Duke University Press, 1989: 271–300.

Lambert, Frank. *Inventing the "Great Awakening".* Princeton: Princeton University Press, 1999.

Le Goff, Jacques. *History and Memory.* Trans. Steven Rendall and Elizabeth Claman. New York: Columbia University Press, 1992.

Lemay, J. A. Leo, and P. M. Zall, eds. *Autobiography of Benjamin Franklin: A Genetic Text.* Knoxville: University of Tennessee Press, 1981.

Linn, John B. and Wm. H. Egle, eds. *Pennsylania Archives.* Rpt. 2nd series. XVII (1890). Harrisburg, PA: C. M. Busch, 1896.

Littlefield, Daniel C. *Rice and Slaves: Ethnicity and the Slave Trade in Colonial South Carolina.* Baton Rouge: Louisiana State University Press, 1981.

Lott, Eric. *Love & Theft: Blackface Minstrelsy and the American Working Class.* Oxford: Oxford University Press, 1993.

Lovejoy, David S. *Religious Enthusiasm and the Great Awakening.* Englewood Cliffs, N.J.: Prentice-Hall, 1969.

Lovejoy, Paul E. "Slavery, the Bilād al-Sūdān, and the Frontiers of the African Diaspora." *Slavery on the Frontiers of Islam.* Ed. Paul E. Lovejoy. Princeton: Markus Wiener Publishers, 2004: 1–21.

Lovejoy, Paul E., ed. *Slavery on the Frontiers of Islam.* Princeton: Markus Wiener Publishers, 2004.

Mathews, Donald G. *Religion in the Old South.* Chicago: University of Chicago Press, 1977.

Matory, J. Lorand. "Rival Empires: Islam and the Religions of Spirit Possession among the Oyo-Yoruba." *American Ethnologist.* 21.3 (Aug. 1994): 495–515.

Maultsby, Portia K. "Africanisms in African-American Music." *Africanisms in American Culture.* Ed. Joseph E. Holloway. Bloomington: Indiana University Press, 1990: 185–210.

McLoughlin, William. *Revivals, Awakenings, and Reform: An Essay on Religion and Social Change in America, 1607–1977.* Chicago: University of Chicago Press, 1978.

Montana, Ismael Musah. "Ahmad ibn al-Qādī al-Timbuktāwī on the *Bori* Ceremonies of Tunis." *Slavery on the Frontiers of Islam.* Ed. Paul E. Lovejoy. Princeton: Markus Wiener Publishers, 2004: 173–98.

Mott, Frank Luther. *American Journalism, A History: 1690–1960*. 3rd ed. New York: Macmillan, 1962.

Nash, Gary. *The Urban Crucible: Northern Seaports and the Origins of the American Revolution*. Cambridge, Mass.: Harvard University Press, 1986.

Norton, Mary Beth, *et al. A People and a Nation: A History of the United States*. 2nd ed. Boston: Houghton Mifflin, 1986.

Parrinder, Edward Geoffrey. *West African Religion: A Study of the Beliefs and Practices of Akan, Ewe, Yoruba, Ibo, and Kindred Peoples*. London: The Epworth Press, 1961.

Pennington, Edgar Legare. *Thomas Bray's Associates and Their Work Among the Negroes*. Worcester, Mass.: American Antiquarian Society, 1939.

Philips, John Edwards. "The African Heritage of White America." *Africanisms in American Culture*. Ed. Joseph E. Holloway. Bloomington: Indiana University Press, 1990: 225–39.

Piersen, William D. *Black Yankees: The Development of an Afro-American Subculture in Eighteenth-Century New England*. Amherst: University of Massachusetts Press, 1988.

Pinn, Anthony B. "African Americans and Humanism." *Down by the Riverside: Readings in African American Religion*. Ed. Larry G. Murphy. New York: New York University Press, 2000: 273–86.

  Terror and Triumph: The Nature of Black Religion. Minneapolis: Fortress Press, 2003.

Purifoy, Lewis M. "The Methodist Anti-Slavery Tradition." *Abolitionism and American Religion*. Ed. John R. McKivigan. New York: Garland, 1999: 19–32.

Raboteau, Albert J. *A Fire in the Bones: Reflections on African-American Religious History*. Boston: Beacon Press, 1995.

  "'The Rule of Gospel Order': Religious Life in the Slave Community." *Down by the Riverside: Readings in African American Religion*. Ed. Larry G. Murphy. New York: New York University Press, 2000: 49–57.

  Slave Religion: The "Invisible Institution" in the Antebellum South. New York: Oxford University Press, 1978.

Rutman, Darrett B., ed. *The Great Awakening: Event and Exegesis*. New York: John Wiley & Sons, 1970.

Ruttenberg, Nancy. "George Whitefield, Spectacular Conversion, and the Rise of the Democratic Personality." *American Literary History*. 5.3 (Fall 1993): 429–58.

Simpson, George Eaton. *Black Religions in the New World*. New York: Columbia University Press, 1978.

Singer, Milton. *Traditional India: Structure and Change*. Philadelphia: American Folklore Society, 1959.

Smith, D. E. Huger, and A. S. Salley, Jr. *Register of St. Philip's Parish, Charles Town, or Charles Town, S. C., 1754–1810*. Columbia: University of South Carolina Press, 1971.

  The South-Carolina Gazette. Ed. Elizabeth Timothy. Charles Town. 1738–46.

Spengelman, William. *A Mirror for Americanists: Reflections on the Idea of American Literature.* Hanover, N.H.: University Press of New England, 1989.

Spillers, Hortense J. "Changing the Letter: The Yokes, the Jokes of Discourse, or, Mrs. Stowe, Mr. Reed." *Slavery and the Literary Imagination.* Ed. Deborah E. McDowell and Arnold Rampersad. Baltimore: John Hopkins University Press, 1989.

Stout, Harry S. *The New England Soul: Preaching and Religious Culture in Colonial New England.* New York: Oxford University Press, 1986.

Stuckey, Sterling. "African Spirituality and Cultural Practice in Colonial New York, 1700–1770." *Inequality in Early America.* Ed. Carla Gardina Pestana and Sharon V. Salinger. Hanover, NH: Dartmouth College, 1999: 160–81.

Thomas, Edgar Garfield. *The First African Baptist Church in North America.* Savannah: By the Author, 1925.

Thompson, Robert Farris. "Kongo Influences on African-American Artistic Culture." *Africanisms in American Culture.* Ed. Joseph E. Holloway. Bloomington: Indiana University Press, 1990: 148–84.

Turner, Lorenzo Dow. *Africanisms in the Gullah Dialect.* Chicago: University of Chicago Press, 1949.

Turner, Richard Brent. "Pre-Twentieth Century Islam." *Down by the Riverside: Readings in African American Religion.* Ed. Larry G. Murphy. New York: New York University Press, 2000: 69–78.

Turner, Victor. *From Ritual to Theatre: The Human Seriousness of Play.* New York: Performing Arts Journal, 1982.

Twesigye, Emmanuel K. "The African Origin of Humanity, Monotheism and Civilization." *God, Race, Myth and Power: An Africanist Corrective Research Analysis.* Ed. Emmanuel K. Twesigye. New York: Peter Lang, 1991: 13–37.

von Linne, Carl. *Systema Naturae: A Photographic Facsimile of the First Volume of the 10th Edition (1758).* London: British Museum of Natural History, 1956.

Weir, Robert W. *Colonial South Carolina: A History.* Millwood, N.Y.: KTO Press, 1983.

Wesley, John. *Free Grace: A Sermon Preach'd at Bristol.* [Boston]: Bristol printed, Philadelphia Rpt. by Ben. Franklin, Boston again rpt. and sold by T. Fleet, 1741. Library of Congress. Rare Book/Special Collections Reading Room.
Thoughts upon Slavery. London. Rpt. Philadelphia: Joseph Cruckshank, 1774. Library of Congress. Rare Book/Special Collections Reading Room.

Westerkamp, Marilyn J. *Triumph of the Laity: Scots-Irish Piety and the Great Awakening, 1625–1760.* New York; Oxford: Oxford University Press, 1988.
Women and Religion in Early America, 1600–1850: the Puritan and Evangelical Traditions. London: Routledge, 1999.

Whitefield, George. "Christ the Best Husband: Or an Earnest Invitation to Young Women to Come and See Christ." *The Works of the Reverend George Whitefield.* London: 1771–2.

Wilmeth, Don B., and Christopher Bigsby, eds. *The Cambridge History of American Theatre.* Vol. 1. Cambridge; New York: Cambridge University Press, 1998.

Wilmeth, Don B., and Jonathan Curley. "Timeline: Beginnings to 1870." *The Cambridge History of American Theatre*. Ed. Don B. Wilmeth and Christopher Bigsby. Vol. 1. Cambridge; New York: Cambridge University Press, 1998: 20–109.

Wood, Peter H. *Black Majority: Negroes in Colonial South Carolina from 1670 through the Stono Rebellion*. New York: Alfred A. Knopf, 1974.

"Jesus Christ Has Got Thee at Last." *Bulletin*. 3. Center for the Study of Southern Culture and Religion (November 1979): 1–7.

CHAPTER 2

Revolutionary Women Critics: Performing Rational Christianity, Patriotism, and Race

Let sin, that baneful evil to the soul, / By you be shunn'd ... An *Ethiop* tells you 'tis your greatest foe.

> Phillis Wheatley, "To the University of CAMBRIDGE, in NEW-ENGLAND"

And may each clime with equal gladness see / A monarch's smile can set his subjects free!

> Phillis Wheatley, "To the KING's Most Excellent Majesty"

By Liberty, by Bondage. I conjure you .... e'er we'll be *slaves*, we'll pour our choicest blood.

> Mercy Otis Warren, *The Adulateur*, 29, my italics

During the pre-Revolutionary War period, the furor of the Great Awakening subsided as Americans battled King George III's invasive new regulations, from the Stamp Act of 1765 to the customs and taxes precipitating the American Declaration of Independence in 1776. Pennsylvania and Massachusetts, centers of colonial opposition to British oppression, proved particularly congenial training grounds for women critics. Often justifying their behavior through the new theory of natural rights, Northern women sought expanded access to public debates from the 1730s to the 1780s. Like female exhorters, they hoped to unlink visibility and identity. They adopted host bodies to protect themselves as they helped shape and critique the tangle of politics, religion, and race. Many adopted "patriot" host bodies to lambaste British imperialism. Others created a composed, "rational Christian" host body, building upon Enlightenment notions of the rational citizen. There were many ways to inhabit this rational Christian body, and some involved an attempt to validate a local culture. African American critics, for instance, adopted judicious Christian bodies to appear as conversationalists, balladeers, courtroom defendants, and poets. They aligned a refined Christian American host body with a figural, "cultured Ethiop" body as they addressed Revolutionary politics. "Alice" (fl. 1700s), an African American Episcopalian, parlayed her job on a Pennsylvania ferry into an opportunity to act as a local historian. Lucy Terry Prince (Luce Bijah, *c.* 1725–1821) wrote a commemorative ballad uniting her Congregationalist community even as she commented critically on it. She pressed for land rights and access to higher education for blacks. Phillis Wheatley (Peters) (*c.* 1753–84) shaped and critiqued colonial culture through poetry readings in Boston and London salon settings, publishing a volume of her poems through a transatlantic missionary connection. She linked rational Christianity to both African and European American culture as she performed her patriotism. European American critics also assumed a rational approach, often based more in Revolutionary politics than religion. They continued to appear as performance critics, often adopting pseudonymous or anonymous "patriotic bodies." Just thirty-six miles from Wheatley's Boston, for instance, Mercy Otis Warren (1728–1814) entered public debates in Gloucester, Massachusetts, as an anonymous (and presumed white male) "patriot," dashing off theatrical satires and critiquing British tyranny through political commentaries, verse dramas, and poems. Nearby, other European American women critics laminated their rational Christian bodies to local culture: Quakers circulated poetry pseudonymously in handwritten commonplace books, while a handful of women in New York and Maryland published theatrical commentaries under feminine pseudonyms.

European Americans often appeared pseudonymously as performance critics, just as Elizabeth Timothy did, but they expanded their options by working within political parties and by creating more individuated pseudonyms. They also led petition drives, war fundraising efforts, and street protests. Mercy Otis Warren, a leading critic, initially published anonymously and pseudonymously, articulating her performance of Americanness through natural rights rather than Christian discourse. Unlike her predecessors, who tried to perform religion as "race," she tried to perform politics as "race": Whig patriots, in her view, were an enslaved "race," held in chains by the monstrous English. Like many exhorters, she borrowed a "black" body: she performed Whig American-ness as abjection so that she could claim the redemption offered by soldiering toward a free Revolutionary America.

African and African American women often appeared as performing critics, formulating their own conception of "blackness." The most prominent, Phillis Wheatley, fashioned multiple host bodies to protect herself. She performed within a "rational Christian" body, imagining an

ideal space where God, like Death, was the great leveler, freeing all
African and European Americans. Through transatlantic Christianity,
Wheatley aligned herself not only with Africa and America but also with
England, where she traveled as a legally "free" woman. Wheatley also
donned a patriot body to lobby for American independence and an end
to slavery. And she linked her Christian and patriot host bodies to a
cultured body: she called herself an "Afric," positing Africa as a literate
nation existing within classical and Biblical as well as eighteenth-century
time frames. By performing in multiple time frames and host bodies,
Wheatley transformed herself from a slave girl into a classical author,
supported by the Muses and by fellow African writers. She looked particularly to Publius Terentius Afer (*c.* 195 or 185–158 BC), a Roman slave
who, when freed, became the successful playwright, Terence. She also
associated herself with Scipio Moorhead (*c.* 1750–), a Boston neighbor,
fellow slave, artist, and poet. She imagined all "climes" within a common
Christian community where "Ethiops" voiced superior moral insights,
demonstrating the illogic of slavery. Wheatley and her predecessors, Alice
and Lucy Terry Prince, performed whiteness as rational Christian purity
and simultaneously claimed blackness as civic insight and artistry.

SITES OF ACCESS

Through seemingly reasonable Christian host bodies, Alice, Luce Bijah,
and Phillis Wheatley gained opportunities to shape civic debates. The
child of Barbadian slaves, Alice serves here as an example of how thousands
of ordinary women performed criticism: by embracing a denominational
body and molding local cultures and histories. As "a worthy member of the
[E]piscopal society" during the Great Awakening, she demanded respect.
She made a name for herself by issuing "judicious remarks on the population and improvements of the city and country," and "pertinent
remarks" on the Bible as she collected fees on Dunk's Ferry near
Philadelphia.[1] She was described as "sensible" as well as "intelligent."
These adjectives are intriguing, because they reveal the savvy strategy that
Alice developed to capitalize upon the performativity of identity.

Alice revealed enough to demonstrate her knowledge of current events,
local history, and the Bible, but couched her oral critiques in such a way
that her caution, her astute judgment of what was sayable and what was
not, became immediately apparent. Her listeners were thus placed in the
uncomfortable position of noticing that some things were, in fact, off
limits in polite company, and that one must be "judicious" to avoid

them. Her ancestors' and neighbors' enslavement, for example, was unmentionable. And Alice judiciously and sensibly did not talk directly about it. But that does not mean that she did not make it felt: the very fact that folks described her as "sensible" means that she reminded them of what she did not say as well as what she did.

Alice functioned as a griot, a repository of cultural and social histories: she shaped the ways in which her community remembered their own past, nudging them toward conceptualizing their histories from her viewpoint. By adopting New Light Anglicanism (Americanized as Episcopalianism during the Revolutionary years), she gained the trust of her community, which enabled her to help shape their memories and attitudes. Possessing an extraordinary memory throughout her 116 years, she crafted "acceptable anecdotes" for local residents, teaching them what to recall. She helped shape Pennsylvania history and folklore, revealing her lived knowledge of and everyday resistance to the grand narratives of Pennsylvania colonization. She forced listeners to regard her as a well-established Christian critic rather than simply a laborer.

Public spaces such as ferries, markets, inns, and taverns were useful sites of access for African American women critics. One of Alice's contemporaries, Lucy Terry Prince, parlayed her workspace, a public inn and tavern, into a platform for cultural critique. Terry was a talented storyteller and "great mimic" with a "strong memory" and knowledge of the Bible: "few indeed could repeat more scripture."[2] In 1746 Terry composed a thirty-line ballad, "Bars Fight," which is, in part, a commemoration of fellow villagers' "valient" fight against Native Americans who attacked them in the "bars" or meadows a couple of miles south of Deerfield, Massachusetts. It is also a veiled critique. In its seemingly fanciful nature as a ballad, it serves as an example of an everyday practice of resistance, similar to Alice's conversational forays. As Saidiya Hartman explains, "these pedestrian practices illuminate inchoate and utopian expressions of freedom that are not and perhaps cannot be actualized elsewhere" (Hartman, *Scenes*, 13). Terry could say and do in a ballad what she could not say or do any other way. Her music gestured toward a utopian world beyond her words. Such everyday practices as Terry's articulate what Paul Gilroy calls a politics of transfiguration: through "the mimetic, dramatic and performative," these practices surpass structures of direct political action and create a counter culture. This counter culture builds its own "critical, intellectual and moral genealogy ... in a partially hidden public sphere of its own" (Gilroy, *Small*, 134). Terry and fellow African Americans, in full view of European American townspeople, performed a quotidian act of resistance through Terry's ballad, transforming a local massacre into an opportunity for solidarity as well as critique.

The Deerfield raid took place on 28 August 1746, and Prince's ballad survived through the oral tradition for over a century.[3] It is composed of seven stanzas: the first stanza sets the scene of the ambush, and each successive stanza describes, briefly, one or two of the eight white townspeople killed, captured, or left for dead in the raid. The rhythm and rhyme are catchy: "August 'twas the twenty-fifth, / Seventeen hundred forty-six; / The Indians did in ambush lay, / Some very valiant men to slay." (In actuality, several of the dead were children, one a girl of thirteen.) Terry's townspeople may have initially sung or recited the ballad with her because she was a fellow Christian mourning their common dead, but her lyrics, which do not disclose her gender or race, hint at an effort to distinguish her Christianity from theirs. They conceal a critique of a white Christian culture that countenanced kidnapping children into slavery and placing restrictive petticoats on teenage girls in the wilderness.

Kidnapped in West Africa by slavers who sailed to Bristol, Rhode Island, Terry may have been purchased in 1730 by an Enfield, Connecticut, landholder named Samuel Terry.[4] Around age five, she was sold to Ebenezer and Abigail Wells of Deerfield. Perhaps she remembered African traditions such as spirit possession, recitation, and praise singing. When the Awakening swept through Deerfield in 1735, Terry was one of five slaves baptized. By 1744 she was old enough to join the Congregational Church, under the tutelage of Reverend Jonathan Ashley (1712–80). Ashley drew upon the astounding success of his Northampton neighbor, Jonathan Edwards (1703–58), who launched the Awakening there in 1734 and preached his famous "Sinners in the Hands of an Angry God" sermon (painting humans as spiders hanging by a thread over the pit of hell, doomed unless they converted), in 1740.

Terry may have been converted during the Awakening, but she adopted a rational and even critical attitude toward Christian conversion, as is signaled by the name she adopted as a married woman. When she married local free black Abijah Prince in 1756, she started calling herself Luce Bijah. Abijah means father, possessor, or worshipper, but it also is the name given the mother of Hezekiah, who is mentioned several times in the Bible, most notably in Second Chronicles 29: 1. Terry's knowledge of the Bible was legendary, and there is every reason to believe that she was familiar with the story of Abijah and her son. Abijah's son was a king who renewed his subjects' faith, telling them: "yield yourselves unto the

Lord ... that the fierceness of his wrath may turn away from you, for *if ye turn again unto the Lord, your brethren and your children shall find compassion before them that lead them captive, so that they shall come again into this land* " (2 Chronicles 30: 8–9). Terry's belief was genuine, but it was also strategic and performative: saying "I accept God" meant that her "brethren" and her family would "find compassion" in the face of those who would try to hold them captive. Through Christianity, they could hope to "come again" – not just into a heavenly recompense but also into a re-imagined, considerate America as well as a diasporic Africa.

Terry's obituary called her a "remarkable woman" with "an assemblage of qualities rarely to be found among her sex" and noted that "her speech was not destitute of instruction and education." Her acquaintances "respected" her and "treated her with a degree of deference."[5] At her funeral the prominent Reverend Lemuel Haynes (1756–1836), usually viewed as the first black minister of a predominantly white American congregation, gave an oration. White New Englanders' response to Haynes sheds light on their reaction to Terry's Christianity. The illegitimate son of a white mother and black father, Haynes worked his way out of indenture to assume a Rutland, Vermont, posting as a minister in 1783. There, like Lucy Terry Prince's son Festus, he married a white woman.[6] Although he did not preach anti-racism directly, he preached it through his very carriage, through his everyday presumption of equality. One historian tells of a reluctant parishioner who, after listening to Haynes preach, called him "the whitest man I ever saw" (Cooley, *Sketches*, 73). It would be easy to see this comment as evidence of Haynes's selling out to white culture, but this parishioner tells us nothing about Haynes's own sense of his mixed heritage or his performance. It does reveal that Haynes, like Terry, was regarded as a part of a small but significant "rational Christian upper-class," within which whiteness meant performing Christian righteousness rather than sporting "a fairer skin and sharper nose." Performing Christianity did not discount their simultaneous performance of African American-ness. In fact, the phrase "fairer skin and sharper nose" is lifted from an anti-slavery poem published following Terry's obituary in the *Vermont Gazette*. The poem celebrated Terry's performance as "their sable mother" and viewed her life as an anti-slavery statement and critique of the Missouri Compromise.[7]

Terry was one of seventeen slaves in Deerfield in the 1740s. New Englanders at that time would have viewed Terry as a young "servant for life," possessing a soul for which her owners, the Wells, and Reverend

Ashley, her minister, were responsible. Although Ashley professed a more liberal theology than Jonathan Edwards, he was more conservative than the rival "White Church" Unitarians in Deerfield. He preached obedience rather than liberation (Proper, *Lucy*, 22–23). Terry's membership in Ashley's church nonetheless cemented her standing in the community, and prompted her to read and interpret the Bible independently. Her owners, a childless couple with one other slave, managed an inn and tavern that still stands on Deerfield's main street, so she worked in a common meeting place where she could easily have recited her ballad, probably to musical accompaniment. When she married and left the tavern, she set up her home as a gathering place for artistic types, black and white – her sons and daughters became talented musicians, and Festus was especially well known as a fiddler – so she continued to create opportunities to comment on her culture.

She drew from disparate performance traditions. Through "Bars Fight," she linked her Christian body with African orature, the American captivity narrative, and the European ballad form. Orature is literature that is composed verbally and aimed for public performance (Mugo, *African*). Ngugi wa Thiong'o uses this term to highlight the ways in which oral and print messages intertwine to the point of inseparability: verbal performances shape print discourse and vice versa in a tangled web of influence and borrowings (*Decolonising*). Terry's borrowings span continents as well as literacies. Like most Deerfield residents she had probably read or heard about the wildly popular local captivity narrative, Reverend John Williams's *The Redeemed Captive Returning to Zion* (1707), but she also recalled the African tradition of the griot, the musical historian who accompanied praise songs about past leaders with banjo-like instruments, routinely updating recitations to include new contexts and audiences. Terry melded these traditions within a typical eighteenth-century American ballad, telling an action-packed story about a local event through rhyming iambic tetrameters divided into four- to six-line stanzas. "Bars Fight," like most colonial ballads, ended inconclusively. It revealed its European as well as its African performance traditions: American ballads emerged from funeral narratives performed in Western Europe during the medieval period, and the form, like the praise song and elegy, was meant to be repeated to honor the memory of the deceased (Coffin, *British*).

Terry claimed authority within her ballad through various strategies: she articulated English colonial interests while registering her resistance to them; she promised to give an accurate account of the raid; and she refused to mark her body by race, gender, or age.[8] She also questioned who had the right to Christian redemption and thereby imagined a particular vision of American-ness. When she composed her poem, the Connecticut River valley served as a home to a number of different cultures in conflict – the English, French, African, Wobanaki, Kanien-kehaka (Mohawk), Wendat (Huron), Iroquois, and Algonkian – and clearly the ballad served English rather than French and Native American interests. When she sang her ballad at Wells' tavern, she acted as a performing critic. However, by refusing to identify herself within her lyrics as an African or African American slave girl, Terry paradoxically gained authority when the ballad circulated on its own, anonymously. Those who assumed the composer was a white male had to readjust their perceptions after they discovered her authorship.

In fact, Terry's invisibility in the lyrics enabled her to reach dual audiences. Terry's ballad could be shared as a record of local heroism, a poem which "conveys genuine sympathy for the white men and women who died in the fight" (Gates and McKay, *Norton*, 137). Or, focusing on the closing couplet which describes how Samuel Allen, a 44-year-old father, was viciously kidnapped by the Native Americans, one might read "Bars Fight" as a critique of *any* culture that kidnaps men, women, and children – including the white American culture that had kidnapped, terrorized, and enslaved *her*. The ballad ends inconclusively, negotiating between sympathy for the Deerfield citizens and a refusal to mourn them.

Church services were designed to teach Terry to identify with European American Christians instead of "unconverted" Native Americans. This identification was crucial to the smooth management of the English colonies, and Terry's ballad demonstrates its effects as well as her resistance. Native Americans are pictured as "awful creatures" who lay "in ambush" for the innocent and virtuous settlers. Actually, a hunter named Eleazer Hawks surprised a band of sixty Abenakis with the report of his gun and touched off their deadly attack. The French and Native Americans had just captured nearby Fort Massachusetts and the Abenakis were searching for more hostages to generate redemption payments, but upon hearing a gunshot, they killed most of their intended hostages. One villager escaped, but Terry does not mention that, nor does she focus on Eunice Allen's survival, for these facts would undermine her story. Part of the cultural work conducted through Terry's ballad, then, was the uniting of English and Africans against Native Americans. Terry represented a bloody skirmish in an ongoing land dispute between Native Americans and English colonists as an Indian raid, pure and simple. Some free blacks, such as Abijah Prince, Terry's husband, owned land in New England, so Terry's identification with the settler's land "rights" prepared her for her future role as the free wife of a landowning American farmer. In one sense, then, "Bars Fight" may be viewed as a type of captivity narrative.[9]

Significantly, Terry's ballad enabled Deerfield residents to keep alive their resentment against Native Americans despite the fact that this was the very last raid on the town, after decades of attacks and counterattacks. The ballad took the place of the real thing. The most devastating raid, called the "Deerfield Massacre" and still taught as a part of Massachusetts history, occurred on 29 February 1704: French and Native Americans took 56 lives, captured 112 men, women and children, and burned dwellings. Reverend John Williams's 1707 book, reprinted into the twentieth century, tells the tale of a forced march into Canada and a fierce Congregationalist battle against the Catholic Jesuits to save Deerfield parishioners' souls. Reverend Williams's own daughter, Eunice Kanenstenhawi Williams (1696–1785) was kidnapped, and he failed to "save" her: she decided to marry into the Kanienkehaka tribe. Eunice's decision was counted a sore defeat for Reverend Williams (Reverend Ashley's predecessor) and for Deerfield as a whole. Eunice visited Deerfield in 1740, 1741, and 1743, reminding townspeople of their defeat even as she demonstrated that the "massacre" was not the work of evil people, but rather part of a war over land and culture. Terry's ballad offered residents in 1746 a means of keeping their fear and anger alive, despite Eunice's efforts to thwart it, in the hiatus before the 1757 French and Indian (Seven Years') War.

While Terry claimed an equal stake in her frontier community and in American-ness through "Bars Fight," she simultaneously critiqued it through what she omitted from her account and through her manipulation of the opening and closing lines. If, indeed, the ballad survived without major cuts, she departed radically from the white captivity narratives that preceded her ballad. Souls are not at issue here, nor is evangelical redemption. Terry left out images of heavenly recompense for those whites who died. Not one of the victims meets his or her Maker or receives a final benediction other than Terry's own equivocal one. Furthermore, the ballad opens and closes with a reference to "young Samuel Allen," who was kidnapped in the raid and carried away to the Abenakis' village.

Through this poem, then, Terry negotiates the tension between the two major events that shaped her own early life: conversion and kidnapping. While her conversion encouraged her to identify with white propertied residents in hopes of eventual inclusion in their ranks, Terry herself – like Samuel Allen who opens and closes her ballad – was kidnapped as an infant and carried to another land. Unspeakably, the next step for Allen – and by extension, for Terry – was "servitude." By recording the unmentionable horror following Allen's capture, Terry signaled the injustice of her own capture.

Lorenzo Greene argues that "slavery in New England was comparatively more humane because of the Puritans' religious concept of bondage, which was based on the Old Testament and the Hebrew Mosaic law. Slaves were regarded as persons and part of the family 'divinely committed to their stewardship'" (Shockley, *Afro-American*, 4). As a convert in a settled New England church, however, Terry was still a slave. She did not own her own body, she sat in a back pew at church, she was told to obey her master as she obeyed God, and she received only a rudimentary education. Though she studied the Bible and was a lifelong Christian, she hints at her disaffection from the Deerfield church and its parishioners through her omission of any heavenly comforts for the victims of the Deerfield incident. At moments in the ballad, in fact, she seems particularly distanced from the victims of the raid: "Simeon Amsden they found dead / Not many rods from Oliver's head."[10] Simeon was a nine-year-old boy from a prominent family. Of course, it is possible that through the oral transmission of the ballad, references to heavenly compensation were dropped, but if we grant Terry the most fully developed artistry and intelligence, the ballad stands as it is, both an elegy and an act of cultural criticism.

Terry suggests her emotional investments in the ballad not just through what is missing from it, and through its equivocal tone, but also through the weight and placement granted to specific figures. She reveals that gender constrictions could prove fatal. She devotes six lines, not just two or four as with the other victims, to describing the lone female victim of the attack, thirteen-year-old Eunice Allen. Eunice could "see the Indians coming, / And hopes to save herself by running." "Had not her petticoats stopt her," the "awful creatures had not catched her" (Proper, *Lucy*, 18–19). Terry, an active young woman, bristled at having to wear the customary petticoat and gown of the period, indicting the societal custom in her song.

Terry also grants the most powerful spot, the final lines of the song, to the captured Allen: "Young Samuel Allen, oh! Lack-a-day, / Was taken and carried to Canada" (Proper, *Lucy*, 19). Atypically, she uses a caesura – "oh! lack-a-day" – to emphasize the sudden grief and particular injustice of this "youth's" kidnapping, and yet its everyday status. Imagine Terry herself publicly reciting, perhaps singing, those catchy lines in the Wells' tavern or on the church square. There is a tension between her invisibility in the lyrics and her visibility in performance – a gap marked by the caesura, the "oh!" – which suggests that those lines voice her unspeakable feelings about her own kidnapping as well as Allen's. She orchestrated a moment of aporia in which she appears at a loss about how to speak of her knowledge or act on the basis of that knowledge even as she levels her fiercest criticism at the whites around her. Thus, while she shared her community's grief over Samuel Allen's fate, she also found a means through which to signal her anger and grief about her own situation. The ballad's double meaning helped insure its survival, and as time passed and the underground railroad emerged, the closing lines about being "carried to Canada" took on another layer of meaning.

Terry's husband, Abijah Prince, was the only free black in town, prosperous and some twenty years older than Terry. Either Terry talked her master into manumitting her upon her marriage, or Prince purchased her freedom. The two lived for a time on a corner of the Wells' property. According to her obituary, they had seven children, though we know only about six, all with carefully chosen Biblical names, all baptized in the church. The Prince family purchased land in two Vermont towns, and their homes became gathering places for locals, particularly for boys the same age as their children who wanted "to hear Lucy talk."[11]

Terry's next recorded appearance as a performing critic followed years later. The Williams College Board of Trustees rejected her son's application for admission, claiming that he was ill-prepared. She was "indignant" and lobbied the Board in hopes of reversing their decision through "a most powerful appeal of three hours['] duration. She laid open to them the whole volume of inspirations, quoting verse after verse." One of the founders of the college, Clark Williams, "an old acquaintance," also represented her interests, but neither her rational Christian plea nor his power could sway the Board.[12] Proper dismisses this story as fiction, because there is no evidence of it in the Williams College archives, but it seems unreasonable to demand verification through the records of College officials who were "not a little discomforted and perplexed" by Terry's demands and by their colleague's defection (Proper, *Lucy*, 31). In fact, the lack of a printed report might augment the story: the Trustees thought it troubling or wished it beneath notice. They could not, however, deter her.

When Terry moved to Guilford, Vermont, possibly as early as 1765, she reentered the public arena, again acting as a performing critic. She and Abijah owned land abutting the property of a prominent landowner and Vermont legislator named John Noyes, who continually harassed them, tearing down their fences and burning their crops. So Terry requested a meeting with the Governor, Lieutenant Governor, and six members of the state council, and presented a petition to them. The meeting took place in Norwich on 7 June 1785. Terry appeared in court in her rational Christian body and convinced the panel that she and her husband had a valid claim. After an investigation, the Governor wrote to the Guilford town selectmen, requiring them to protect the Prince family, who were "greatly oppressed & injured by John and Ormas Noyce," warning that otherwise they would "fall upon the Charity of the Town."[13] The combination of Terry's performance of Christian rationality and the townspeople's self-interest tipped the land dispute in her favor.

She continued to perform as a free, rational, Christian American, critiquing the illegal practices of whites: when the Princes faced another land dispute with neighbors in their new home in Sunderland, Vermont, she presented her case before the US Circuit Court in Bennington in May 1796. Supreme Court Justice Samuel Chase was presiding. Chase reportedly informed her she "made a better argument than he had heard from any lawyer of the bar of Vermont," elevating her status as a cultural critic and insuring that even though she started out as a "servant for life," she earned as much space in Josiah Holland's *History of Western Massachusetts* as eight Deerfield luminaries all put together.[14]

Like Lucy Terry Prince, Phillis Wheatley was kidnapped from her family, probably from the coast of Senegal or Gambia, and sold to a New England family. Arriving in Boston in July 1761 at age seven or eight, Wheatley was one of approximately 600 "servants for life" living there at the time. Unlike chattel slaves, "servants for life" possessed certain legal rights: they could, for example, launch civil suits and own land, bequeathing it to their heirs. Typically held by elite families, only one or two to a household, these slaves were viewed as a reflection of the families that owned them, as in Deerfield. Reverend Cotton Mather (1663–1728) had called Yankee slaves "more clearly related to us than many others are" without a hint of irony[15]. Newspapers reported slaves' court cases alongside anti-slavery letters lambasting slave-owning Whigs who railed about being "enslaved" by the English.

Wheatley was surrounded by a political debate about the "natural rights" of Americans, and she capitalized on the ways in which that debate intersected with transatlantic Christianity and diasporic African-ness. The natural rights debate emerged as Americans embraced the ideas of Enlightenment philosophers such as John Locke (1632–1704). Locke pictured humans, in their natural state, as rational, tolerant, and happy, capable of enjoying life, liberty, and the pursuit of happiness. In nature, he argued, people followed natural laws and possessed natural rights, independent of legal jurisdictions or localized restrictions. However, because a small group of people ignored natural laws and thereby denied others' freedom, individuals had to create a social contract. Within this contract, persons became citizens of a state, and the state guaranteed the rights of all. The host body of the citizen offered protection. Difficulties arose, however, as Wheatley was keenly aware, when implicit local notions of race, gender, and class hampered the abstract quality of that host body. Henry Louis Gates, Jr., traces the history of American human rights theorists such as James Otis (1725–83) and Philadelphia physician Benjamin Rush (1745–1813), who both believed that "colonists are by the law of nature free born, as indeed all men are, white or black."[16] But women critics also contributed centrally to the natural rights debate, and Phillis Wheatley and James Otis's sister Mercy were among them.

Wheatley gained access to public debates both as a performance critic and as a performing critic, by writing as well as reciting neoclassical poetry. Neoclassicism enabled her to inhabit not simply a Christian but also a pagan Roman world where she elevated her performance as an "Ethiop" or "Afric," even as she expanded notions of Christian practice. Her mistress and master, along with their teenage daughter Mary and her twin Nathaniel, encouraged her literary work within certain limits, and – partly to demonstrate their own status as transatlantic Christians – ushered it into publication under the patronage of the Englishwoman Selina Hastings (1707–91), the Countess of Huntingdon, one of Whitefield's patrons.[17]

Wheatley, like Terry, entered colonial debates as a teenager composing poetry. She published in newspapers, magazines, and broadsides: her 1770 elegy "On the Death of the Rev. George Whitefield" appeared in London and American broadsides. It captured the attention of the Countess of Huntingdon, who helped publish her *Poems on Various Subjects, Religious and Moral* in London in 1773.[18] Wheatley's 1779 subscription call for a second book publication was unsuccessful, and her last published poem appeared in *The Boston Magazine* in September 1784. She died in poverty on 5 December that same year.

In March 1774, just weeks after Wheatley's mistress's death, Reverend Samson Occom (1723–92), a well-respected Native American minister, published one of Wheatley's letters. Through it, a newly freed Wheatley revealed directly the politics hidden in her poetry. Embracing Occom's critique of Christian slaveholding, Wheatley agreed that blacks possessed "natural Rights." She claimed the common Christian American "we": "in every human Breast, God has implanted a Principle, which *we* call Love of Freedom." Then she linked that Christian American freedom to diasporic Christian freedom: "and by the Leave of our modern Egyptians I will assert that the same principle [of freedom] lives in us." The "divine Light" was "chasing away the thick Darkness which broods over the Land of Africa," transforming chaos into order and revealing "civil and religious Liberty," which are "inseparably united." Traditionally, this passage, like the poem "On Being Brought," has been read as a comment about how Africa was Christianized, moving from pagan darkness toward light, from African chaos toward European order. However, perhaps for a nineteen-year-old with memories of the Middle Passage, the dark chaos brooding over Africa was the sinfully dark confusions of the slave trade rather than the "sinful" paganism of the Africans. The divine Light of diasporic, rational Christianity, Wheatley suggested, was chasing away the darkness of the slave trade, "converting" all to a "beautiful Order" in which religious and civil freedoms flowered. Wheatley stopped short of calling for insurrection, but she asked God to convince Americans "of the strange Absurdity of their Conduct" and dryly concluded, "How well the Cry for Liberty, and the reverse Disposition for the exercise of oppressive power over others agree[,] I humbly think it does not require the penetration of a Philosopher to determine."[19]

Poetry provided Wheatley's primary access to the public sphere, but it was not without dangers. The Wheatley parlor, arguably, functioned as a scientific laboratory in which an invited public investigated Wheatley's capabilities and contemplated the humanity of all slaves. It was also an intimate theatre in which a curious and voyeuristic few could experience the thrill of watching a young slave girl feel and think. For some, it was one step away from pornographically viewing the "Negro girl" in Mr. Potatfelt's parlor in Charleston. But everyone had to acknowledge Wheatley's literacy and education, which complicated matters considerably.

Wheatley's access as a critic depended heavily upon her ability to maintain her owners' interest in educating her. Reportedly she often popped awake at night, inspired to write a poem, for which reason she was granted a candle. Perhaps she also stayed awake to study English and neoclassic poetry, to insure her astonishing progress and thus her increasing access to literacy. Mary and then Susanna Wheatley tutored Phillis, offering her lessons in Biblical literature, classics, history, British literature, and geography. Justifying their work as a religious duty, they also derived a sense of accomplishment through her achievements. They saw slaves as a "bodiless souls" rather than "soulless bodies" (Earl, *Dark*, 23).

Wheatley showed a marked interest in learning, but she downplayed her ambitions to dispel fears of her rebellion. According to her Preface, she wrote for her own "Amusement" (*Poems*, 147–48). John Wheatley's statement followed the preface, explaining her status as a slave and the circumstances of her education. This letter is of some interest, because two versions exist. Susanna Wheatley, Phillis's mistress, dictated the first version to Phillis, though Nathaniel Wheatley signed it. The second version, the better known one, is in actuality Phillis's *revision* of the first letter, signed under John Wheatley's name and printed in the 1773 publication of her poems (*Phillis*, ed. Robinson, 403, 149).

These two letters reveal the gap between the performance that Susanna Wheatley sought through her dictation and the performance that Phillis herself staged through her revision. Both versions noted that "as to her Writing, her own Curiosity led her to it"; but Phillis added the phrase "she learnt in so short a Time," thereby making her accomplishment more extraordinary. Both versions also reported that "Phillis was brought from *Africa* to *America,* in the Year 1761, between Seven and Eight years of age," thereby side-stepping the issue of her enslavement through the euphemism "brought" (*Phillis*, ed. Robinson, 149).

However, in her revision Phillis added the fact that "she has a great Inclination to learn the Latin Tongue, and has made some Progress in it," as if to insure that she would be allowed to continue her studies despite the Wheatley family's opposition (*Phillis*, ed. Robinson, 149). Interestingly, Latin was one of the few subjects denied her white contemporary, Mercy Warren. The language of the Roman pagans gave Wheatley access to the work of the Latin playwright, Terence, whom she clearly regarded as an African mentor.

Aware of the dangers of audacity, Wheatley added the following italicized words to Susanna Wheatley's letter:

Without any Assistance from School Education, *and by only what she was taught in the Family,* she, in sixteen Months Time from her Arrival, attained the English Language, to which she was an utter Stranger before, to such a Degree, as to read any, the most difficult Parts of the Sacred Writings, to the great Astonishment of all who heard her. (*Phillis*, ed. Robinson, 149)

Through this additional phrase, Phillis carefully performed her gratitude to the Wheatley family. She simultaneously held up their practice as a political model, a challenge to other slaveholding families who should also educate their "servants for life." She modestly deletes the modifier "perfectly" from the phrase "attained the English Language."

Wheatley's deft negotiation of the shoals of the slave–mistress relationship reveals her keen sense of her own performance of self and its relationship to the performance she is encouraged to enact. She is aware of her own performativity. For her, servitude itself was a performance of sorts, mapped by a jumbling of oppression and carefully delineated "privilege." She was often excused from all but light housework because of her lifelong ill health and her status as a special pupil. She was not allowed to fraternize with the other servants, except for her correspondence with Obour Tanner, who may have shared the Middle Passage with her (Wheatley, *Collected*, 317).

In the 1770s the beginnings of a transatlantic host network of women cultural critics was forming, although it would be decades before free black and white women critics would work together within anti-slavery organizations. Susanna, Mary, and Phillis Wheatley relied upon the Countess of Huntingdon to validate Phillis's poems in England. They caught the attention of readers like Mercy Otis Warren, who shared books with Englishwomen like Catharine Sawbridge Macaulay Graham (1731–91), a celebrated historian. American women critics were gaining access to each other's work, and to a common discourse of patriotic rebellion: Phillis Wheatley and Mercy Warren favored the same Whig newspaper, *The Massachusetts Spy*, which published Warren's 1772 *Adulateur* as well as Wheatley's 1774 letter to Occom.[20]

Wheatley also enjoyed her correspondence with Obour Tanner, an equally devout black Christian. "Let us be mindful of our high calling," Wheatley warned Tanner, "continually on our guard."[21] Like most converts, Wheatley was wary of slipping back into sin. But her warning also suggests that she knew that her performance was a highly visible one, tied to the project of liberating slaves in this life as well as the next. Borrowing Hortense Spillers's notion of a "writing community," Bassard sees Wheatley as writing for Tanner and the "other" within herself rather than for her master and mistress, building on the tradition of the African spiritual to create a self-reflexive "African Americanism."[22] Wheatley also retained evangelists' interest in linking civil and religious freedoms. Clearly Wheatley perceived herself as a part of a community of rational African and Native American Christians, as well as European American

Christians who were not always rational. She claimed an African culture that stretched back to Terence and included her neighbor, Scipio Moorhead.

Phillis Wheatley was herself viewed as a part of a transatlantic circle of women writers of genius: Mercy Otis Warren included Wheatley in her reading circle, despite her comment that Wheatley was "barbarian." This linking of "barbarism" to African-ness (instead of to American slave-holders) marks the limits of Warren's sense of connection to her fellow poet, but since Warren did not issue praise liberally, her admiration for Wheatley's accomplishment is worth noting. She valued Wheatley's *Poems* more than a volume by a white contemporary, arguing that, considering the circumstances, Wheatley was "best entitled to the claim of original genius."[23] As Warren and her female relative discussed the relative merits of Wheatley's poetry, they performed their sense of being a part of a larger conversation of cultured American women, which included Wheatley. This performance of an imagined circle of transatlantic women writers offered critics varied avenues of access to the public sphere.

METHODS OF ACCESS

At a time when many European American women critics published anonymously or pseudonymously, Wheatley, like Alice and Lucy Terry Prince, often appeared in person to recite her poetic criticism. When Wheatley did publish her poems, she signed her own name. African and African American women critics may very well have published anonymously or pseudonymously during the Revolutionary era, but it would have been difficult for them to do so before the emergence of the anti-slavery and black press in the late 1820s. Wheatley's name and status are printed multiple times in her *Poems on Various Subjects*: within the frontispiece engraving, on the title page, in her master's preface and letter to the editor, and in the statement attesting that she was the author of the poems. The Countess also required that a likeness of Wheatley accompany her poems. Wheatley had to turn her visibility – in print as well as in person – to advantage. She did so through a variety of strategies. She tried to shield her identity even as she constructed her host bodies. She crafted these bodies by meshing disparate words and gestures, pasting Christian catchphrases alongside references to Africa and natural rights. She adopted multiple host bodies: the rational Christian body; the Biblical "Ethiop" body stretching her hand to God; the patriot body claiming natural rights; and the cultured, diasporic body living in a classical as well as an eighteenth-century frame. She linked this transatlantic body to England, where she was legally free. These host bodies enabled Wheatley to perform whiteness as rational Christian patriotism and simultaneously claim blackness as moral insight and artistry. Curiously, Reverend Whitefield was central to Wheatley's transatlantic reach.

Susanna Wheatley probably took Phillis to hear Reverend Whitefield during his August 1770 appearances in the Old South Congregational Church in Boston, just the week before his death. And because of their connection with the Countess, the Wheatleys may have housed Whitefield in their home. By the 1770s, however, much of the radical potential of his sermons had disappeared: he was no longer a dissident preacher speaking to a diverse group of congregants milling around outside in a fluid, dynamic, and partially unanchored denominational setting. He was firmly ensconced in a settled, indoor, carefully regulated sanctuary. Listening to his sermons in the gallery or back pew of the church, Phillis nonetheless latched onto the subversive potential of his words. Upon his death, she composed a eulogy, widely distributed throughout New England and London on broadsides, in newspapers, and in pamphlets in variant forms. The eulogy reveals her early strategy for gaining access to publication as well as the ways in which her "productions" helped make the case for the moral intelligence, and therefore the humanity, of the "race" of Africans and African Americans. Advertised in Boston in October 1770, the eulogy was billed as "a Consolatory *Address*" to the Countess and Whitefield's "Orphan Children in GEORGIA" ("An Elegiac Poem," *Phillis*, ed. Robinson, 370). This eulogy is more than an address, however. It is a demand for the Countess to expand Whitefield's patronage of the dispossessed. A year after Wheatley published the eulogy, she joined the church.

In the last stanza of the eulogy, Wheatley calls out "Great COUNTESS!" and warns her future patron that Americans will weep on Whitefield's urn until "life divine re-animate[s] his dust" (Wheatley, "On the Death of the Rev. Mr. GEORGE WHITEFIELD," *Poems*, 24) in the Countess and others who must take up the orphans' – and the Africans' – cause. Wheatley repeats this kind of directive in her 1778 poem on the death of General Wooster, whose widow she urges to follow her husband's anti-slavery lead: "'Tis thine fair partner of his life, to find / His virtuous path and follow close behind" (Wheatley, "On the Death of General Wooster," *Collected*, 150). Zafar analyzes the way in which Wooster serves as a "cover" for Wheatley's abolitionism, but the general's living wife is the primary target of Wheatley's attention (Zafar, *We*, 35). In her poems on Whitefield and Wooster, Wheatley turns her visibility in print into an advantage. She dons a rational Christian body to exhort the wealthy to advocate anti-slavery and anti-racism.

Unlike Lucy Terry Prince, who refused to identify herself in her lyrics, Wheatley did not – and, in fact, could not – remain unmarked. If she did not appear in parlor settings or refer to her "clime" or "Sable race" within her poems, others mentioned her slave status, as if to insure her continuing enslavement even as they signaled its inhumanity. Wheatley's visibility meant that she served as one of the African and African American others through which American national identity was forged, but she understood the power of performative moments, and used them to force her audiences to rethink their strategies for interpreting her work and their concepts of "black" and "white." She used her *visibility* to prompt political change. Even when she did not mention slavery, her performance of literacy constituted an attack on it.

Valerie Smith has argued that a "marked" position might be useful at times: she has recognized "the strategic need to claim racial, gendered, sexual, and class identities as meaningful in specific ways in the name of struggle and resistance to institutional violence and exploitation ... for some audiences and moments, the certainties of stable notions of identity and community perform more useful ideological work than does the free play of subjectivities posited within cultural studies" (Smith, *Not*, xvii–xviii). Since Wheatley's access to the public sphere was often mediated in person, through parlor performances of her poems, it was crucial for her to develop ways to make visibility work on her behalf.

Partly because of increased slave agitation in the Boston courts and newspapers, Phillis Wheatley's visibility – her embodied literacy and intelligence – vexed American culture at its very heart. Her mistress, Susanna Wheatley, could not find an American publisher for Wheatley's poems, partly because she advertised her project in an unpopular Loyalist newspaper, but more importantly because she could not locate 300 subscribers who wanted to believe in the "authenticity" of Wheatley's text. As lawyer John Andrews explained the matter, she "could not sell it by reason of their not crediting ye performances to be by a Negro." Another reason for a London publication, according to Andrews, how-ever, was that Wheatley was "made to expect a large emolument, if she sent ye copy home [to London] which induc'd her to remand it of ye printers & also of Capt [Robert] Calef."[24] It is unclear how Wheatley's manuscript reached Archibald Bell, a religious publisher in London. Calef sailed regularly from Boston to London for the Wheatley family and may have delivered the manuscript. In any case, necessity and a hope for economic reward fueled Wheatley's efforts to publish her "performances" in London.

Wheatley's American readers, however, required a live and visible performance, or a written account of one, before they would believe in her authorship. Consequently, John and Susanna Wheatley marshaled a large group of men from both sides of the political spectrum and from the highest rungs of Boston society, to quiz Wheatley in person and to attest to the "authenticity" of her voice. Henry Louis Gates, Jr., explains that Europeans believed that if the Africans could master "the arts and sciences," they were "fundamentally related" to Europeans; if not, the African was "destined by nature to be a slave" (Gates, "In Her Own," ix–x). Through her live performance in front of white Bostonians, Wheatley forced Americans to admit once again the limits of their strategy of reading identity through purportedly visible signs. Gates imagines this 1772 test of Wheatley's skills as occurring all at once "in a room in Boston," with the eighteen examiners "perhaps gathered in a semicircle" around Phillis to test her knowledge of Greek and Latin, Milton and Pope (Gates, "In Her Own," viii). He envisions a large enough room to hold comfortably around twenty people: perhaps a public room, then, for an eighteenth-century orals examination.

But this scenario would have been extremely difficult for the Wheatleys to stage. Setting aside the challenge of finding such a public room and finding a date and time that eighteen ambitious men would set aside their own private concerns to validate the work of a young slave girl, one must still confront the fact that the men who "authenticated" Wheatley's volume were divided by fierce political animosities. They were Whigs as well as Tories. In 1772 it would have been a Herculean task to gather them together in one place for any endeavor. By that time, the crown's seizure of John Hancock's sloop had caused a riot, Governor Hutchinson had placed James Bowdoin on the Massachusetts Council to prevent his joining the Assembly, and Joseph Green had begun to shift his allegiance from the patriots to the loyalists, with whom Mather Byles had staked his claim. The Honorable Thomas Hubbard had been a slave dealer (and most of the examiners were slaveholders), while the Reverend Andrew Elliot was an abolitionist. In order to prove Wheatley's literacy, the Wheatleys had to secure the signatures of these men, who detested one another. Furthermore, the Wheatleys appear to have acted in ways that alienated all sides: they attended a church that housed patriot rallies but published Phillis's original subscription notice in an out-of-favor loyalist newspaper. They allowed Phillis to write patriotic verses, but probably billeted British soldiers in their home. It is doubtful that the Wheatleys possessed the social clout to bring together in one meeting the diverse luminaries listed in "To the Publick."

There is another, more likely, performance possibility. Many of the signatories had already met Phillis at one time or another, either in the Wheatley home upon a social visit, or at religious services or in the marketplace. She had been publishing individual poems in the newspapers and performing her poetry for small gatherings for some time. So it would have been possible for the Wheatleys to ask those who already knew Phillis's abilities well to sign the attestation without a public trial or reviewing of her skills. Those who had not yet observed Phillis might have received invitations to the Wheatley home, where Phillis might have been ushered into the parlor to demonstrate her skills to one or two visitors at a time, in the same fashion as recorded in her interview that same year with Thomas Wooldridge, emissary to Lord Dartmouth.

Although this is a more likely scenario, it is a messier one, because it merges a public act, a "thesis defense," with a more private act, conversing about literature. And it invites into the domestic, social space of the parlor the more public spaces of the schoolroom, courtroom, and church, not to mention the auction block and wharves, where in Boston and New York free black and white prostitutes had begun to eke out a living. Phillis's grilling in front of a few examiners in an intimate space (at a time when the closest performance parallel was the questioning of students at a graduation exercise or the interrogation of female defendants at a trial) was, in part a performance of cultured domesticity, a claim on American-ness through femininity. It was also an intellectual torment. It was a heady version of the sadistic torture of slaves in the market. By placing a woman barely eighteen in their parlor and inviting strange men to probe her skill as a poet, the Wheatleys were staging their own version of Christian sadomasochism, of pornography.

As Marcus Wood explains, Edmund Burke argued in 1756 that watching someone subjected to pain produced sublime feelings in the spectator. He also believed that the visual sight of a black body shocked the eye (qtd. Wood, *Slavery*, 137). The Christian slaveholders – judges, lawyers, ministers, merchants – who examined Phillis Wheatley were given access to a grotesque intellectual torture, designed to make them feel intensely. And there was yet another performance memory at work when the examiners met with Wheatley: the memory of such displays as the "WHITE Negro Girl" who was "SHEWN" in the home of a Charlestonian in 1743, who though "of Negro Parents" was "as white as any *European*" (*South-Carolina Gazette*, 30 May 1743: 3). The question as these men looked at and listened to Phillis Wheatley was not only *was* she literate but also *should* she be literate – in their view "as white as any European"? Could they re-imagine this performance as something other than pornographic sadism? Could they imagine it as Phillis's own staging of her intelligence, *her own production*?

Wheatley's literacy suggested ambition to those who witnessed it, another reason that the Wheatleys may have wished to lessen the impact of their staging of Phillis's literacy by producing private scenes rather than a single public trial. In 1774 John Andrews, a Boston tradesman, wrote a letter to his brother-in-law, informing him that he had purchased Wheatley's volume of poems but felt somewhat cheated: "there don't seem to be near all her productions" in the book, he protested. He continued, "she's an artful jade, I believe, & intends to have the benefit of another volume" (*Phillis*, ed. Robinson, 123). Andrews's diction is telling: "artful" at that time meant "versed in the liberal arts, learned, wise" but also "skilful in taking an unfair advantage, using stratagem, wily, cunning, crafty, deceitful" and "artificial, imitative." In acknowledging her liberal education, Andrews is also damning her willfulness and suggesting that she is mimicking others' art. A "jade" is not only an unusual gem but also "a contemptuous name for a horse . . . of inferior breed, e.g., a cart- or draught-horse as opposed to a riding horse . . . a vicious, worthless, ill-tempered horse." In one word Andrews calls forth both an image of beauty and an image of the eighteenth-century newspaper advertisements that pictured slaves and horses side by side. In addition, a "jade" was "a term of reprobation applied to a woman, also used playfully, like hussy or minx."[25] So Andrews, like the "Two Gentlemen of the Navy" with whom Wheatley engaged in a poetic exchange, was keenly aware of Wheatley's sexuality and his own stirrings of desire for her or the idea of her. As Wheatley herself seemed to recognize in her poem warning Harvard students about momentary passions, her literary presence stymied this arousal.

Wheatley's appearance before the Boston luminaries – however it was staged – was only part of her performance of literacy. She expanded this performance over the years, launching a performance tradition of African and African American women critics journeying overseas: first to England, later to Europe, and finally to Africa, demonstrating their literacy and power. Through her very visible and embodied movement to

England and her return to the States, she forced American audiences to see her material body, her textual body, and the body of "that class of Americans called Africans" in a new light.[26]

When she performed her literacy in London in 1773, she proved that skin could not act as a valid marker of literacy, humanity, or rights, any more than it could mark one as a "visible saint." In fact, by the time of her appearance in London on 17 June 1773, British Lord Mansfield's 1772 Somerset court decision was in place, dictating that slaves who set foot on English soil were free and could, as James Somerset did, refuse to return to bondage in the colonies. So when Wheatley read her poems aloud in London, she was legally free – as long as she stayed there. When she returned to Boston, it was as a woman who had possessed the legal power to refuse to return to Susanna Wheatley's side. Her return so powerfully proved her moral superiority that the Wheatleys were virtually forced to manumit her shortly after her return. Through her transatlantic performance, she prompted her own emancipation, on her own terms – a rational Christian foundation – and demonstrated that slaves possessed not only souls but also intellect and moral sensibility, a demonstration crucial to the thorny but important development of anti-slavery sentiment.

Wheatley often used her own performativity to turn the trap of visibility into an opportunity. In 1772 Wheatley was commissioned to write a poem commemorating the Earl of Dartmouth's appointment as "His Majesty's Principal Secretary of State for North America." She had reason to believe that he would lobby for fewer restrictions on the colonies (Wheatley, *Collected*, 287). In addition, she had reason to believe that he would be a friend to races other than his own. He was an active member of the transatlantic Methodist community and had chaired a fundraiser for the Moor's Indian School in Connecticut, where her Native American correspondent, Samuel Occom, had studied. Dartmouth was, Wheatley immediately realized, a powerful and potentially sympathetic reader. Before long, in fact, he was placed in charge of coordinating British alliances with enslaved blacks and Native Americans.

So when Wheatley sat down in front of Dartmouth's emissary, Thomas Wooldridge, to respond to his request for a poem in honor of Dartmouth, she not only expressed the general hopefulness that accompanied his appointment, but also boldly, and atypically, called direct attention to her kidnapping and her enslavement. She suddenly invited Dartmouth and other readers to imagine "What pangs excruciating must molest, / What sorrows labour in my parent's breast?" She condemned the "steel'd . . . soul" that kidnapped her. She reminded Dartmouth that it was in his power "to sooth the griefs, which thou did'st once deplore" ("To the Right Honourable WILLIAM, Earl of Dartmouth," Wheatley, *Poems*, 74–75).

This performative effort to enlist his aid on behalf of slaves demonstrates that Wheatley recognized and seized the power granted her by the enforced visibility of her performances as a poet-critic. She realized that once her performances began, her mistress could not easily control their outcomes. Even if her plea on behalf of slaves made her mistress anxious, Susanna Wheatley could not alter the shape of her performance once it had begun: she had to listen to Wheatley, she had to let Wooldridge listen, and she had to allow him, if he wished, to deliver the poem to Dartmouth, who would doubtless circulate it more widely.

Furthermore, Wheatley's lines suggest her awareness of the growing sentimental discourse of pain that would, in painting the black body as victim, stir her listeners' hearts and prompt them to act: she pictured sorrowful parents being accosted by "excruciating" pains. In fact, Wheatley's line enables slave-owning readers such as Susanna and John Wheatley to imagine their own heartstrings being "molest[ed]" by exquisite pangs of guilt, even as they stand witness to a scene of sadism. But, tellingly, she refuses to place *herself* in the position of the miserable victim of the pain inflicted by slavery. She does not give Wooldridge or Dartmouth or her owners the voyeuristic pleasure that sentimental anti-slavery fiction later offered its readers. She does not paint herself as a half-naked child near death on the slaver *Phillis* but rather forces readers to consider the sorrow felt by her parents, the same sorrow that she tries to soothe through her eulogies comforting Boston area parents whose children died young.

She is aware that her white contemporaries actually believe that slaves deserve their slavery because they supposedly do not fight for freedom and do not possess the feelings and exquisite moral sensibilities of whites. So she puts questions into Dartmouth's mind, questions about what prompted her "love of *Freedom*" from which such "wishes for the common good" flow. Such wishes, she acknowledges, are "by *feeling* hearts alone best understood." It was her kidnapping, she explains, that made her hate not only British tyranny but any tyranny: "can I then but pray / Others may never feel tyrannic sway?" ("To the Right Honourable WILLIAM, Earl of Dartmouth," *Poems*, 74). Wheatley creates in this poem a feeling but rational Christian American body that must strive to widen its vision to hers, one which incorporates African-ness (and European-ness) as well as American-ness and imagines a fluid bridging of the two types of identifications. She is more Christian, more American than anyone, her logic goes. And yet there she sat, demurely poised to do Wooldridge and her mistress's bidding of composing a truly Christian poem. This is a complicated performance combining audacity with humility, invisibility with visibility.

Perhaps Wooldridge's response is emblematic of other whites who witnessed Wheatley's skilled performances. In a letter to Dartmouth, he explained that, having heard of Wheatley's eulogy on Whitefield, he "visited her Mistress, and found by conversing with the African, that she was no Imposter; I asked if she could write on any Subject; she said Yes." He then asked her to write the poem on Dartmouth's new appointment as "Secretary of State," and "she immediately wrote a rough Copy of the inclosed [*sic*] . . . I was astonish'd, and could hardly believe my own Eyes. I was present while she wrote, and can attest that *it is her own production.*"[27]

Socialized to see Africans and African Americans as visibly outside of the sphere of privileged white culture and class, Wooldridge was forced to reassess his reading strategies. He was forced to see that Wheatley could direct crucial aspects of her own self-presentation, despite her slave status. He had to see Wheatley as a part of the literate class, and therefore a member of that class of Americans designated as worthy of the privileges attached to "whiteness." Wheatley, clearly, attached these privileges to "blackness" as well as "whiteness." Wheatley's African American readers could see in her work not only a poet forced to display her neoclassic form, but also a critic providing a model of performative subversion. Furthermore, they could see her broader view of Christianity, her more inclusive vision of America. Literacy, as Wheatley's life demonstrated, established a path to freedom, a path which was, at least in Wheatley's case, dependent upon being visibly intelligent. Within four months of her London success, she was finally granted her freedom.

Another example of Wheatley's use of her visible presence within her work may be useful. Wheatley's poem "To the University of CAM-BRIDGE, in NEW-ENGLAND" is typically read as an exhortation to the young men of Harvard University to take advantage of their "privileges *while they stay*" (*Poems*, 17) and to embrace Christian salvation. Bassard reads it as an attack on the sin of slavery (*Spiritual*, 42). But the poem may hide another, more specific warning, linked to its general advice to avoid sin and its castigation of slaveholders. When she wrote the poem, Phillis was thirteen years old, and when she revised it for publication in 1773, she was seventeen. On Boston streets, as Robinson notes, "there was, as Phillis must have noticed, such a bustling of so many peoples, white skinned, coppery skinned, swarthy, black skinned" (*Phillis*, 8). "Mulattoes" were much in evidence, which necessitated on some level an acknowledgment of interracial sexual contact. Even before Lord Chesterfield's infamous letters were published, the doctrine of "seeming virtue" was used to justify young white men's unwanted advances toward black women and white women of the lower classes. A precocious teenager, Wheatley surely was aware of this sexual double standard, and perhaps she glimpsed the prostitutes populating the wharves near the market.

Within her poem, Wheatley reminded the reader not once but twice that it was an "*Egyptian*" or "*Ethiop*" who was warning teenage boys against sin. As Zafar explains, through her "repeated interjections of nationality and race," Wheatley sought to "denature or make positive" commonly held notions of blackness (*We*, 20). The first reference signals that a literate black is critiquing their squandering of the privilege of an education and a full Christian life. This first reference to Wheatley as "Egyptian" creates a positive vision of blackness as Christian rationality and classical African wisdom. But the second reference, when Wheatley refers to the speaker of the poem as an "*Ethiop*," marks the speaker more specifically as a young black *woman* speaking to the white boys. "Ethiop" figures in the second case as *womanly* African nation. She warns the American manchildren of the "immense perdition [that] sinks the soul" which yields to the "transient sweetness" of a variety of sins, including, surely, those of a sexual as well as those of an imperialist nature.

In Wheatley's revised version of the poem, "the sable monster" of sin becomes instead "the deadly serpent."[28] Her revision specifically rejects the traditional Christian imagery linking blackness with sin and monstrosity. It replaces that imagery with traditional phallic imagery which connects the "deadly serpent" to sin, specifically to the sinfulness of sexual knowledge. To insure that her message was clear, Wheatley positioned this poem immediately following the poem "On Virtue," which argues that while "wisdom is higher than a fool can reach," "*Virtue* is near thee." Virtue is a queen leading "celestial *Chastity* along," and the speaker of the poem begs, "attend me, *Virtue*, thro' my youthful years!" ("On Virtue," *Poems*, 13–14). By warning Harvard boys about the "transient sweetness" of the "deadly serpent" of sin, Wheatley was telling those in charge of the "University of CAMBRIDGE, in NEW-ENGLAND," as well as rowdy white college boys (and their families) that a literate, intelligent black woman was watching them, and that black women, like black men, were not to be trifled with. These Harvard boys had better avoid "false joys" and "transient sweetness." Wheatley claims her place as a part of the Christian "human race" within which the boys "bloom" ("To the University of CAMBRIDGE," *Poems*, 16). In a truly Christian nation and "race," each person was granted respect; each person's genius was recognized. To imagine her recitation of this poem for parlor gatherings – her direct address to visitors young and old – is to recognize the boldness of her critical intelligence.

PERFORMING CRITICISM/PERFORMANCE CRITICISM

Unnerved by Wheatley's visible intelligence, colonists developed counter-strategies to circumscribe it. In Massachusetts her eulogy on Whitefield was advertised as written "By PHILLIS, a Servant Girl of 17 Years of Age, belonging to Mr. J. Wheatley of Boston – And has been but 9 Years in this Country from Africa," while in London it was simply "Compos'd in *America* by a Negro Girl Seventeen Years of Age" (*Phillis*, ed. Robinson, 370–72). The American version emphasizes the poet's African slave status, to insure its continuance and to applaud "Mr. J. Wheatley," as if the accomplishment of literacy were his.

This same negotiation about Wheatley's status is evident in the introductory material published in her volume of poems. The frontispiece engraving describes her as a "Negro Servant," but she erases the racial term in her dedication to the Countess: "much obliged, Very humble, And devoted Servant, Phillis Wheatley." In the preface and John Wheatley's letter of attestation, she is referred to as an "Author" working under disadvantageous circumstances but also, familiarly, as simply "Phillis." In the letter of attestation signed by eighteen Boston gentlemen, she transforms from a respectable "young Negro Girl" into a reformed "uncultivated Barbarian from Africa" into a "Slave" – but one qualified to write neoclassical poetry. She descends from Girl to Barbarian and then, the logic of the sentence structure argues, to the more elevated status of Slave Author. Through these shifts in naming, the anxiety about her literacy and its effect on her identity becomes palpable.

Because of the political implications of her public display of intelligence and the forced reassessment of reading strategies that it occasioned, Wheatley's contemporaries often labeled her a black "genius," positioning her as unique within her "race" rather than a representative of its potential or its achievements. It was important then and now, of course, to acknowledge and celebrate Wheatley's genius, but the reiteration of this term had serious implications.

Simultaneously exalting and domesticating her talent, those who called her "genius" avoided having to acknowledge the shifting class basis of racial formulations. They kept Wheatley safely ensconced as an oddity, "an uncultivated Barbarian from *Africa*" who in a matter of months became a poet not through an educational process applicable to every slave and free black's situation, but rather through "the Strength of her own Genius."[29] Her remarkable talent and achievements could not easily be duplicated if they were based on "genius." A French statesman, for example, regarded Wheatley as "one of the strangest creatures in the country and perhaps in the whole world," and Archibald Bell, her London publisher, billed her work as "one of the greatest instances of pure, unassisted Genius, that the world ever produced."[30]

While Wheatley certainly bore the burden of embodied womanhood, she was, paradoxically, spoken of more as an "African" than as a "woman" genius. Even though Mary Wheatley taught Phillis, Susanna Wheatley acted as her literary agent, and Selina Hastings served as her patron, their work as women together was obscured as Phillis was introduced to the general public. It was John Wheatley and seventeen other men who, as representatives of white culture, "authenticated" her abilities. They wanted her to serve not as an emblem of womanly achievement, but of African and Christian obedience guided by white men. They thwarted any attempt that might be made to represent black and white women working together on a project, even within the slave–mistress relationship. They also diverted attention from the transatlantic collaboration between women such as Susanna Wheatley and the Countess, the kind of collaboration that would characterize nineteenth-century women's abolition and reform efforts. And they did not perceive Wheatley's careful maneuvers within the framework of this transatlantic body of Christian women.

They dealt with the increasing colonial anxiety about controlling black men by foregrounding a seemingly malleable black woman as the black "type," even as they refused to focus on her womanliness. And despite the advertising references to her genius, many of their cohorts simultaneously dismissed her poems as "merely imitative" rather than inventive (*Poems*, ed. Mason, 25). In an oft-quoted passage in his "Notes on the State of Virginia" (1787) Thomas Jefferson not only denied her the title of genius but also the title of poet: "Religion, indeed, has produced a Phyllis Whately [*sic*]; but it could not produce a poet." Jefferson saw misery and love as the parents of poetry, but thought blacks were mired in rather than inspired by misery. He viewed them as incapable of the kind of love that fired the imagination to create poetry. He dismissed Wheatley's work as "below the dignity of criticism," arguing that she ranked as far below the wretched poetasters of Alexander Pope's "The Dunciad" as Pope himself, a crippled diminutive, ranked beneath that physical wonder, Hercules. Jefferson's comparison, however, thwarted his objectives: his comments, in fact, constituted a criticism of her work. That fact positioned her poetry as art (as well as cultural criticism), generating a public backlash against Jefferson's assessment of her.[31]

Wheatley positioned herself not just as a Christian but also as an "Afric" or "Ethiop" – as a writer with a classical, literary attachment as well as a material connection to Africa. She was a part of the African diaspora that Isidore Okpewho traces, a part of the triangulating, hybrid cultures that Gilroy calls the Black Atlantic. Through her poems she linked herself to America, England, and Africa. She clearly drew strength from Scipio Moorhead, the neighboring African artist who engraved her likeness for the frontispiece to her book. She forged a tie to Terence, the classical African dramatist who wrote refined drama for the privileged classes. Unlike his contemporary Titus Maccius Plautus (*c.* 254–184 BC) – whose plots provided the model for Shakespeare's earthy comedies for the masses – Terence chose to compose refined scripts for the discriminating. He typically depicted a good, clever servant who masked his efforts at freedom so that he could snatch it in the final scene – a useful scenario for Wheatley.

In "To Maecenas," the opening poem of Wheatley's volume, it was Terence (as well as John Wheatley, the poet Mather Byles, and Alexander Pope) who served as Wheatley's patron, her Maecenas. As she pictured Terence reading non-African poets' work, she asked him – and by extension, herself: "What felt those poets but you feel the same? / Does not your soul possess the sacred flame? / Their noble strains your equal genius shares / *In softer language, and diviner airs*" ("To Maecenas," *Poems*, 9, my italics). Wheatley's speaker is not just claiming equality here; she is claiming superiority for herself as a part of the African diasporic world she imagines into being. Like Terence, she writes "diviner airs." The speaker performs Wheatley's own sense of her Black Atlanticness, articulating and lobbying for an awareness of her soulful humanity and imaginative power. She speaks with Maecenas/Terence, claiming a rational, creative body as her own. By focusing "On Imagination," she "can surpass the wind . . . and grasp the mighty whole," – all the world, all the Black Atlantic – "Or with new worlds amaze th' unbounded soul."[32] Just as Terence claimed superiority to the rougher Plautus, she claims a place for herself, but within an "unbounded" soul that refuses to be limited to national affiliations. When she asks the Muses "why this partial grace, / To one alone of Afric's sable race," and says she'll "snatch a laurel" from Terence's crown while he "indulgent smile[s] upon the deed" ("To Maecenas," *Poems*, 11–12), she is lobbying for a place in transatlantic literature on her own terms, as a representative of the Black Atlantic, an African, a rational Christian American woman.

Wheatley creates within the world of neoclassical verse a kindly African literary father who will "defend [her] lays" ("To Maecenas," *Poems*, 12). This thoughtful African warns whites that their crimes will not be forgotten, that they are not safe despite their Goliath-like power. As Wheatley cautions the young white woman who suggested that she write the poem "On Recollection," the goddess of memory or remembrance is implacable: "But how is Mneme dreaded by the race, / Who scorn her warnings, and despise her grace? / By her unveil'd each horrid crime appears ... Hers the worst tortures that our souls can know" ("On Recollection," *Poems*, 63). This poem is (among other things) an anti-slavery critique. Wheatley's anti-slavery writing is, like the Night she described in "Thoughts on the Works of Providence," covered by a "sable veil" which "conceals effects, but shews th' *Almighty Cause.*" In these poems the emerging notion of an idolatrous "Ethiopia" suffering the punishment of slavery is upended by an awareness of the evils of theodicy: one should not use God to ignore political culpability.[33] In the era before the white-led colonization movement prompted many blacks to shift strategically from identifying as Ethiopian or African to claiming status on American soil as "free colored" or simply "American," Wheatley imagined a mythic and supportive African space for her performance as a critic and cantilevered it against the more fluid space of the Black Atlantic.

One early commentator, atypically, highlighted Wheatley's compositions as produced not by an African but by a specifically *womanly* poetic genius. Jane Dunlap (fl. 1771), read Wheatley's broadside on Whitefield and responded with a Sheaf of poems: "Shall [Whitefield's] due praises be so loudly sung / By a young Afric damsels virgin tongue? / And I be silent!" (Dunlap, *Poems*, 4). The edge in Dunlap's 1771 publication not only reveals a race-based competition but also proves that Wheatley served as a model for other women poets and critics. She provided an altered social code, in which enslaved people were educated, encouraged in Christian pursuits, and eventually freed.

In the 1770s most women, let alone enslaved women, did not enjoy the opportunity to meet collectively to consider their needs as women.

However, women do appear in various guises and relationships in Wheatley's poems. They appear as mothers, wives, daughters, sisters, as the building blocks of Christianity; and as abstract principles such as Freedom and Reason, as the building blocks of the Black Atlantic and of American-ness. Her last publication, "Liberty and Peace" (1784), for example, represents freedom as a woman who "comes" in a perpetual present moment.[34] Christian womanhood, Wheatley argued, is reasonable and through love creates freedom, on earth as it is in heaven. When Wheatley chooses to appear as a thinly veiled speaker in her poems, she performs as an intelligent, virtuous girl; a lively and talented Ethiop; a wise and knowing "Afric" capable of serious and damning judgments, and a generous-hearted Christian American and member of the black Atlantic. Each of these performances expanded the pathways open to women critics, but also raised anxieties about her work.

American colonists were more anxious about Wheatley's achievements than the British were, because her achievements signaled the intelligence and natural rights of the enslaved and of women. She critiqued Enlightenment notions of liberty as circumscribed and cramped. An anonymous London reviewer for the *Gentleman's Magazine and Historical Chronicle* called it "disgraceful" that Wheatley was still held as a slave after the publication of her poems. Another critic pointed out the irony of the fact that Wheatley was enslaved in Boston, the cradle of liberty. Ignatius Sancho, a former slave who became a merchant, playwright, and well-known correspondent in London in the 1770s and 1780s, bemoaned the fact that those who testified to Wheatley's "authenticity" as a poet "all knew – and perhaps admired – nay praised Genius in bondage – and then ... passed by – not one good Samaritan amongst them."[35] Authenticity on American soil did not guarantee freedom, but traveling to England as an individual conversant with multiple cultures was useful: Wheatley's London contacts lobbied for her release from slavery, which was granted about six months before her mistress's death. Wheatley's visible literacy, particularly her expertise in neoclassical literature, demonstrated to many whites her intelligence and therefore her humanity and right to freedom. It provided blacks with a glimpse of one way to identify as a part of a transatlantic culture, not just African or American, but cultured and Christian.

Wheatley developed her own notion of Christianity. As Zafar explains, "the refusal to recognize the liberating possibilities of Protestant Christianity and the supposition that Wheatley must want to be 'white' because she is a confessed Christian have fostered simplistic critiques of her work" (*We*, 17). Through her eulogies, in particular, she tried to convert others to her vision of a free Christian America embracing all (overlapping) nations, races, and cultures. Her idea of a rational Christian love is often aligned with pagan images from classical times, as in "Thoughts on the Works of Providence": Reason gives birth to a Goddess of Love that reveals Godhead. It is this same rationality that Wheatley calls on in "On being brought from AFRICA to AMERICA," widely regarded as a problematic poem because it seemingly posits slavery as a necessary step toward Christian redemption. But it is possible to imagine a different reading. Picture the fourteen-year-old Wheatley reciting, in a seemingly obedient tone to her owners, "'Twas mercy brought me from my *Pagan* land, / Taught my benighted soul to understand / That there's a God, that there's a *Savior* too: / Once I redemption neither sought nor knew." And then consider a shift in tone as she speaks directly to fellow Africans and African Americans: "Some view *our* sable race with scornful eye" ("On being brought from AFRICA to AMERICA," *Poems*, 18, italics mine).

The next line plays in various ways by virtue of the fact that it is set in quotation marks: "'Their colour is a diabolic die.'" Often this line is interpreted as if spoken by a scornful white who views black skin as a sign of African Americans' status as Hagar's vengeful children. But it may also be read as if it is spoken by an African or African American, denouncing the *whites*' color as a hellishly evil "die." It can be read as a critique of *whiteness*. (The line also calls to mind the indigo "die" harvested by blacks in the South, a crop which died their skin dark blue and led to numerous health problems; this reference, again, critiques whites.)

The final two lines, which sound like a threat as well as a reminder, liken Christian repentance to the refining of sugar cane: "Remember, *Christians, Negros,* black as *Cain,* / May be refin'd, and join th' angelic train" ("On being brought," *Poems*, 18). The comma between "Christians" and "Negros" is customarily read as a colon: Wheatley is pictured reminding (white) Christians that blacks can be refined and reach Heaven. But a more complex performance is demanded if the comma remains a comma: Wheatley stood in front of her largely white audiences in the parlor of her master's house and reminded them that all those who were sinful or "black as *Cain,*" *including (white) Christians and "Negroes,"* had the opportunity to repent and join the angelic train leading from life to death and redemption. Wheatley compares Christian slaveholders to Cain, who steals his brother's birthright and therefore is "black" with sin. Errant whites and blacks can be refined through a rational Christianity.

As Jennifer Fleischner explains in her psychological study of later slave narratives, "one does not readily forget, though one may travel far from, the lessons of identity learned in childhood": Wheatley does maintain her Christian performance, but she also transforms it, "humbly" pointing out the ludicrous viciousness of Christian slaveholding (*Mastering*, 1).

Wheatley was raised as a Congregationalist in the Old South Church in Boston, a church founded by conservatives who believed that childhood baptism (instead of a "born again" experience of spirit possession) should be the basis for church membership. The largest building in town, the Old South Church regularly hosted town meetings when they overflowed Faneuil Hall. Election sermons were delivered there (Bacon, *Boston*, iv). It also served as a center for patriots' resistance to the crown. On the anniversary of the Boston Massacre, for example, restive crowds gathered to hear Joseph Warren (1741–75) speak there; on 16 December 1773, patriots gathered there to protest the new tea tax, dashing from there to the harbor to stage the Boston Tea Party. In 1775 the British ripped out the pews, dumped dirt on the expansive floor, and established their cavalry practice there, with a tavern handy in a lower gallery.

Late eighteenth-century Christianity, as practiced by the Old South congregants, was a site of contestation for political ideas about who had rights and who did not, who was a slave and who was not. From 1780 to 1784, the Methodists and Baptists condemned slavery, passing regulations at their conventicles against buying, owning, and selling slaves. Wheatley was doubtless aware of the early rumblings that led to these developments, perhaps overhearing them as she ran errands with other slaves in the Boston market, or as she sat for her portrait by Scipio Moorhead. Even in the late 1770s there were independent African American preachers with black as well as "mixed" congregations, and they were "interpreting the stories, symbols, and events of the Bible to fit the day-to-day lives of those held in bondage," in ways that did not seek validation from whites (Raboteau, *Fire*, 24). Wheatley joined in this project of interpretation.

Roughly a third of Wheatley's published poems were eulogies, and it seems that she pursued this performance of the "muse to the bereaved" with multiple objectives. Through her eulogies, she insures that her poems will be read and offers comfort to herself as well as others. She also creates a Christian heaven as a restorative intellectual space of equality where she can feel and perform her subjectivity. It becomes her ship, her mode of travel. Wheatley calls this restorative space into existence in the here and now: to imagine a (Christian) utopia is to re-imagine reality.

Wheatley's eulogies have multiple roots, deriving from European neo-classical tradition as well as from the African tradition of the praise song, designed to honor the spirits of those who have died. Perhaps Wheatley remembered the praise songs of her youth and tried through the eulogies to keep some vestige of them alive. But she also had a very pragmatic reason for writing eulogies: important people *had* to accept her eulogies and read them. When she composed a eulogy for Massachusetts Lieutenant Governor Andrew Oliver's wife, she noted that Oliver could not "assent refuse / To heav'nly tidings from the *Afric* muse." Through her "advent'rous lays" ("To His Honour the Lieutenant-Governor, on the Death of His Lady," *Poems*, 117) she exhorted one of the most powerful men in the colony to help her create a rational Christian heaven on earth. She pictured Death as a great leveler, where "nations mix with their primeval dust." Consider, she asked her listeners and readers, your perilous situation, and act now to secure your future well-being. To be a true Christian, you must see all as Death does: as equal. Even nation-hood, that frenzied goal, is passing. Wheatley imagined a space larger than nationhood. In her eulogies of children, she offered Christian comfort to all parents separated from their children, as if to send a message home to Africa: "Parents, no more indulge the falling tear: / Let *Faith* to heav'n's refulgent domes repair." Her vision of God becomes clearest, perhaps, when she represents the deity telling his Son (or the sun) to "descend to earth" to inspire mankind to "enlarge the close contracted mind."[36] Her rational Christianity frees closed minds.

"Goliath of Gath" and "Isaiah lxiii. 1–8" are the poems most obviously inspired by this Biblical vision. In "Goliath" a cherub warns Goliath that he will lose the battle against the underdog David: Goliath's spear and shield provide no protection against David, armed (like Wheatley) by God. In "Isaiah lxiii" Wheatley warns readers that an abandoned, blood-drenched God plans to avenge those who wronged Him. The Biblical passage reads: "I will tread down the people in mine anger ... and I will bring down their strength to the earth" (63: 3–6). Wheatley voiced her righteous anger against racist Christians in this poem, and linked Christian retribution with American vengeance against British wrongs. The poem ends with a strategy that Wheatley found useful: the speaker lays herself at God's chest, just as Zion (heaven) has done; both smile serenely at their detractors' "cunning," defying "all their force" ("Isaiah lxiii. 1–8," *Poems*, 61).

In her widely distributed eulogy on George Whitefield, Wheatley imagines the minister winging his way to heaven through "vast seas of

day" ("On the Death of the Rev. Mr. GEORGE WHITEFIELD," *Poems*,
22). But his journey is not uneventful: the moon and stars silently observe
that he "wrestled with his God by night" (23). This image is curious,
because it unflatteringly compares Whitefield to Jacob, who also wrestled
with God. It sends knowing readers – perhaps Africans meeting secretly
in hush arbors under "all the stars of light" (23) – an inside message.
Genesis 32 tells how Jacob, the second-born brother, cheats his older
brother Esau out of his inheritance and then years later prays for God's
protection on his fearful journey to reunite with his brother: "Deliver me,
I pray thee, from the hand of my brother, from the hand of Esau: for I
fear him, lest he will come and smite me, and the mother with the
children" (32: 11). A terrified Jacob sends his retinue ahead with presents
to placate Esau, at which point he finds himself wrestling alone in
the dark with an unnamed man. The fight lasts until daybreak, when the
man, seeing that he is not going to prevail against Jacob, touches the
hollow of Jacob's thigh, injuring him even as he grants the blessing Jacob
demands. Jacob concludes that he has "seen God face to face" and
expresses gratitude that his life has been preserved (32: 30).

Jacob's story may be read as a parable of two nations: the younger,
budding Anglo-American nation cheats the older civilization, Africa, out of
its inheritance. As the wealthy younger brother returns to their common
(eternal) home, he fears retribution for the thefts he has committed against
his brother Africa, just as Thomas Jefferson and other white Americans
feared "ten thousand recollections, by the blacks, of the injuries they have
sustained" (*Notes*, query XIV). Anglo-America tries to smooth its way into
heaven with after-the-fact "gifts" (such as black literacy) but is nonetheless
left alone to face God. The budding nation wrestles with God, who marks it
as his own, renaming Jacob "Israel" or "ruled by God." Thus chastened, a
youthful but halt nation lifts up its eyes to see its African brother, who
greets him with Christian forbearance but also with self-sufficiency: "I have
enough, my brother; keep that thou has unto thyself" (Genesis 33: 9). By
this point in the parable, however, Jacob/Anglo-America/Wheatley's white
reader has changed. He acknowledges the godliness of Esau/Africa and is
ready to divest himself of privilege: Jacob urges Esau to take his gifts
"because God hath dealt graciously with me, and because I have enough.
And he urged him, and he took it" (33: 11). Anglo-Americans can change,
Wheatley suggests, they can divest themselves of privilege, acknowledge
Africans, and provide reparations.

Having gestured toward how Christians should treat other Christians,
Wheatley reveals how Whitefield's Christianity implicitly supports

American self-definition: "He pray'd that grace in ev'ry heart might dwell, / He long'd to see *America* excel." He exhorts both "AMERICANS" and "*Africans,*" to accept Christ: "Take HIM, my dear AMERICANS, he said, / Be your complaints in his kind bosom laid; / Take HIM ye *Africans,* he longs for you" ("On the Death of the Rev. Mr. GEORGE WHITEFIELD," *Poems*, 23). The repetition and revision of the directive "Take HIM," coupled with Christ's special longing for African over American converts, elevated African converts into a special constituency. The "Impartial SAVIOUR" enabled all to become "sons, and *kings, and priests* to GOD" (my italics). Her reference to Revelations is clear: a community "out of every kindred, and tongue, and people, and nation," is transformed into "*kings and priests*: and we shall reign on the earth" (Rev. 5: 9–10). In a British broadside version these lines tie Christianity more explicitly to anti-slavery and its freeing effect (not only for blacks but also for whites): Christ "will make you *free*, and Kings, and Priests to God" ("An Ode of Verses on the much-lamented Death of the Rev. Mr. GEORGE WHITEFIELD," *Phillis*, ed. Robinson, 372–73, my italics). In a godly nation, Wheatley argued, all people formed a community in which there was no slavery, no hierarchy of class, language, race, or nation. Wheatley establishes a performance tradition for black Christian women critics by hiding this Biblical parable in her eulogy for Whitefield; black women critics will follow her lead in hiding their critiques in Biblical references, as the next chapter of this study will reveal.

As a slave, Wheatley would probably have been familiar with 1 Peter 2: 13–25, a Biblical passage which catechized slaves into obedience and advocated that they suffer as Christ suffered. Perhaps she heard her minister read, "Servants, be subject to your masters with all fear; not only to the good and gentle, but also to the froward ... for even hereunto were ye called: because Christ also suffered for us, leaving us an example" (1 Peter 2: 18,21). But hearing is not the same as believing, and it is equally probable that she read the preceding passages in 1 Peter 2, which undermine, in advance, the lines advocating obedience. Earlier verses liken some believers to "lively stones" – rejected by men but chosen by God as cornerstones for a newly constituted people, "a royal priesthood, a holy nation, a peculiar people." These people "which in time past were not a people, but are now the people of God," were to serve as "stumbling-stones" for the less godly. This is the kind of vision Wheatley created: African diasporic peoples, gathered into a spiritual home in the Black Atlantic, constituted a holy nation that would trip up those who thought they were godly but were not.

By performing the role of Christian eulogist, Wheatley managed to critique slavery. She wove her public performance of self out of the traditions of African praise songs, Biblical exhortation, neoclassic poetry – and the political rhetoric of "natural rights."

In 1775, when the colonial discourse of "natural rights" was in full swing, Johann Blumenbach translated Carl von Linne's four "types" of homo sapiens into five separate "races": the Caucasian, Ethiopian, American, Mongolian, and Malay, each developing in a different fashion, Blumenbach argued, because of the environments in which they lived. Both Linne and Blumenbach still upheld monogenesis, or the idea that all humans stemmed from one common ancestor. Blumenbach himself even admitted the arbitrary nature of his designations.[37] Within this concept of racial classification, political theorists could argue that every individual, regardless of his "clime," possessed "natural rights."

Wheatley and Warren's understanding of natural rights differed, however. Warren joined her older brother James (the Whig who coined the phrase "no taxation without representation") as a major agitator for the natural rights of (implicitly white propertied) Americans, while Wheatley recognized that the theory of natural rights was invaluable in establishing the groundwork not only for colonial independence from England, but also for slaves' independence from their masters and free blacks' independence from a racist society. Keenly aware of the ways in which the abstract body posited by natural rights discourse was implicitly marked as white, Wheatley tried to refashion the ways in which Americans understood the Enlightenment theory of natural rights.

Wheatley's salon performances helped prove the natural rights of blacks in the face of white American domination, as well as the natural rights of all colonists in the face of British domination. Benjamin Rush referred to her to prove that Africans not only reasoned but possessed ethical power: if their environments were altered, they would flourish (Gates, "[Phillis Wheatley]," 219). John and Susanna Wheatley's house was situated on a major thoroughfare, so that Phillis witnessed many of the altercations preceding the fight for independence. The Stamp Act riots inspired her poem "To the KING's Most Excellent Majesty 1768," which applauds the repeal of the Stamp Act and reminds King George that "A monarch's smile can set his subjects free!" (*Poems*, 17). It is a short distance between an absolute power that "can" and an absolute power that "should" set his subjects free, and since Wheatley obviously remained enslaved even after the repeal of the Stamp Act, the final lines evoked Wheatley's desire that "each clime," including her own, might see freedom. Even as she imagined a Black Atlantic, she positioned herself squarely as a patriotic Whig, a member of the American "race." In the 1768 poem "America," for instance, she built revolutionary sentiment by castigating Britain for acting like an unreasonable mother enchaining her virtuous American son. By indirection, she simultaneously critiqued Americans who held "Ethiopians" not in metaphorical but in real "Iron Chains" (*Phillis*, ed. Robinson, 135–36).

The preponderance of eulogies in Wheatley's corpus may, in fact, suggest more than her preoccupation with Christian transcendence. They may signal her attempt to deal with the death of her seemingly irretrievable ties to her family and her village in Africa, her seemingly irreversible lack of freedom and natural rights. She constructed a graveyard and a heaven through her poems, and that heaven was aligned as much with Africa as America. In a telling poetic exchange with two Navy officers who may have been billeted in the Wheatley home, Wheatley reveals that focus upon Africa as a sacred site. "A Gentleman of the Navy" acknowledges her as "the lovely daughter of the Affric shore, / Where every grace, and every virtue join," and Phillis responds by recalling and reclaiming that shore: "pleasing Gambia on my soul returns ... and Eden blooms again" (*Phillis*, ed. Robinson, 286–87). Africa, not America, figures here as Eden for Wheatley as she defines herself, and – through references to her fellow African poet, Terence – her literary tradition and diasporic community. The well-known image of her first memory, her mother's pouring water libations to the ancestors at dawn, haunts her lines about Eden. Through her elegies imagining a heavenly site of absolute equality, Wheatley mourns her own unspeakable losses as well as others'. She acts as a ventriloquist of the alabastered dead, animating them to promote a rational vision of a Christian nation of equals, all possessing natural rights.[38] Her contemporary Mercy Otis Warren, however, wedged her way into the public sphere through a different notion of nationhood.

SITES OF ACCESS

Mercy Otis Warren also performed as a ventriloquist of sorts, posing as an anonymous (and implicitly white male) patriot, parlaying her family connections into a public resistance to British rule. Her father, an activist lawyer, judge, and justice of the peace in Plymouth, and her brother James, an early revolutionary leader, supported her early education, and her husband, James Warren (1726–1808), eventually the Speaker of the

Massachusetts legislature, admired it.³⁹ John Adams (1735–1826), a close family friend, neighbor, and correspondent, along with his wife Abigail, encouraged her and helped publish her work. After the publication of her first two propaganda plays, Warren's male family members and friends began to request specific poems or plays, in a manner reminiscent of Wheatley's patrons: John Adams requested the poetic "Squabble of the Sea Nymphs" at the Boston Tea Party; her husband expressed a "particular desire" for her satire *The Group*, Harvard professor and friend James Winthrop asked for the satirical pro-boycott poem *Lamira*, and Warren's son Winslowe prompted a drama about *The Ladies of Castile*. It is clear that Warren sought these men's approval. After sending her Tea Party poem to the Adamses, she promised "none Else till I hear how it stands in the inspection of Mr. Adamss [*sic*] judicious Eye."⁴⁰

Mercy's brother James Otis acted as her first intellectual mentor, but she may have affected his thinking, as well. As early as 1764 he asked if women did not have "as good a right to give their respectable suffrages" as men. Warren's literacy was not unusual in Massachusetts – nearly three-fourths of the women could read and write – but she did enjoy unusual access to an advanced education and to public policy deliberations. She hosted political gatherings in which John and Samuel Adams (1722–1803) joined her father, brother, and husband to plot revolution. As her father's age and her brother's deteriorating mental health forced their retirement from politics in the early 1770s, Mercy joined her husband in taking their places. Despite her partisan politics, like Wheatley she represented her poems and plays "as the amusement of solitude."⁴¹

With unalloyed family support for her education, her writing, and her politics, Mercy Otis could, unlike Wheatley, publish her cultural criticism over a lifetime. Her father allowed her to study with her brother, who took her intellectual interests seriously. Their uncle, Yale graduate Reverend Jonathan Russell, tutored them in college-preparatory courses in Greek, Roman, and English literature and history. Mercy's husband, elected to the Massachusetts House of Representatives in the mid-1760s and for many years the Speaker, looked favorably upon women's participation in politics: he even solicited female signatures for his Solemn League and Covenant demanding economic sanctions against England. He expressed pride and pleasure in her literary achievements, calling her "an Author of great Abilities, discernment, and Judgment."⁴² Her sons, George and James, encouraged her to complete her *History*, offering to take dictation and critique drafts of it. When Warren launched her life as a writer, she did so within a supportive family circle that believed fervently that the English were going to "enslave" colonists if they did not all rally to the patriot cause. Warren tried to rally patriots to action by donning a "patriot" host body and imaginatively weaving non-fiction with fiction, thinly disguising current events in what might be called newspaper theatre.

Donning a patriot body was risky outside of her immediate circle. By 1772, many towns were setting up Committees of Correspondence to share information and create a Whig alliance, in some cases an armed alliance, against British rule. There were over two hundred such committees across Massachusetts, many eager to read and perform Warren's propaganda. Her satires were not produced in theatres, but were probably performed in informal readings by patriots in their taverns, homes, and secret gatherings.[43] Warren merged the actual and the imagined in her scripts, to prompt audience members to jump into politics and redirect unfolding events.

Her first play, *The Adulateur, a Tragedy*, as it is now acted *in Upper Servia*, attests to Warren's awareness of "the theatre of political frustration." In March 1772, while Phillis Wheatley prepared to prove her literacy for Boston luminaries, Mercy Warren published the first installment of her anonymous play and announced that it would soon be produced in Boston "at the grand parade in Upper Servia."[44] Readers would have understood that the "grand parade" was the Boston Common, a large park-line tract of land where military training, musters, parades, and public executions had historically taken place. Hundreds of British soldiers had encamped there in 1770, sparking the deadly altercation with townspeople that became known as the Boston Massacre. Savvy readers would also have grasped Warren's point that Tory Governor Thomas Hutchinson (1711–80) was producing pure political theatre on the Common, and that patriots had better stage their own political theatre there if they did not wish to lose their rights. From the first, Warren was more interested in political drama than the theatre; her scripts were ready-made for reading aloud in semi-private political gatherings but were not suited for staging in professional venues, nor was that her intent. The 1774 Continental Congress's ban on "exhibitions of shows, plays, and other expensive diversions and entertainments" did not pertain to her scenes of propaganda.[45]

In *The Adulateur*, Warren launched her crusade to rid Massachusetts of the newly appointed Hutchinson by characterizing him as Rapatio, a despot who sought to enslave the patriot race.[46] By 1772 many colonists held Hutchinson responsible for Boston's woes: its unreasonable taxes, armed occupation, the five citizens killed in the Massacre, and the death of Master Sneider, a twelve-year-old German immigrant killed by customs officer Ebenezer Richardson. Hutchinson had maneuvered himself and his family members into political positions long promised to Mercy's father, so the Otises loathed him. For Mercy Warren, the responsibilities of the daughter and patriot merged: she tried to unveil Hutchinson's monarchical designs and redeem her father as well as the fatherland. Warren's Rapatio/Hutchinson uses promotions to lure patriots to become loyalists and seeks revenge when they do not respond. He lies to colonists and misrepresents their behavior to the crown, so that he can muster more soldiers, who in turn slaughter patriots on sight. He closes down trade and plots the release of Richardson and the loyalists involved in the Massacre. Stripped of their rights, the patriots vow to fight tyranny. Brutus, the Whig hero and stand-in for the ailing James Otis (and Mercy Warren), along with Cassius (Samuel Adams), pledges to fight Rapatio and warns that a Revolutionary War may be imminent (*Plays*, 29).

Warren alternated fiction and non-fiction even more boldly in *The Defeat*, her next Whig propaganda play. She interpolated actual news reportage into her scenes. She depicted thinly veiled British authorities, including Rapatio (Hutchinson), Limpit (Hutchinson's in-law, Lieutenant Governor Andrew Oliver [1706–74]), and the side-switching Proteus (General William Brattle). She opened with the script's production history, wryly explaining that since many "country readers have been out of the way of the theatrical amusements of the last season," they might enjoy "a few extracts from The Defeat, a Dramatic Performance lately exhibited." Many of the "country readers" had been busily organizing their Committees of Correspondence, in fact, and Warren invited them not only to produce her script, but to embody her politics (*Plays*, n.p.).

She again depicted Hutchinson as Rapatio: he calls the Senate together to prevent the Committees of Correspondence from meeting, he bribes patriots away from the cause, he repairs his home with taxes levied on patriots, he unseats new anti-loyalist senators. "Proteus" (Brattle), disturbed by "a spirited Paragraph" resembling Otis's inflammatory *Rights* pamphlet, pledges allegiance to Rapatio, at which point Warren blithely notes: "The Scene closes on Proteus. *After which several Tragical Scenes are exhibited, but we refer the curious to the whole Representation, as acted at the Head Quarters of the Bashaw of Servia, and proceed to the 3rd Act, which opens* SCENE I" (*Plays*, n.p.).

Warren's off-handed dismissal of her own scene called attention to the real political theatre unfolding in Boston, and used real events as a substitute for a second act before drawing readers back into her satire.[47] Nothing I could make up would be as outrageous as what our loyalist Governor is doing, she suggested: watch what is really happening as your second act, and then return to my satire. You will see things in a different light. When Warren's readers did return to her scenes, they witnessed a battle "in which Rapatio, his Abettors and Creatures are totally defeated, after which Freedom and Happiness are restored to the Inhabitants of Servia." A letter follows, warning Bostonians that they had better elect "some new Performers," the Whigs (*Plays*, n.p.). A news report announces that Rapatio is stewing over an impolitic and widely circulated letter. This is a reference to an actual letter that the "real" Rapatio – Hutchinson – had written to Thomas Whately, the former British Secretary of the Treasury and the author of the Stamp Act. In the actual letter, Hutchinson had argued for the necessity of abridging colonists' rights. His incendiary letter fell into Benjamin Franklin's hands in London, and Franklin returned it to the colonies, where, tradition has it, it was first read in Mercy Warren's parlor, then circulated around the colonies (Zagarri, *Woman's*, 59). Many historians regard the 1773 release of Hutchinson's letter as the spark igniting the Revolution. Warren helped fan that spark. By the end of her *Defeat*, both Rusicus (Warren) and Horiensius (Adams) have called for Rapatio's (Hutchinson's) demise, and Rapatio even worries that Brutus (Otis) may kill him.

Interweaving imaginary and actual events, melding classical allusion and Bible stories with politics, Mercy Warren published dramatic satires depicting British power as performative and subject to colonial intervention. In *The Group*, published anonymously as a pamphlet on 3 April 1775, and widely reprinted in New York and Pennsylvania newspapers, she pictured the Tories as locusts and monstrous serpents: the dramatis personae are

attended by a swarm of court sycophants, hungry harpies, and unprincipled danglers, collected from the neighbouring villages, hovering over the stage in the shape of locusts, led by Massachusettensis in the form of a basilisk; the rear brought up by Proteus ... the whole supported by a mighty army and navy, from blunderland, for the laudible purpose of enslaving its best friends. (*Plays*, 2)

In Warren's image, as in the Bible (Joel 1: 1–7), locusts invade the land – and Mercy gives them a leader: Hutchinson, a vicious and chimerical mythical creature whose name, "basilisk," means "little king" in the Greek.

Given the viciousness of her early political propaganda plays, Mercy Warren had to develop a method to disguise her identity. She had to perform "(in)visibly" to launch her career as a cultural critic: she was simultaneously widely read as a patriot and invisible as a woman.

Like many European American women critics, Warren developed a host body to try to maintain her anonymity: she crafted a patriot body that was routinely read as masculine. Between 1650 and 1783 (the year the Treaty of Paris ended the Revolutionary War), European American women, like their male counterparts, usually adopted anonymous host bodies to protect themselves against social embarrassment or legal action. If their work was not published anonymously, it appeared posthumously, pseudonymously, under initials, or through dictation to a male author. Pseudonymous productions enabled white women to create "cultured American" bodies: they tried to claim citizenship through culture, and that culture was implicitly attached to notions of whiteness. Quaker women tried an alternative method of access to the public sphere: they created a body of "Friends" in order to circulate their writings privately through commonplace books – but their host body was equally tied to notions of American culture and whiteness.[48] All these host bodies – the patriot, the cultured American, the Friend – enabled European American women to perform claims on whiteness. By positioning themselves as (implicitly white) male patriots, cultured Americans, or Friends, they asserted their privilege even as they dodged detection or at least provided themselves with a veneer of respectability.

Toward the end of the eighteenth century, white male writers began to abandon anonymity. They started signing their work to establish themselves as authors and paid professionals. Their hold on their intellectual property was intimately tied to emerging concepts of authorship, ownership, and authority within American nationhood: in 1789 the Constitution (Article 1, section 8) granted Congress power to establish copyright protection, and with copyright protection came an awareness of the text as property and profit and an idea of the author as a subject capable of originality. To establish this "new immaterial property" and the authority it conveyed, the first federal copyright statute was passed in 1790. It covered books, maps, and charts. Published play scripts were covered, but not play performances, suddenly prompting male playwrights to publish their scripts and to publish them under their own names. These male writers claimed the new, *immaterial*, national authorial body as their own. Most white women critics, however, still published anonymously, pseudonymously, or under their initials until they could gauge the political and social repercussions of their publications. Sometimes, as will become clear in chapter 3, they worked desperately to protect their anonymity even as they hoped for a limited detection and recognition. Sometimes women critics signed their own names to their work after the initial dangers passed, reaping a certain economic or literary success.[49]

Mercy Warren initially published within an anonymous body or a generically pseudonymous body with a male valence, as a "Columbian Patriot." As a consequence, readers assumed white male authorship of her works. This strategy allowed her to try to protect herself and her family while "the spirit of party runs so high."[50] It also lessened the cultural anxiety surrounding her authorship so that she could publish over a lifetime. By attaching herself parasitically to a host body, she managed to perform maleness and whiteness. And this body acted as a host network as well, connecting her to other like-minded patriots, eager to stage patriotism as Whig (and later as anti-Federalist) whiteness.

Virtually all of the European American women critics with serious ambitions regarding their writing published initially under cover, and they deployed pseudonyms or remained anonymous long after the men had shucked off the custom of remaining invisible. In 1772, when Warren critiqued the British by publishing her play *The Adulateur* anonymously, she was simply following the custom available to all the white male patriots in her circle. However, in 1792, when Judith Sargent Murray (1751–1820) launched her "Gleaner" column, she adopted a masculine pseudonym just as the men were dropping theirs.

Warren's patriotic male host body shielded her from charges of treason and libel. Her dramatic satire, *The Adulateur*, appeared anonymously in Boston's Whig newspaper *The Massachusetts Spy* in 1772 and as a pamphlet in 1773, and was followed by *The Defeat* (1773) and *The Group* (1775), also published anonymously. John Adams sent her "Sea Nymph" poem to the *Boston Gazette* to be published anonymously. Typically, the anonymous *Blockheads* (1776) and *The Motley Assembly* (1779) have also been attributed to her authorship (as in Franklin and Anthony), although recently scholars have contested this claim (Fritz, *Cast*, 318–19; Zagarri, *Woman's*, 70). In February 1788, Warren adopted the generic but implicitly masculine pseudonym "a COLUMBIAN PATRIOT" to publish a pamphlet critiquing the Federalists' newly proposed Constitution. Titled *OBSERVATIONS On the new CONSTITUTION, and on the Federal and State CONVENTIONS* – and attributed to anti-Federalist Elbridge Gerry for many years to come – this influential pamphlet demanded amendments to the Constitution, a lobbying effort that helped lead to the ratification of the Bill of Rights in 1791.[51]

Partly because the Revolution had succeeded by the time she published the bulk of her work, and partly because she had helped justify white women's entrance into the public sphere, she was able to publish her *POEMS* (1790) and her three-volume non-fiction work, *HISTORY of the Rise, Progress and Termination of the AMERICAN REVOLUTION* (1805), under her own name. She signed the former "Mrs. M. Warren," and published the latter under the even more confident label "Mrs. Mercy Warren of Plymouth, (Mass.)." Mercy Warren's path from anonymity through (male-gendered) pseudonymity to a more transparent claim on authorship was not the only path available to European and European American women in the late eighteenth century.

A number published under feminine pseudonyms during this time period, creating a gendered subjectivity. This practice enabled them to retain their class status as gendered "ladies" or "gentlewomen" while obscuring their individual identities. It enabled them to perform whiteness. Their very femininity guaranteed their upper (or upper-middle) class status, as long as it remained generic.[52] Critics working alone often published under general pseudonyms, for example, as "Daughters of Liberty." Women circulating their work within a community of women – authors like Elizabeth Graeme Fergusson (1737–1801), for instance – claimed more individuated pseudonyms, imagining a single and specific bodily shield. They appeared in print or in the salon as English or Roman matrons: as Laura or Martesia, for example.

Women even adopted pseudonymous host bodies in their private letters, which were often carried from place to place by traveling servants, relatives, or friends. Sometimes they tucked poems into the envelope or directly into the text of the letters. Mercy Warren wrote as "Marcia" to her Cambridge friend Hannah Winthrop (Honoria) as well as to Abigail Adams (Portia). The historical Marcia and her husband Hortensius had a daughter who, like her father, became a Roman orator, so this pseudonym indirectly validated Mercy's outspokenness. Warren was anxious about her role as a critic: she initially hid the fact of her public writing even from her son Winthrop, explaining that her desire to be esteemed by those closest to her and her "inability of executing [the writing] in a manner deserving the approbation of the judicious" prompted her concealment. Warren's writings eventually reached far and wide, but she professed that she would be pleased "if enabled by my pen to give pleasure to a little circle of very valuable friends."[53]

She was not alone in expressing this sentiment. The idea of publishing one's writing within a circle of friends was quite widespread in the mid eighteenth century. As a result, commonplace books shared among friends emerged as a popular means of pseudonymous publication, particularly among well-to-do Quaker women in New England. These critics circulated poems, sketches, and letters among themselves, "publishing" in a semi-public fashion while remaining invisible to those outside of their social circle. This was another way in which European American women performed their sense of whiteness.

Many of these poet-critics understood themselves to be occupying the host body of a Quaker "Friend." Milcah Martha Hill Moore (1740–1829), for example, created and circulated a commonplace book which collected miscellaneous writings along with poems by members of her family and by friends, particularly women friends. After circulating her book privately for a couple of decades, Moore published it anonymously. Her elite Quaker culture, centered in Philadelphia and rural Pennsylvania, "was a culture of performance, a culture poised on the verge between oracular effects and printed directives," and indeed, many of the poems in Moore's book were recited in social gatherings.[54] Moore's commonplace book enabled her to collect and distribute the poetic commentaries of Susanna Wright (1697–1784) and Hannah Griffitts (1727–1817) as well as Elizabeth Graeme Fergusson.

Neither Wright nor Griffitts ever married, and their poems demonstrate the ways in which they forged strong same-sex ties of Friendship, using pseudonyms to explore them more fully. They corresponded regularly, and clearly drew strength from liberal Quaker notions about women's importance. As "Fidelia," Griffitts justifies the very act of writing through "An Essay on Friendship": "The Friend requires, & friendship does demand, / At least th' attempt from my inferior Hand" (Moore, *Miscellanies*, 115). Her friend Annis Boudinot Stockton (1736–1801), who authored another early commonplace book, also speaks of "friendships [*sic*] sacred shrine." In Stockton's book, "Laura" (probably Elizabeth Fergusson) celebrated the "steady flame" of female friendship over "love's frail passion," titling her poem "FRIENDSHIP *preferable to* LOVE."[55]

Professions of same-sex love were ordinary at a time when many elite women lived far from one another and expressed their friendship through long letters and poetic inserts, but when those professions surfaced in public venues, they were typically cloaked by pseudonyms to protect the writers from a nascent anxiety about class respectability. Only those forced to try to profit economically or politically from their authorship used their real names. Gentlefolk used pseudonyms. Carroll Smith-Rosenberg explains that strong emotional connections among women were common: "deeply felt, same-sex friendships were casually accepted . . . These relationships ranged from the supportive love of sisters, through the enthusiasms of adolescent girls, to sensual avowals of love by mature women." These bonds among women often evinced a "romantic and even sensual note."[56]

This focus on friendship moved into female academies as commonplace books were adopted as textbooks. Young European American girls were invited to memorize selections, recite them for private audiences, and model speeches and compositions on them. The women who circulated their poems in commonplace books were keenly aware of political events as well, which in turn politicized women's education. Nor was their political critique simple: Griffitts, for example, advocated boycotting British products even as she satirized Thomas Paine and Benjamin Franklin in her poems (Moore, *Miscellanies*, 172–73; 86, 116, 105). In "Meschianza," she lambasted the "Philadelphia girls, dressed as Turkish maidens" who joined British officers in a masque (51–53). These commonplace book critics, in other words, modeled political engagement as well as solidarity among women. Stockton, like Griffitts and others, gained confidence from her writers' circle, and eventually became a very well-known poet. She invented pseudonyms for others as well as herself: Mulford lists seven pages' worth (*Only*, 320–26).

Women who wrote, more publicly, for or about the theatre during this period had to be doubly careful to adopt anonymous or pseudonymous bodies: the crown regarded theatrical satires as treasonous and religionists viewed play-going as lascivious.[57] Despite these disincentives (and years before Warren appeared on the public scene), a handful of women theatre critics faced down prejudice and adopted pseudonyms to defend the stage. In the process, they critiqued the social customs associated with whiteness, not to dismantle but to reshape them. For example, as early as 1756, "Arabella Sly" praised *The Beaux Strategem*, but wondered if it was truly necessary for a lady, while laughing at it, to cover her face with her fan. Sometimes women critics tried to enforce aesthetic standards onstage as well as in the auditorium. For instance, "Clarinda" blasted unruly actors who added crude improvisations to a 1760 *Hamlet* production and then had the audacity to castigate the audience for hissing at them.[58]

Occasionally, a theatre critic directly attacked gender codes. In the 1760s, "Amanda," probably an upper-class white woman, initiated a debate about women and the theatre in the *New York Gazette*, revealing some of the drawbacks of pseudonymity.[59] Amanda critiqued "Philodemos's" diatribe against the theatre and his "scurrilous insinuation" that female theatre-goers lost their reputations at the theatre through "criminal assignations, and lascivious intrigues." Amanda dismissed her presumed lower-class opponent as an "Impudent fellow!" and "in the name of all [her] incented females," she refuted his claim that theatrical performances "so corrupt a female mind, as to make her lose all sense of virtue" (989). She cited evidence from contemporary dramas to prove her point. Amanda's pseudonym failed to protect her fully from Philodemos, however. He castigated her as one of "the playhouse ladies" who had been led to believe that they were "Goddesses, and proper objects of adoration." He suggested that Amanda herself was probably a "strolling player" (990). Luckily, she had published a letter in the newspaper before the theatre troupe came to town, using the same pseudonym, therefore proving she was not an itinerant player (991). Into this pseudonymous exchange walked "Dolly Blithe," a satirist posing as a "female friend" to Amanda, who ridiculed Amanda's defense of the theatre so soundly that the editor announced that he would not publish the rejoinder (probably by Amanda) (993). What this exchange reveals is that when "unlicensed" women critics like Amanda spoke through pseudonyms, men often tried to materialize their imaginary host bodies, to "blacken" the critic and her work. And men were not above "blithely" appearing as women in order to malign women critics. For that reason, Mercy Otis Warren took care to remain invisible and license her writings as "lessons of morality" (Warren, *Plays*, 11).

Performing anonymity may have been necessary in the 1770s, but it also held dangers. For instance, Warren could not easily protect her intellectual property or shield her work from unwanted collaboration and plagiarism. On 26 March and 23 April 1772, excerpts of *The Adulateur* appeared in the *Massachusetts Spy*. Then, as Warren explained, "before the author thought proper to present another scene to the public, it was taken up and interlaced with the productions of an unknown hand. The plagiary swells *The Adulateur* to a considerable pamphlet."[60] The unseen collaborator added scenes of the Boston Massacre to the play, and Mercy could not excise them.

Anonymity was also difficult to maintain. Offering Warren access to her largest audience yet, her 1775 play *The Group* was such a success that it threatened her invisibility. She wrote *The Group* at the request of her husband, tucking the first half of it into a letter to him, perhaps without anticipating that he would forward it to John Adams. Adams published it immediately and asked for more. The play was reprinted in Boston, Philadelphia, New York, Jamaica, and London, and Whigs *and* Tories wanted to know who wrote it. James Warren confided to John Adams that Mercy was "much Concerned at hearing it is reported that She wrote the Group," and asked Adams to speak to a mutual friend to see if he had informed "Parson Howe [who] told A large Company at Table that She was the Author of it." He urged Adams to staunch the rumor. For her part, Mercy "Wished the World Might not have suspected [her author-ship]: Considering how Cruel and Vindictive Mankind Generally are."[61]

Suddenly Mercy Warren began to fear not just official retribution but also the reaction of friends. She wondered if she could occupy both a politically partisan and a Christian host body: "Is it Consistant with the Benevolent system of Christianity to Vilify [*sic*] the Delinquent, when we only Wish to Ward of[f] the fatal Consequences of his Crimes?" she asked John Adams. Furthermore, could she occupy a political and a feminine body at the same time? If she wrote political satire, would not her "Female Character suffer"? "Will she not be suspected as Deficient in the most Amiable part of that Candour and Charity which Ensures her both Affection and Esteem"? By way of apology, she noted that her husband had prompted her "to indulge A satirical propencity [*sic*]," despite her feeling that there might be something shameful about it. She wanted to be useful to the Whig cause and closed her letter to John Adams by asking his advice and encouragement.[62]

Both John and Abigail Adams hastened to reassure Warren that the patriot cause required her pen. Abigail called *The Group* "meritorious" and reminded her that satires promoted change where "Lectures of morality have failed." She echoed Warren's own defense of Molière's satires: Mercy had argued that "the Follies and Absurdities of Human Nature Exposed to Ridicule ... may often have a greater tendency to reform Mankind than some graver Lessons of Morality." John Adams added his approval: he told James Warren it would be "criminal" for Mercy not to use her talent. It was her patriotic duty to speak the truth, and Christian prophets and apostles had validated "Satyr of the Sharpest Kind." Satire, "more than Laws" curtailed wrongdoing.[63] *The Group* was indeed wildly successful as a rallying point for patriots and their overseas sympathizers: politicians actively sought out copies and discussed it in their letters.

The Adamses encouraged Mercy Warren until their viewpoints diverged from hers, at which point Warren quickly learned about more disadvantages attached to anonymity. With only a few secret allies, anonymous authors could not be certain that others would protect their good names over time. By 1807, her camaraderie with John and Abigail Adams had eroded. While the Adamses had joined John Hancock and others to support a stronger Federalist government with a new Constitution, James and Mercy Otis Warren, along with Samuel Adams, joined the radical Old Republicans of the anti-Federalist camp to oppose what they perceived as a secretive, aristocratic move to divorce the government from the larger group that they identified as "the people." Mercy Warren thought her old friends had abandoned the Revolutionary goal of establishing a "true" democracy. To her, Adams's Presidency (1797–1801) revealed an ideological shift toward monarchy.[64]

The Adamses, for their part, thought that their old friends the Warrens had supported the uprising known as Shay's Rebellion, retired too quickly from the responsibilities of leadership, and circulated slanders that ousted John from the Presidency. Newly stripped of his power, protective of his legacy, Adams was enraged that Mercy Warren, a friend, a woman, had represented him in her *History* as having veered from the path of democracy instead of having forged it. Abbé Raynal had published a new chapter on the Revolution for his multi-volume history, without even mentioning Adams. George Washington and John Hancock had already passed away and Adams himself was not planning on writing a history. Who would tell his story? He regarded her critique as a personal betrayal and responded to it in a series of escalating, furious attacks, to which she retorted, "is not every one at liberty to draw inferences according to his own ideas of truth?"[65]

Anonymity also opened the door for wrongful and embarrassing attribution: in the 1780s, Warren's name was linked to a play about card-playing, dancing, and lax morals. In 1784 her son George asked if she had authored the anonymous, sexy romp titled *Sans Souci, alias, Free and Easy, or, An Evening's Peep into a Polite Circle*. The play satirized the carefree Boston social circle presided over by Perez Morton (1750–1837) and his wife Sarah Wentworth Apthorp Morton (1759–1846), whose sister had reportedly had an affair with Perez, produced a son, and taken her own life. (Adams publicly defended the husband in the 7 October 1788, *Massachusetts Centinel*, casting the report aside as scurrilous.) Warren explains the confusion about the *Sans Souci* authorship as follows: "from the honourable mention of my name in the Farce and my particular acquaintance with Mrs. Macaulay, some ill natured persons suggested to her that your mama was the author."[66] She did not write *Sans Souci*, but her earlier tradition of anonymity left her open to such charges of mean-spiritedness and immorality, even from those she had counted among her best friends.

Perhaps the most poignant danger Warren faced in deploying an anonymous "patriot body" as a shield was that she could not easily prove, after devoting years to writing propaganda plays and poems, that she had contributed to the Revolution. At age eighty-six, in the year of her death, Warren was still fighting her claim to authorship. She had to swallow her pride and write to John Adams on 4 August 1814, requesting his assistance in establishing her intellectual property. By that time, Eldridge Gerry had brokered a peace between the two old friends. Abigail and Mercy had exchanged locks of hair, woven into a handkerchief pin and ring.[67] Mercy wrote John, "Do you remember who was the author of a little pamphlet entitled *The Group*? . . . A friend of mine who lately visited the Athenaeum saw it among a bundle of pamphlets, with a high encomium of the author, who, he asserted, was Mr. Samuel Barrett. You can, if you please, give a written testimony contradictory of the false assertion." A week later she intensifies her request: "If the author of [the 1775 satire] *The Group* ever deserved half the encomiums you have lavished on her talent, it ought to be rescued from oblivion. This little work was committed to the press by yourself the winter before Lexington battle."[68] These passages reveal Warren's continuing and tenuous reliance on her political connections for access to the public sphere, a safe reputation, and credit for her own work and no more.

The authorial challenge over *The Group* was not an isolated incident. Warren chose, during her lifetime, not to disclose her authorship of her powerful and widely disseminated critique of the Constitution, OBSER-VATIONS *on the New* CONSTITUTION, *and on the Federal and State* CONVENTIONS. Consequently, the Quadrangle Books 1962 reprint of Richard Henry Lee's 1788 *Letters from the Federal Farmer*, still circulating within university libraries, contains no notice that the "Columbian Patriot" who wrote the "Observations" was Mercy Otis Warren. Warren disclosed her authorship of this essay in an 18 December 1787, letter to Catharine Macaulay, the celebrated British historian, but until 1932 the work was widely thought to be by Elbridge Gerry, another leading anti-Federalist. One of Warren's descendants, Charles Warren, finally proved her authorship.[69]

The challenge of proving authorship in light of initial anonymity is profound: *The Defeat* – despite almost two hundred years of being solidly linked to Warren's authorship and despite its stylistic and character-based connections to *The Adulateur* – is, scrupulously, listed in *The Cambridge History of American Theatre* only as "possibly by Mrs. Warren." And *The Group* is described as "the only play acknowledged by Mrs. Warren" – though Warren published the 1790 dramas *The Ladies of Castile* and *The Sack of Rome* under her own name (Wilmeth and Bigsby, *Cambridge*, 41–42). Seven plays altogether are associated with Warren's authorship, in varying degrees of contestation.

The authorship of *The Blockheads* (1776) and *The Motley Assembly* (1779), often attributed to Warren in the past, is now hotly debated, which shows that Warren's anonymous mask may also have invited unwanted and perhaps unwarranted attribution. Such a dilemma was not uncommon: Annis Stockton, for example, complained that "they lay a great deal to me that I never did" (qtd. Mulford, *Only*, 10). *Blockheads* and *Motley Assembly* differ from Warren's earlier pieces in that they lack the fierce anger of *The Adulateur* and the incisive, imaginative stage directions of *The Defeat*. Written in prose instead of verse, farce instead of satire, in a contemporary rather than a classical setting, they also demonstrate a greater interest in dramatic structure and female characters. Their sexual explicitness and crude language mitigate against attributing them to Warren, but her loathing for the Tories and the shield of anonymity argue for her authorship. Perhaps Warren wrote part of the scripts, which were then, like her other works, embellished by others. This debate over Warren's authorship, however, finally reveals more about contemporary historians' notions of eighteenth-century women than about Warren's actual literary output.

A serious drawback of performing anonymity and gaining "invisible" power is that it is difficult to reverse that invisibility, to claim one's own work and prove that one has, in fact, contributed to the building of a republic. Furthermore – and this is important – since the identity of the author has been erased, the identity category occupied by the writer, in this case "white womanhood," remains unexamined and uncontested. The privilege of Warren's anonymity prevented her from being held accountable for her part of the thorny legacy of the Enlightenment, its separation of legality and morality, its implicit standard of propertied whiteness. She remained within a tight circle of family members and political associates and was not forced to engage seriously with the work of such writers as Phillis Wheatley. She was not forced to see the limits of her own intellectual path through womanhood. And despite certain common goals, Warren and Wheatley were not able to identify one another as public allies. Warren benefited from the advantages of invisibility: she could write freely about a range of subjects, avoid libel charges, and reach a wide audience that would take her "productions" seriously, but she paid a price for these benefits.

At age sixty-two, Warren started making herself visible. She began publishing under her own name, constructing a rationale for women's participation in the public sphere, and enjoying newfound pleasures provided by her visible claim to authorship. Not the least among these pleasures was the pride of authorship and a secure claim to her intellectual property. In 1790 she secured her first copyright for her POEMS, *Dramatic and Miscellaneous*, published by "Mrs. M. Warren." She referred to it as " 'the only thing' she could 'properly call her own,'" and bequeathed it to her favorite son, Winslowe (qtd. Anthony, *First*, 163).

As a critic publishing under her own name, Warren drew strength from other European American women's participation in public discourse and from their responses to her work. She created another kind of host body, a network of transatlantic connections with other "cultured" women. This host body solidified her position as an Anglo-American but also marked her status as the once-colonized American. Sometimes, as with Warren's *History*, this gave her an advantage. Catherine Macaulay clearly viewed Warren as an expert on American history and their correspondence clearly granted Warren self-confidence. In fact, Warren transcribed passages from her letters to Macaulay directly into her *History*.[70] Warren had replaced her brother James as Macaulay's correspondent when his health failed, and had found in her an eager sounding board. When she read Macaulay's *Observations on the Reflections of the Right Hon. Edmund Burke on the French Revolution* (1791), she immediately contributed a preface to the pamphlet and published it in Boston. Macaulay, in turn, honored Warren's work through a visit to Mercy's home in 1784. As late as 1791, Macaulay was encouraging Warren.[71] In the mid 1780s, Warren's transatlantic correspondence also included Abigail Adams, who sent from London a copy of Mrs. Elizabeth Robinson Montagu's *Essay on the Writings and Genius of Shakespeare*. This volume impressed Mercy so much that she opened her "Miscellaneous Poems" with a verse dedicated to Montagu (1720–1800), in hopes that the author would "across the Atlantic stretch her eye ... Then let the critic soften to the friend."[72] In addition to her transatlantic correspondence, Warren also exchanged letters with essayist and dramatist Judith Sargeant Murray.

Writing to and for each other and the wider public, late eighteenth-century European American women published their criticisms with a keen sense of speaking "to posterity – perhaps very far remote" (Warren,

History, 1, v). Their sense of building a host network transcending time enabled them – dangerously – to claim the momentum of history for themselves, to cast others into the past and refuse them a future. In her poem "To Mrs. Montague," Warren wrote that she was going to ignore those outraged at her authorship: "secure I'll walk, and placid move along, / And heed alike their censure or their song."[73] Warren's sanguinity stemmed not only from her focus on future audiences, but also from her rock-solid belief in her own – if not all others' – natural rights.

PERFORMING CRITICISM/PERFORMANCE CRITICISM

Mercy Otis must have watched her brother James with particular interest as he challenged British warrants or "writs of assistance" in 1761.[74] Instead of simply arguing his case on the basis of civil law or precedent, Otis innovatively drew upon Enlightenment rhetoric and claimed that the writs were an offense to what he called "natural" law, which was prior to and superior to English law. Although Otis's novel natural rights argument failed to sway judges in 1761, it became a major political tool for the disenfranchised for years to come. It also became a major weapon used against the disenfranchised, because of the way in which, through nationhood, it implicitly connected citizenship, (European) culture, and (the white) "race." In discussing this tangle, Appiah makes the important point that the Enlightenment notions of liberalism that combined natural rights, Constitutions, elections, and safeguards for private property in a new way in the eighteenth century were a heterogeneous set of practices more than a unified philosophy (Appiah, *Ethics,* ix–xi). A set of practices, unlike a philosophy, is a site of contestation. Mercy Warren's performance as a liberal critic marks her participation in a rowdy debate over American-ness, and it also reveals the faultlines within natural rights discourse.

Warren explains in her history that by 1767 James Otis had found American patriots receptive to the concept of natural rights, furious as they were over royal taxes on tea and the continuing use of writs of assistance. She credits her brother with "laying the foundation of a revolution." In his 1764 pamphlet, Otis had argued that government was not founded on grace (the notion of the elect), force, social compact, or property, but on the "will of God." Drawing from John Locke but rejecting Deism, Otis contended that the "author of nature" created individuals and the societies they elected to join. God granted that each individual had a "natural right to think and act and contract for himself," a right that no one could rescind. Democracy was the system closest to God's plan, Otis continued, as he linked colonial freedom to slaves' emancipation, arguing that "colonists are by the law of nature freeborn, as indeed all men are, white or black":

Will short curled hair like wool instead of Christian hair, as 'tis called by those whose hearts are as hard as the nether millstone, help the argument? Can any logical inference in favor of slavery be drawn from a flat nose, a long or a short face? ... a [slave] trade that is the most shocking violation of the law of nature, has a direct tendency to diminish the idea of the inestimable value of liberty, and makes every dealer in it a tyrant.[75]

In this passage Otis reveals the radicalism of and the challenge facing Wheatley's project of articulating a rational Christian human "race" that would end slavery: the competing construction of Christianity as "race" linked a biological notion of race to religion and nationhood, arguing that only Europeans could be Christians and true Americans. Christian apologists for slavery called their very *hair* Christian. The passage reveals another difficulty: slavery was a clear threat to everyone's natural rights because it made nonsense of patriot's calls for liberty. As Warren explained, democracy depended upon equal conditions among all people: a wealthy elite class "and a train of domestic slaves naturally banish a sense of general liberty," and lead to aristocracy (*History*, 1, 22). Otis and Warren argued against slavery because it made democracy more tenuous, not (as Wheatley argued) because it was immoral, unChristian, and illogical. They introduced anti-slavery into the emerging notion of American-ness, but collapsed racial oppression into a means of establishing natural rights theory. In fact, Warren feared that if slaves were freed, they would join the English and "enslave" the Whigs. A Whig newspaper echoed that anxiety: "now the [British] soldiers are come, the Negroes shall be free, and the Liberty Boys slaves."[76]

Warren regarded Anglo-American Liberty Boys as a separate and "intrepid race" whose love of freedom drove them to establish the colonies, where they could pass "the privileges of Englishmen" on to their posterity. As "a race of self denying heroes," they were rightfully Anglo-centric, in her view, reverencing English law and waging war against the English only to avoid "slavery."[77]

After the Revolutionary War, Warren's racial anxieties expanded to include Europeans "not originally from the stock of England," who had fled monarchies to live in the colonies. She feared that as the French and Germans assumed leadership positions in the government, they would move the United States away from its republican roots (*History*, III, 249). In fact, she perceived federalists such as John Adams as catering to this constituency, and believed that the new Constitution codified their privilege and the end of a wider democracy.

Warren's vision of a wider democracy was directly linked to her performance of "genius." Genius, in her view, was evidence of a drive toward American freedom. American scientific and artistic productions dramatized "a determination to be free." When Thomas Jefferson noted her "high station in the ranks of genius," and when John Adams praised her "real genius," comparing her to Alexander Pope, she believed they were recognizing her natural rights.[78] The major theorists of genius – Kant, Rousseau, Jefferson – all, with different rationales, left women out of their definitions of genius, but Alexander Hamilton wrote that "in the career of dramatic compositions at least, [Warren's] female genius has outstripped the Male."[79]

Warren's genius is described differently from Wheatley's, however. Warren was never described as a strange anomaly within her sex, or called a "white" or a "Caucasian" genius. Warren's husband referred to her "Masculine Genius," but he understood how writing informed Mercy's sense of identity through her patriot host body: "I advise you to sit down and write a Satire ... I am sure the remedy will succeed and you will feel a laudable pride." Those who knew of Warren's publications valued her satirical attacks, so pivotal to the Whig cause. During the war, John Adams referred to her as a "good Lady, whose manners, virtues, genius, and spirit will render her immortal."[80] Just as Phillis Wheatley's genius proved that slaves could produce literature and ought to be free, Warren's genius proved that colonists could produce art and politics and ought to be free. The recognition granted these women vexed the relationship between American genius and freedom from the start, because their very performances as critics suggested that Revolutionary notions of American-ness and Christianity fell far short of creating a true republic.

Of the various definitions of "republic" circulating during the Revolutionary War era, Warren embraced a relatively liberal one, though Wheatley's idea of American-ness, like her idea of Christianity, was far more inclusive. There were three main concepts of republicanism circulating in the colonies during the 1770s and 1780s. The upper class, often educated in England, believed that republics "could succeed only if they were small in size and homogeneous in population," and that their citizens had to be particularly virtuous and subordinate to the "'natural aristocracy,' men of talent who had risen from what might have been humble beginnings to positions of power and privilege."[81] In return, the people would purportedly receive equal opportunity. John and Abigail Adams came to espouse this notion. The second concept of the republic, championed by men like Alexander Hamilton among the elite and by "skilled craftsmen" as well, held that the most important thing was for individuals to pursue their own economic self-interest: the government's job was to support private interests to spur a dynamic economic explosion rather than the development of a virtuous submission to a common ideal. The final definition of republicanism most closely articulates Warren's view: a republic meant a broad-based engagement in political activities and a rejection of the idea that the upper classes were capable of speaking for others (here Wheatley would agree but with a broader vision of who the "others" were). Warren espoused this anti-federalist, agrarian concept of the republic, a view supporting what Schloesser calls a "radical *delegate* theory of representation": people elected delegates to represent their viewpoints, and if that representational process failed, citizens had the right to redress (Schloesser, *Fair*, 90).

Warren's democratic vision stemmed more from a distrust of newly wealthy "pseudo-aristocrats" than from a desire to embrace the "rude peasants" of the Carolinas, however. She believed that "the subordination of Civil Society" was necessary to quell the chaos of the emerging republic, and she was appalled by the bald ambition for riches and titles that followed the war. Shortly after George Washington took office, she worried that Americans were "too poor for Monarchy, too wise for despotism, and too dissipated[,] selfish[,] & extravagant for Republicanism."[82]

Even after the Revolutionary War ended and the May 1787 Constitutional convention had been held, Warren remained determined to perform her critique of American-ness. As "A COLUMBIAN PATRIOT" she published her 1788 "Observations" on the proposed Constitution. Her pamphlet was disseminated in Boston and published in newspapers in New York and adjacent states. Distressed by the secrecy of the Constitutional convention, she argued in her "Observations" that the delegates had reinvented American governance without consulting the people. The newly proposed federal government, because of "the undefined meaning of some parts, and the ambiguities of expression in others," was "dangerously adapted to the purposes of an immediate *aristocratic tyranny.*" She disliked the idea of an upper as well as a lower legislative body. Fearing that the new post-Revolutionary War "monarchists" would "enslave" patriots, she reminded readers that "the origin of all power is in the people, and that they have an incontestible right to check the creatures of their own creation . . . to reject their decisions . . . or to demand further time for deliberation on matters of the greatest moment."[83]

Chief among her concerns was the fact that there was no Bill of Rights in the new Constitution – no guarantee of free speech and press, no trial by jury, and no protection against illegal searches and seizures. With no imprimatur from the people, the conveners had drastically diminished individual states' power, and rashly increased judicial power, in her view. The executive and legislative branches were too close, and a single legislature for such a large land mass impracticable. The Constitution held no provision to rid the country of a standing army, nor any term limits set for those in governmental offices, who should, Warren felt, face election annually, as in the past. She argued that Congress should not set its own salaries, and held that the Senate was organized in such a way that Senators were, in effect, lifetime office-holders. Despite these wide-ranging concerns, Warren ended her critique with a note of moderation and a plea for peace. Warren sought a limited direct democracy. Although she was certainly not alone in criticizing the newly proposed Constitution – indeed, her husband Warren, among many others, also published a response – she was one of the more democratic.

Revolutionary concerns and connections, rather than Christian missionary contacts, provided Mercy Otis Warren's access to the public sphere, but she did hope that her performance was a Christian one. She regarded Christianity as the "best cement of society," crucial to the maintenance of an engaged but hierarchical republic. For Warren, Christianity also provided a justification for womanly ambition. Self-subordination within the family did not mean inferiority, in her view, because a Christian woman was intelligent and virtuous, ready for the judgment day.[84] Heaven itself was a well-ordered democracy, where diversity existed and reason and self-subordination meant harmony: the virtuous ruled with a light hand, everyone kept their place – and women in patriot host bodies contributed to political debates.

Mercy Warren's performance within a "patriot body" modeled the notion that women should become politically engaged. Accepting John Adams's offer of correspondence in 1770, she bemoaned the fact that "the sphere of female life is too narrow to afford much entertainment to the wise and learned." Like Abigail Adams, Warren asked Adams to validate the idea of woman as citizen and critic. She cleverly warned him that posterity would judge male patriots "and censure or applaud" according to their "magnanimity" to women. Mercy Warren and Abigail Adams developed their own political theories: they shared books, critiqued them, and dedicated themselves to educating their families. "Confined to the Narrower Circle of Domestic Care," they tried to educate their sons, in particular, in "the divine Science of the Politicks." When John Adams sought Mercy as well as James Warren's advice as he left for the First Continental Congress, Mercy's suggestion was that he meet with local townspeople for a "preparatory Conference."[85] She was consistent in her political vision of a direct democracy that incorporated women's views if not their suffrage.

Sometimes Warren's performance of American womanhood irritated the very men who had encouraged her to write. The most notable instance of this is John Adams's critique of her *History*, but another gentleman, whose identity Mercy obscured in her archives, also lambasted her. The gentleman, who identifies himself as someone Mercy occasionally consulted about her writing, wrote her "unasked" after the publication of her *Poems* in 1790. He sent her pages of criticism. He announced that he would not attempt "an impartial and general criticism." He pronounced *The Sack of Rome* and *The Ladies of Castile* "immortal," then accused her of plagiarism, vulgarity, mediocrity, and presumptuousness, for starters. He faulted her for portraying sham virtue as "a state machine," missing her critique of empire altogether in "To Torrismond." He condescendingly advised her to avoid abstruse subjects because poets who discuss philosophy "risk their character."[86] He framed his critique in language with a moral and class-bound valence, using words like "vulgarity" and warning her she was jeopardizing her "character," as if the very act of a woman's writing about philosophy and politics was immoral.

Living at a time when homes were routinely transformed into barracks and headquarters, however, Warren – and colonial women in general – could not escape politics. Warren believed that to insure a healthy democracy in the new republic, intelligent women had to disseminate their views. Others seemed to agree: when Adams introduced Mercy Warren to Catharine Macaulay, he noted that Warren was "not the less amiable for being attentive to public affairs."[87] Warren accepted traditional gender roles, "certain appropriate duties assigned to each sex," but argued that since "every domestic enjoyment depends on the unimpaired possession of civil and religious liberty ... a concern for the welfare of society ought equally to glow in every human breast" (Warren, *History*, 1, iv). In this passage, the term "domestic" has a double edge, referring not just to home but also to nation, as in "domestic affairs." For Warren, patriotism and womanhood were inseparable.

In a revealing response to a young woman hurt by the "aspersions" men cast on women, Warren confided that while women often brought the criticism upon themselves, the origin of their behavior was "the different education bestowed on the sexes" rather than an "inferior contexture of female intelligence."[88] Her poems, later plays, and history all included women as speakers, characters, and participants. Her letters are full of gender concerns. She represented European American women as intelligent, politicized citizens in poems such as "A Political Reverie" and "To the Hon. J. Winthrop, Esq.," all the while insisting that they fulfill their obligations as wives and mothers. In an early letter to Macaulay, Warren articulates her view of the inextricable and unavoidable relationship between women and political action:

You see, madam, I disregard the opinion that women make indifferent politicians. It may be true in general, but the present age has given one example at least to the Contrary, and pray, how many perfect theorists has the world exhibited among the masculine part of the human species, either in ancient or modern times? When the observations are just and honorary to the heart and character, I think it very immaterial if they flow from a female life in the soft whispers of a private friendship or whether thundered in the Senate in the bolder language of the other sex. Nor will the one be more influential than the other in the general conduct of life or the intrigues of statesmen in the Cabinet so long as private interest is the spring of action which is indeed so often the Pole Star that governs mankind from the King to the Cottage.[89]

Warren does not refute but "disregards" detractors, naming Macaulay (who had already published a theory of democracy) as an exemplary political thinker. She theorizes that "private" discourse is just as influential in terms of political power as "public" debate, intertwined as the two performative realms are: through the social realm, women's commentaries equally affect the construction of public policy.

This view is bolstered by eighteenth-century practices regarding women's performances as correspondents. In Warren and Macaulay's world, social connections led to politicized epistolary exchanges – and people frequently published the letters they received, often pseudonymously, in newspapers as well as books. Women also routinely circulated the letters they received from or wrote to others, and sometimes they acted as each other's agents. Warren, for instance, shared with Abigail Adams a letter that she had written to her son, a critique of Lord Chesterfield's view of women, and Adams promptly forwarded it to the Boston *Independent Chronicle* for publication. Upon occasion, Warren sent John Adams copies of her letters to Macaulay. Abigail sent copies of *The Group* to London for a

British bookseller, to market.[90] Sometimes both Abigail and Mercy were quite aggressive in their requests for access to each other's letters; Mercy, in particular, wanted to read John Adams's letters to Abigail. Occasionally they worried over unreturned letters, fearful that they would reach the wrong hands and see publication.[91] So European American women quietly appeared as political theorists through their often pseudonymous letters, satires, poems, and prose, while men appeared not only there but also in the Senate, "thundering" their views. Warren's private friendship with Macaulay and Adams, her dinners with generals, her engagement in daily conversations shaping James Otis's views and her husband's, made her feel like a politician shaping America. Her private friendships ushered her political plays and poems into print, where her pseudonymous performance carried as much weight as any man's essay or speech.

Warren's early plays and poems do not represent female characters, but she was deeply interested in gender issues. Like Wheatley, Warren tried to control the construction of masculinity, not only by trying to shape patriotic politicians but also by advising young men to avoid sin. She, too, castigated Harvard students for licentiousness and disorder. When her son James left home she cautioned him about the "sallies of passion" and when Winslowe left, she warned him about Lord Chesterfield's letters, which in her view replaced Christian ethics with a Machiavellian code of seeming virtue that was especially detrimental to women. Echoing Wheatley's admonishment that Harvard boys avoid transient pleasures, Warren criticized Chesterfield for sometimes sacrificing "all the moral feelings to a momentary gratification."[92]

Women's concerns began to figure more prominently in Warren's later plays. Tellingly, in *The Sack of Rome* and *The Ladies of Castile*, respectively, Warren staged a tragic and a triumphant woman warrior. Both *Sack* and *Ladies* reveal the workings of patriarchy through "the interactions, the limitations, and the inhibitions of the female characters." They indict rapacious, unscrupulous politicians like Valentinian in *Sack* and Don Velasco in *Ladies*, and paint courageous women such as Edoxia, who tried to save Rome, and Maria, who exacted vengeance upon the enemy that killed her husband during the Spanish Civil War. When Maria's brother attributes her patriotic fervor to her "manliness," she explains that "men rail at weaknesses [they] themselves create, / And boldly stigmatize the female mind, / As though kind nature's just impartial hand / Had form'd its features in a baser mould."[93]

In *The Group*, Warren expanded her critique of Tories to attack their treatment of women. Once again, she opened with a "production history" of the play, noting that it was printed "as lately acted, and to be re-acted to the wonder of all superior intelligences, nigh head-quarters at Amboyne." To the amazement of all Whigs, she intimated, Tory idiocy continues. Warren's primary gender concern in *The Group* was to exhort Tories like Simple and Crusty to switch sides and become "manly" Whig soldiers. Simple, Crusty, and the other esquires who had followed Rapatio (Hutchinson) out of greed or stupidity are represented as suddenly full of doubt. Simple worries about his wife, acknowledging that his feckless "ambition beggars all her babes." Crusty sees that Rapatio has used them as "wretched tools." When Hateall tells them that the Tories will win through brute force, they seem unconvinced, but they follow him anyway. "Monsieur" does so for a title. Simple turns his home into a barracks, casting away his concerns not only about his wife but also about his children. His superior, Hateall, celebrates the practice of wife-beating. Loyalists abuse women as they abuse patriots – and John Adams surely was not the only reader who knew precisely who served as a model for each of Warren's characters.[94] In the final moment of *The Group*, a woman related to one of these Tory characters champions Whig patriotism, as Warren all at once shows how women and men should act.

In Warren's *History*, women emerge variously, as brave, politically savvy, or ravished objects of pity. Lady Ackland, for example, bravely follows her husband to war. The flawed Catharine of Russia invents a smart policy of armed neutrality, and the women of Charleston petition the release of Colonel Hayne, an American who escaped from a British prisoner of war camp to see his dying wife. An unnamed lady defeats a parliamentary candidate's hopes after he brags of having "ravished more women, than any man in America." These portraits appear in Warren's letters as well: soldiers rape young women and even the dead are not safe.[95]

Mercy Warren strove to validate her own performance as a woman critic: she sought safety in collapsing the woman into the patriot. The unflattering description of Warren which accompanies her portrait in the *Adams Family Correspondence*, however, suggests the challenge she faced. The author suggests that Warren forced her letters and poems upon the Adamses, when in fact they initiated both the correspondence and some of the poetic endeavors. Abigail looked to her older neighbor Mercy for support, particularly in the 1770s: "I must entreat you to write to me every opportunity," Abigail pleaded.[96] A late-nineteenth-century evaluation of Mercy is reprinted in the *Adams Family Correspondence*, calling her pen "never quiet" when in fact she stopped writing many times in her long life and shied away from satire the moment her name was publicly associated with *The Group*. She is painted in the reprinted portrait as "untroubled by logic, reason, or perspective, furious in her prejudices," guilty of a "confident and assertive correspondence" which made everyone pity her husband.[97] Judging from this harsh depiction, Warren did not fully succeed in collapsing the woman into the patriot, but she did irritate, for generations, those who felt that women should have no part in public debates.

Over the course of the mid to late eighteenth century, Revolutionary women critics developed complicated new strategies for entering the public sphere and designating the private sphere as public. As performing critics and as performance critics, they tried, like their predecessors, to keep the basis of identity invisible. They created host bodies to shield themselves from charges of inappropriate behavior. These substitute bodies, initially anonymous, became the means through which they forged a notion of womanhood and individuated it. Paradoxically, they deflected attention away from women's material bodies even as they appeared within the abstract body of citizenship.

Revolutionary women critics developed new performance strategies: instead of shielding themselves through a feeling host body possessed by spirit and enmeshed in seemingly pornographic desires, they embraced a "rational Christian body" enmeshed in patriotic desires, though they did not always agree about what reason dictated or Christianity required. They linked "whiteness" and "blackness" to varied religious, political, and cultural claims. Rational Christian bodies protected women critics: Alice was "judicious" despite her rewriting of Pennsylvania history; Terry Prince was "much respected" for her ballad and legal initiatives; Wheatley and Warren could even claim "genius." Patriotic host bodies provided another new layer of protection as Revolutionary fervor emerged. These bodies were posited as equally logical. Mercy Otis Warren escaped censure as a "Columbian Patriot," and Wheatley often aligned herself with a reasonable American-ness. In fact, from the 1740s through the 1780s, women critics gradually began to perform as if they, like men, possessed certain natural rights: the right to history, education, political engagement, and equitable treatment, no matter what their "clime." The patriotic rhetoric of American natural rights was forged by female as well as male, "black" as well as "white" critics, and was linked to the performance of Christianity in a variety of ways.

Pseudonyms flourished. Quakers and literary amateurs signed their commonplace book poems behind names like "Laura" or "Flora," or hid more generically and securely as "Patriotic Daughters." Warren used a female pseudonym even in letters with close friends. Elite theatre critics also experimented with female pseudonyms, but with a different goal in mind: they hoped to defend women's right to the arts, to theatre-going, to the pursuit of pleasure, experimentation, and self-reflection. Both Quakers and theatre critics, however, hoped to claim cultured "whiteness." They wanted to inhabit American letters.

European American critics wrote plays, broadsides, political diatribes, poems, and histories, while African and African American women critics circulated their views as historians, singers, poets, Biblical scholars, and activists. All Revolutionary women critics were less likely to pose as abject and more likely to figure themselves or be figured in heroic terms. Alice outdistanced all local historians; Lucy Terry Prince lobbied more eloquently than any competitor in the boardroom and courtroom; Phillis Wheatley soared as a larger-than-life Ethiop; Mercy Warren figured as a "Daughter of Liberty"; the Quakers were lifelong "Friends"; and the theatre critics stood as representatives of the cultured class. Metaphors of slavery were tinctured with outrage and rebellion rather than sinfulness and abjection. Metaphors of ravishment were, for the most part, replaced by direct appeals for legal or political action or by metaphors of (sometimes heavenly) liberation by the supreme political leader, the "Almighty Governor."

Wheatley and Warren appeared, respectively, through an "Ethiopian" rational Christian American body and an anonymous patriotic body. Both hosts presented certain advantages and disadvantages. Wheatley's identity was linked to "African-ness" in a manner that kept her visibly at the margins, and yet she manipulated her performances to prove that she possessed literacy and, by extension, humanity. She forged a notion of "African American" literary culture and simultaneously claimed American-ness. She adopted unlikely allies, and took advantage of the performativity of her own identity, acting as a visible model of subversion for other Africans and African Americans. In contrast, Warren's strategic anonymity enabled her to present her political views forcefully and to quell the cultural apprehensions surrounding her appearance in print, but she could not then protect her intellectual property, nor easily establish public alliances with other women. Nor could she be held accountable for her views. The professional critics who emerged in the next generation reimagined these host bodies, revising notions of Christianity and culture as "race" and pursuing not only life and liberty but also moral and artistic superiority.

NOTES

1 See *Eccentric Biography*, 9. Subsequent quotations from same page, same source. For a commentary on "Alice," see Foster, *Written*, 2–3.

2 George Sheldon, a Pocumtuck Valley farmer, reported that his mother once "acted out Lucy"; this drawing room blackface comedy suggests not just a white woman's desire to appropriate Terry's "various positions," but also a certain anxiety about Terry's own performance as a subaltern. Terry clearly wished to participate in American culture, to engage in what Homi Bhabha calls colonial "mimicry," adopting the colonizer's normative behavior. She wanted to own land, send her son to college, and reap the benefits of capitalism. Bhabha argues that the subaltern's mimicry of the colonizer is always perceived as partial: it signals the same and yet also signals something not quite the same. In this way, it both mirrors colonial power back to the colonizer and mocks that colonial authority to its face. Terry highlighted this process of mimicry by routinely staging that slippage and mockery: in parlor performances, she set aside a theatrical space and time in which to mimic – and therefore comment upon – white townsfolk. The effect of mimicry on the authority of colonial discourse, as Bhabha notes, is profound and alarming, because it creates a critique of Enlightenment notions of freedom and civil society. It suggests another definition of freedom and civility. Bhabha "Of Mimicry." See Letter from Rodney B. Field to George Sheldon, Guilford [Vermont], 15 February 1879, Field Family Papers, Box 1, Folder title "Letters to Geo. Sheldon," Pocumtuck Valley Memorial Association Library, Deerfield, Massachusetts, and Letter from Giles B. Bacon to Rodney B. Field, Sunderland, [Vermont], 27 February 1877 (forwarded to George Sheldon), Prince Family Papers (Misc.), PVMA Library, Deerfield.

3 J[osiah] G[ilbert] Holland published Terry's ballad in his 1855 *History*, and Sheldon reprinted it in his 1895–99 *History*. See Shockley, *Afro-American*, 13–14; Foster, *Written*, 23–30. Katz restored the following lines to the end of the first four-line stanza: "'Twas nigh unto Sam Dickinson's mill, / The Indians there five men did kill"; Proper prints the full poem (Katz, "Second Version," 183–84; Proper, *Lucy*, 18–19). The term "Bars" in the title "Bar's Fight" may refer to a gate in the fence dividing the meadow as well as the meadow itself.

4 Proper offers the fullest account of Terry's life, and I draw on his work here. He reassessed Sheldon's 1895 biography, based on Sheldon's correspondence with Rodney B. Field: Field relied upon conversations with those who had known Terry. As a result, some of the biographical information that has circulated for years (such as Terry's presentation before the Supreme Court, which, in fact, never met in Vermont) requires revision.

5 *Vermont Gazette* (Bennington, Vt.), 13: 51 (11 May 1796): 2.

6 Giles B. Bacon to Rodney B. Field, Sunderland [Vermont], 27 February 1877 (forwarded to George Sheldon), Prince Family Papers (Misc.), PVMA Library, Deerfield. The context of Haynes's indenture is unclear.

7 *Vermont Gazette* (Bennington, Vt.), 13: 51 (11 May 1796): 2. The full text of the poem is also published in Proper, *Lucy*, 26–27.
8 See Foster for a discussion of her contract with the audience and her invisibility (*Written*, 25, 29).
9 Narratives such as the 1682 *Narrative of the Captivity and Restoration of Mrs. Mary Rowlandson* represented Native Americans as savages – at a time when Native American women functioned as treaty negotiators (Gundersen, *Useful*, 143).
10 Arms, "History," 34. Often this line is reproduced inaccurately as "not many rods from his head."
11 *Ibid.*, 31.
12 *Ibid.*, 38–39. Arms qtd. Proper, *Lucy*, 31. See also Field correspondence (1888).
13 Records of the Governor and Council of the State of Vermont, ed. and pub. by Authority of the State of Vermont, vol. III (1782–91) Montpelier, Vt., 1875. Qtd. Proper, *Lucy*, 27–28.
14 Arms, "History," 32. Arms reports: "a lawyer drew for Terry the pleadings, and she argued the case against Stephen R. Bradley, who had been States Atty. and Royal[l] Tyler (?), afterwards Chief Justice of State of Vermont." The Princes eventually returned to Guilford, where Abijah died in 1794. Terry returned to Sunderland around 1808, perhaps to live with her eldest son, Caesar. She remained active until her death, although her eyesight failed.
15 On servants' rights, see Akers,"'Our Modern,'" 162; Bethel, *Roots*, 37–38. Mather qtd. Pierson, *Black*, 26.
16 Otis, *Rights*, 1764 qtd. Gates, *Critical Essays*, 219.
17 Susanna sought out Christians such as the Countess along with English philanthropist John Thornton (1720–90) and William Legge, the Earl of Dartmouth (1731–1801), His Majesty's Principal Secretary of State for North America.
18 See Wheatley, *Collected*; *Phillis*, ed., Robinson, and Robinson, *Critical*; *Poems*, ed., Mason.
19 Phillis Wheatley, letter to "Reverend and Honoured Sir" [Samson Occom], 11 February 1774, in Wheatley, *Collected*, 176–77. Wheatley was freed by 18 October 1773. The Occom letter appeared in the *Connecticut Gazette* on 11 March 1774, and was reprinted in at least eleven other New England newspapers.
20 See Robinson, *Phillis*, 26, *Poems*, ed., Mason, 185–86.
21 Wheatley's letter to Tanner, dated 19 July 1772, qtd. Wheatley, *Collected*, 166.
22 Bassard, *Spiritual*, 23, 27–29.
23 Mercy Warren to Sarah Hesilrige, 1773, Mercy Warren Papers, Microfilm Reel 1, 81–82, Massachusetts Historical Society, Library of Congress Manuscript Reading Room, Library of Congress; quoted in Richards, *Mercy*, 42. Subsequent quotations from the same source. Hereafter this microfilm is referred to as MOW Papers with a Reel number noted.

Warren's Letterbook, however, is not a timely kept record: organized by correspondent instead of date, it is not written in her hand. An unknown editor has sometimes altered or added bits of text or incorrect dates. When possible, I have checked these letters against other sources. Some letters, however, are only extant in the Letterbook.

24 John Andrews to William Barrell, Boston, 29 May 1772, "Letters to William Barrell" [transcriptions], 1772–76, Massachusetts Historical Society, Boston, Massachusetts; qtd. Robinson, *Phillis*, 27.

25 Oxford English Dictionary Online, Oxford University Press, 2004, *http:// dictionary.oed.com*, 15 August 2004.

26 See Child, *Appeal*. For instance, in the early to mid nineteenth century, Zilpha Elaw (*c.* 1790?–?) took her ministry to England; Sarah Parker Remond (1826–87?) delivered anti-slavery speeches across Britain, then studied in France, and set up a medical practice in Italy; slave fugitive Ellen Craft (1826–91) and her husband William fled to England, where they spoke out against slavery. They eventually set up a "free cotton" business in Africa.

27 Letter from Thomas Wooldridge to the Earl of Dartmouth, New York, 24 November 1772, Earl of Dartmouth Papers, County Record Office, Stafford, England; qtd. Robinson, *Critical*, 20–21, my italics.

28 Wheatley, *Collected*, 16, 197, n. 280–81.

29 [Ezekiel Russell?], "[First Proposals for Phillis Wheatley's Volume of Poems]" "Reprinted from *Boston Censor*, February 29, 1772, p. 2. Repeated in the same newspaper for 14 March and 11 April 1772, the proposals were rejected." The recipient of Wheatley's poem "Recollection," sent it to the *London Magazine* because it revealed "a most surprising genius," and George Washington, in a 1776 letter, referred to Wheatley's poetic "genius," to cite sample references (Robinson, *Critical*, 19, 21–22, 35).

30 Letter, Marquis de Barbé-Marbois, 28 August 1779. Rpt. *Morning Post and Advertiser*, London, 3 September 1773. Qtd. Robinson, *Critical*, 37, 28.

31 See Jefferson, "QUERY XIV The administration of justice and description of the laws?" *Notes*; qtd. Robinson, *Critical*, 42–43. I thank my Georgetown University colleague Dennis Todd for his insights into the Pope reference.

32 Wheatley, *Collected*, 66, 68.

33 *Ibid.*, 63, 45. See Tilley, *Evils*. I am very grateful to my daughter, Anna Francesca Cima, for introducing me to the concept of theodicy.

34 Wheatley, *Collected*, 155. After her marriage, Wheatley published as "Phillis Wheatley Peters." She and her husband had three children, two of whom died very young. Wheatley died giving birth to the third child, who survived her only hours.

35 Qtd. Robinson, *Critical*, 29–31, 37.

36 "Nations mix" in "To a Gentleman and Lady on the Death of the Lady's Brother and Sister, and a Child of the Name *Avis*, aged one Year," Wheatley, *Collected*, 84. "Parents" in "On the Death of J. C., an Infant," *ibid.*, 93. "Descend" in "An Hymn to Humanity. To S. P. G. Esq.," *ibid.*, 96.

37 Witzig, "Medicalization," 675. Blumenbach, *Elements*.

38 After writing this passage, I read Bassard, who uses the same term, "ventriloquism": she views the elegies as a process of "self-ventriloquism," in which Wheatley stages "an important 'spiritual interrogation' that serves to bring into focus a central facet of her diasporic religious experience – the desire to speak beyond the 'grave' of separation to those she left behind" (Bassard, *Spiritual*, 70).

39 Warren's husband's ancestors had landed at Plymouth Rock in 1620, and she and her husband still lived on "estates first purchased of the natives" (Warren, *History*, 1, 404). See Brown, *Mercy* for an early biography and Kern, "Mercy Otis Warren" for a useful overview.

40 John Adams's request was conveyed in a letter to James Warren, 22 December 1773, Boston, Adams, *Papers*, 2: 3; James Warren to John Adams, 19 December 1774, Adams in *Warren-Adams Letters*, 1, 36; Zagarri, *Woman's*, 73; Warren, Preface to *Ladies* in *Plays*, 99. Mercy Warren (MW) to Abigail Adams, Plimoth, 27 February 1774, Butterfield, *Adams Family*, 1, 99.

41 Otis, *Rights*, 6; Warren, *Poems*, iii.

42 James Warren to MW, 28 June 1790, Plymouth, MOW Papers, Reel 11, qtd. Zagarri, *Woman's*, 20; Box 1 (1790) MOW Papers, Massachusetts Historical Society (MHS).

43 Scholars debate this point, but Wilmer offers credible evidence that Warren's work was read aloud "in clandestine gatherings," noting James Warren's request that John Adams prepare the first two acts of *The Group* for publication "if you think it worth while to make any Other use of them than a reading" (Wilmer, *Theatre*, 46; Adams, *Papers*, 2: 214). The "use" of Warren's scripts was their ability to conscript patriots, and since reading snatches of propaganda in patriot gatherings was commonplace, it is logical and likely that Whig leaders seized opportunities to grant Mercy's scripts impromptu staged readings as well as newspaper publication.

44 "Theatre of political frustration" in MW to Catharine Macaulay, 28 September 1787, Milton, Mass., MOW Papers, Reel 1. "Grand parade" in *Massachusetts Spy* (rpt. in *Connecticut Courant*) 26 March 1772: 152–54; 31 March–7 April 1772: 23, 31. On 23 April the *Spy* reported that "the publick not long since had presented to them a few scenes from The Adulateur."

45 "Resolution Passed by the Continental Congress, Philadelphia, 1774," Mahard "1750–1810" in Witham, *Theatre*, 1, 20.

46 Warren, *Plays*, 26. All subsequent references to Warren's plays and poems are from this facsimile edition. *The Defeat* is unpaginated. See Wilmer, *Theatre*, 39 on Hutchinson's nepotism.

47 MW to Catharine Macaulay, Milton [Massachusetts], 28 September 1787, Gilder Lehrman Collection 1800.3, p. 3, Pierpont Morgan Library; "Digital History," 20 June 2004, *http://www.digitalhistory.uh.edu/exhibits/dearmadam/letter4.html*.

48 Only two American women, both "white," are widely known to have published initially under their own names between 1650 and 1783: Martha Wadsworth Brewster, who published her poems in 1757, and Jean Lowry,

whose captivity narrative appeared three years later. Sarah Goodhue, Mary Rowlandson, Sarah Fiske, Jane Colman Turell, Bridget Richardson Fletcher, Sarah Prince Gill, and Elizabeth Sampson Ashbridge were all published posthumously. Intriguingly, a Mercy Wheeler published her thoughts by claiming the status of the dead.

49 For example, Sophia Hume published her *Exhortation* under her initials in 1748, her name in 1771. Male patriots and political thinkers adopted pseudonyms or published anonymously: Thomas Paine's *Common Sense* (1776) was "Written by an Englishman"; Benjamin Rush's anti-slavery address (1773) was published anonymously. Male playwrights followed suit: William Dunlap published *The Father, or American Shandy-ism* (1789) anonymously, while Royall Tyler's *The Contrast* (1790) was published "by a citizen of the United States." As late as 1806 John Howard Payne printed his first effort, *Julia, or The Wanderer*, anonymously. Eventually, however, these men began to claim their own intellectual property: Rush, for example, signed his work as early as 1778, Dunlap by late 1789, Paine by 1794. Payne soon followed their lead. Not until 1856 were unpublished plays granted copyright protection.

50 MW to Hannah Winthrop, February 1775, MOW Papers, Reel 1.

51 Warren's political criticism reached her public through circuitous routes. Excerpts of *Adulateur* appeared in Isaiah Thomas's *Spy* on 26 March and 23 April 1772, and in pamphlet form the following year, expanded by an unknown hand. *The Defeat* was published in the *Boston Gazette* on 24 May and 19 July 1773. The following year Mercy sent John Adams the Tea Party poem he had requested, and he sent it to the *Gazette*, where it appeared anonymously on 21 March 1774. In 1775 James Warren tucked Act 1 and Act 2, scene i of *The Group* into a letter to Adams, who gave them to the *Gazette*, where they appeared on 23 January. They were reprinted in the *Massachusetts Spy* on 26 January. On 15 March Mercy sent the rest of Act 2, scenes ii and iii, to Adams, and the entire script was published as a pamphlet, still anonymously. The 3 April *Gazette* advertised it. The partial version was later reprinted in New York and Philadelphia newspapers, based upon the Jamaican version of it. See Butterfield, *Adams Family*, 1, 186 for citations of relevant letters. Until the publication of *The Group*, only a handful of insiders knew of Warren's authorship. See Zagarri, *Woman's*, 120–23. See Brown, *Theatre*, 191–92 n. 19 for a further list of scholars claiming for Warren the authorship of *The Blockheads* and *The Motley Assembly*.

52 Anne Dudley Bradstreet's male relative published her poems "By a Gentlewoman" in 1650. Sarah Osborn (Haggar) (1714–96) published under a generic feminine pseudonym, and poet Anne Steele (1717–78) likewise sought cover as "Theodosia." Elizabeth Graeme Fergusson (1737–1801) signed her work "Laura," and Jane Dunlap called herself "a Daughter of Liberty and Lover of Truth." Fergusson's salon protégée, Anna Young Smith, circulated her occasional poems as "Sylvia," and Esther de Berdt Reed (1746–80) signed her work as "an American Woman." Fergusson held

"literary evenings" on her estate for friends from Philadelphia's Christ Church.

53 MW to Mrs. Hannah Winthrop, February 1773, Plymouth, Mass., MOW Papers, Reel 1.

54 [Milcah Martha Hill Moore], *Miscellanies, Moral and Instructive, in Prose and Verse, collected from various authors, for the use of schools, and improvement of young persons of both sexes* (Philadelphia: Printed by Joseph James, 1787), Rare Book/Special Collections Reading Room, Library of Congress. Subsequent in-text references, unless otherwise noted, are to the widely available 1997 Blecki and Wulf edition of this work. "Culture of performance" in Mulford, *Only*, 8.

55 Quakers "believed that one of the lessons to be learned from the Edenic experience was that before the Fall, men and women were 'helpsmeet,' or equal partners, and that subsequent generations should strive to achieve the state of equality that existed before the Fall." Quaker women traveled in the ministry and were valued independently of their marital status (Wulf in Blecki and Wulf, *Milcha*, 10–12). "Love's frail", in Mulford, *Only*, 71, 5.

56 Smith-Rosenberg, "Female," 156, 168.

57 In 1746, for example, a religious fanatic denounced "the Lewdness or Impiety of most of the Plays . . . the infamous Characters of the Actors and Actresses . . . the inhumanly impudent Dances and Songs" between the acts. Anonymous, "On Theatrical," 356.

58 It is possible, but not, I think, probable, that these female pseudonyms were assumed by males. That practice surfaced in reaction to women's success in the marketplace and as a way to model appropriate feminine behavior. None of those contexts is present here. On *Strategem*, see Latta, "Lady," 227. On Clarinda see *Maryland Gazette*, 6 May 1760.

59 I thank Odai Johnson for introducing me to Corry, *Performing Arts* and to the *New York Gazette* exchange. See Johnson and Burling, *Colonial*, 2001. Subsequent quotations regarding Amanda's critique are from the *New York Gazette & Weekly Post Boy*, 17 December 1761: 32 (989), 24 December 1761: 31 (990), 31 December 1761: 31 (991); and 14 January 1762: 32 (993). In-text references are linked to these parenthetical numbers, which are item numbers on the Corry *Performing Arts* CD. For a history of colonial and US dramatic criticism in periodicals, see Wolter, *Dawning*.

60 Fragments, MOW Papers, Reel 11. Warren wrote most of the script. Three sections of the 1773 pamphlet version of *Adulateur* are definitively hers: iv.ii, v.i, and v.ii–iii, except for the last ten lines. See Fragments and Franklin's discussion in Warren, *Plays*, viii.

61 James Warren to John Adams, 20 February 1775, Plymo. [*sic*], Adams *Papers*, 2: 394. MW to Abigail Adams, 25 February 1775, Plymouth, Butterfield, *Adams Family*, 1, 187.

62 MOW to John Adams, 30 January 1775, Plimouth, Adams, *Papers*, 2: 389–90.

63 Abigail Adams to MW, 3? February 1775, Braintree, Butterfield, *Adams Family*, 1: 185–86. MW to Abigail Adams, 19 January 1774, Plymouth,

Butterfield, *Adams Family*, 1: 93. John Adams to James Warren, 15 March 1775, Braintree, Adams, *Papers*, 2: 404. John Adams to MW, 15 March 1775, Braintree, Adams, *Papers*, 2: 408. On the public success of *The Group*, see Samuel Swift to John Adams, 31 March 1775, Adams, *Papers*, 2: 409.

64 MW to John Adams, 28 July 1807, Plymouth, Adams, *Correspondence*, 361.

65 On Adams's accusations, see MW to John Adams, 1 August 1807, Plymouth, Adams, *Correspondence*, 397. On Adams's rage at Mercy's critique of his concept of democracy, see Adams, *Papers*, 10: 405, note 1. Adams confided to James Warren that he dreaded Mercy's *History* "more than that of the Abby": John Adams to James Warren, 9 December 1780, Amsterdam, Adams, *Papers*, 10: 405. For Mercy's retort, see MW to John Adams, 1 August 1807 and 27 August 1807, Plymouth, Adams, *Correspondence* 394–99, 479–91. Macaulay had anticipated Warren's *History* as "the most authentic account of that grand event," Catharine Macaulay to Mercy Warren, Binfield [Berkshire], March 1791, Gilder Lehrman Collection 1800.05B, p. 3, Pierpont Morgan Library; "Digital History," 20 June 2004, *http://www.digitalhistory. uh.edu/exhibits/dearmadam/letter7.html.*

66 MW to George Warren, 7 March 1784, Milton, MOW Papers, Reel 1.

67 Abigail Adams to MW, 30 December 1812, Quincy, Adams, *Correspondence*, 501–02.

68 Qtd. Anthony, *First*, 243.

69 MW to Catharine Macaulay, 18 December 1787, Plymouth, MOW Papers, Reel 1. Charles Warren, "Federal Constitution," 143–64.

70 MW to Catharine Macaulay, 7 September 1786, Milton, MOW Papers, Reel 1.

71 Catharine Macaulay to MOW, Binfield [Berkshire], March 1791, Gilder Lehrman Collection 1800.05B, p. 3, Pierpont Morgan Library; "Digital History," 20 June 2004, *http://www.digitalhistory.uh.edu/exhibits/dearmadam/ letter7*.html.

72 On Macaulay's letters and Warren's *History*, see MW to Catharine Macaulay, 7 September 1786, Milton, MOW Papers, Reel 1. On Macaulay's encouragement, see Catharine Macaulay to MOW, Binfield [Berkshire], March 1791, Gilder Lehrman Collection 1800.05B, p. 3, Pierpont Morgan Library; "Digital History," 20 June 2004, *http://www.digitalhistory.uh.edu/ exhibits/dearmadam/letter7.html.* Montagu, *Essay*; Anthony, *First*, 190; Warren, *Plays*, 181.

73 On speaking to posterity, see Warren, *History*, 1, v. Kwame Anthony Appiah defines as "historicality" the process through which a given group – say European Americans such as Warren – claims historical momentum by consigning another group to a past and leaving them without a future. See Appiah, *Ethics*, 64: "historicality is a modern notion in that it presupposes a *politics* of time: making connections between ontology, nationality, and theories of racial difference. It is associated not only with the idea of authenticity and the national principle but with the elevation of 'race' to a determining position in theories of history." My contention here is that

despite an anti-federalist vision and an emerging sense of gender solidarity, Warren wrote herself into history through an Enlightenment notion of whiteness that claimed timelessness for itself. On "To Mrs. Montague," see Warren, *Poems*, 182.

74 These writs mandated duties on certain items. Some merchants attempted to escape the duties by smuggling goods into the country, which in turn prompted unreasonable searches and seizures of merchants' homes and warehouses.

75 On "foundation," see Warren, *History*, I, 47; "will" see Otis, *Rights*, 3; "author" see Otis, *Rights*, II; "hair" see Otis, *Rights*, 29.

76 Southern patriots played upon this fear, drawing whites to the revolutionary cause by suggesting the power of the British and their collusion in slave rebellions. But many blacks, especially free Northern blacks, joined the patriot rather than the British cause, because at first it was not clear which path led to further rights. Otis, *Rights*, 38. Akers, "Our," 167. Mercy charged Virginia Governor Lord Dunmore with "inhumanity" when he promised to grant slaves freedom and "arm them against their masters" if colonists revolted (Warren, *History*, I, 201). In Georgia and South Carolina, Dunmore's call prompted some 55,000 slaves to seek asylum with the British (Norton, *People*, 148).

77 MW to Catharine Macaulay, 9 June 1773, Plymouth, MOW Papers, Reel 1. Loyalists, in contrast, were "a race of creatures who have thus forgot their origen [*sic*]." Mercy Warren to Mrs. Bowen Lady of Governour Bowen [*sic*], 25? April 1775, Plymouth, MOW Papers, Reel 1. MW to Catharine Macaulay, 29 December 1774, Plymouth, MOW Papers, Reel 1. 1: 22, 41.

78 On "determination" see MW to Catharine Macaulay, 17 February 1777, Plymouth, MOW Papers, Reel 1. "High station" qtd. Zagarri, *Woman's*, 63–64, xv; Thomas Jefferson to James Warren, 21 March 1801, Jefferson, *Writings*, x, 232. John Adams to James Warren, 9 April 1774, Boston, Adams *Papers*, 2: 82–83: "May a double Portion of her Genius, as well as Virtues, descend to her Posterity, which united, to the Patriotism &c &c &c of &c &c &c, will make _____." Adams marks this compliment as a pro-forma one that links genius and patriotism.

79 Harris, *American*, 227–29; qtd. Zagarri, *First*, xv; Alexander Hamilton to Mercy Warren, 1 July 1791, *Warren–Adams Letters*, II: 326.

80 James Warren to MW, 6 June 1779, *Warren–Adams Letters*, II: 101; qtd. Anthony, *First*, 120. Adams qtd. in MW to John Adams, 27 August 1807, Plymouth, MOW Papers, Reel II.

81 Norton, *People*, 156.

82 On Warren's vision, see Warren, *Plays*, 252; *Poems*, 249; *History*, III 280–87, 250. On "subordination," see MW to Catharine Macaulay, Plimouth, New England, 24 August 1775, Gilder Lehrman Collection 1800.2, p. 3, Pierpont Morgan Library; "Digital History," 20 June 2004, *http://www.digitalhistory. uh.edu/exhibits/dearmadam/letter3.html*. On "too poor," see MW to Catharine Macaulay, Plimouth, 20 September 1789, Gilder Lehrman

Collection 1800.4, p. 2, Pierpont Morgan Library; "Digital History," 20 June 2004, *http://www.digitalhistory.uh.edu/exhibits/dearmadam/letter5.html*.

83 On reinventing governance, see Warren, *History*, III 227; Warren, "Observations," 12. On aristocratic tyranny, see Warren, "Observations," 4. On legislative bodies, see MW to Catharine Macaulay, April 1790, Binfield [Berkshire], Gilder Lehrman Collection 1800.05A, p. 2, Pierpont Morgan Library; "Digital History," 20 June 2004, *http://www.digitalhistory. uh.edu/exhibits/dearmadam/letter6.html*. On the origin of power, see Warren, "Observations," 4.

84 On Christianity, see Warren, *History*, I 17. To "My dear Miss," n.d., MOW Papers, Reel I.

85 On female sphere, see MW to John Adams, March 1770, Plymouth, MOW Papers, Reel I. On woman as citizen, see Abigail Adams to John Adams, 31 March 1776, Braintree, Butterfield, *Adams Family*, I: 370: in an oft-quoted passage, Abigail asked her husband to "put it out of the power of the vicious and the Lawless to use [women] with cruelty and indignity[,] with impunity." Abigail wrote to Warren from Braintree on 27 April 1776, confiding that she had raised the issue of "Female Grievances" with her husband. She playfully suggested they petition Congress (Butterfield, *Adams Family*, I: 397.) Warren did not reply; her son James, Jr., had just arrived home in a "disordered" state of mind. Abigail Adams to John Adams, 5 August 1776, Boston, Butterfield, *Adams Family*, II: 80. On confinement, see MW to Abigail Adams, 28 January 1775, Plimouth [*sic*], Butterfield, *Adams Family*, I: 182. On "divine Science," see John Adams to James Warren, 25 June 1774, Ipswich, Adams, *Papers*, 2: 100. On educational methods: Abigail Adams to MOW, 16 July 1773, Boston, Butterfield, *Adams Family*, I: 84–85. On advice and suggestions: John Adams to James Warren, 25 June 1774, Ipswich, Adams, *Papers*, 2: 100; James and Mercy Warren to John Adams, 14 July 1774, Plymo., Adams *Papers*, 2: 108.

86 Unknown author to MW, 26 November 1790, Winslow, MOW Papers, Reel II.

87 John Adams to Catharine Macaulay, Boston, [Mass.], 28 June 1773, Gilder Lehrman Collection 1786.4, p. 2, Pierpont Morgan Library; "Digital History," 20 June 2004, *http://www.digitalhistory.uh.edu/exhibits/dearmadam/ letter1.html*.

88 "My dear Miss," n.d., MOW Papers, Reel I.

89 MW to Catharine Macaulay, 29 December 1774, Plymouth, MOW Papers, Reel I.

90 On sharing letters: John Adams to James Warren, 3 January 1775, Braintree, Adams, *Papers*, 2: 208. On sharing books: Abigail Adams to Edward Dilly, 22 May 17[75], "America, New England," Butterfield, *Adams Family*, I: 202.

91 On Warren's part, see, for instance, her letter to Abigail Adams, II December 1775, Plimouth[*sic*], Butterfield, *Adams Family*, I: 339, when she asks for access to Adams's journals, a request Abigail wisely denied. Or see her letter to Abigail Adams, 3 July 1776, Plimouth [*sic*], when Warren asks her friend

to return or destroy certain shared letters. This request was reiterated several times (Butterfield, *Adams Family*, 11: 33).

92 On Harvard students, see Warren, *History*, 11: 45. MW to James Warren, 1773, Plymouth, MOW Papers, Reel 1. Mercy Warren to Winslowe Warren, 24 December 1779, Plymouth, MOW Papers, Reel 1.

93 On "interactions," see Detsi-Diamanti, *Early*, 48; Maria in Warren, *Plays*, 114.

94 Warren, *Plays* 1, 3–4. See Seilhamer, *History*, 6 for Adams's list, which he jotted down in his copy of the play.

95 On Ackland, see Warren, *History*, 11: 32–33. On Catharine, see Warren, *History*, 11: 206–08. On Charleston women, see Warren, *History*, 11: 337. On the candidate's hopes, see Warren, *History*, 11: 197. On portraits, see MW to Mrs. Washington, Lady of General Washington, 1776, Plymouth, and MW to Catharine Macaulay, 15 February 1777, Plymouth, MOW Papers, Reel 1.

96 Abigail Adams to MW, 2 May 1775, Braintree, Butterfield, *Adams Family*, 1: 190.

97 Butterfield, *Adams Family*, 1: xiv.

WORKS CITED

Adams, Charles F., ed. *Correspondence between John Adams and Mercy Warren*. New York: Arno Press, 1972.

Adams, John. *Papers of John Adams*. Ed. Robert J. Taylor *et al*. Vols. 1–x. Cambridge, Mass.: Belknap Press, 1977–96.

Akers, Charles W. "'Our Modern Egyptians': Phillis Wheatley and the Whig Campaign Against Slavery in Revolutionary Boston." *Critical Essays on Phillis Wheatley*. Ed. William H. Robinson. Boston: G.K. Hall & Co., 1982: 159–71.

Anonymous. "On Theatrical Entertainments." *The American Magazine and Historical Chronicle* (1743–1746); August 1746; American Periodical Series Online, p. 356.

Anthony, Katharine Susan. *First Lady of the Revolution*. Garden City, N.Y.: Doubleday, 1958.

Appiah, Kwame Anthony. *The Ethics of Identity*. Princeton: Princeton University Press, 2005.

Arms, Pliny. "History of Deerfield." ms. *c*. 1819. Arms Family Papers. Box 13, Folder 17. Pocumtuck Valley Memorial Association Library, Deerfield, Massachusetts.

Bacon, Edwin M., ed. *Boston Illustrated*. Rev. ed. Boston: Houghton Mifflin, 1886. 22 June 2004, *http://www.kellscraft.com/bostonillustrated/bostonillustrated04a.html*.

Bassard, Katherine Clay. *Spiritual Interrogations: Culture, Gender, and Community in Early African American Women's Writing*. Princeton: Princeton University Press, 1999.

Bethel, Elizabeth Rauh. *The Roots of African-American Identity: Memory and History in Antebellum Free Communities.* New York: St. Martin's Press, 1997.

Bhabha, Homi K. "Of Mimicry and Man: The Ambivalence of Colonial Discourse." *The Location of Culture.* London, New York: Routledge, 1994: 85–92.

Blecki, Catherine La Courreye, and Karin A. Wulf, eds. *Milcah Martha Moore's Book: A Commonplace Book from Revolutionary America.* University Park: Pennsylvania State University Press, 1997.

Blumenbach, Johann Friedrich. *Elements of Physiology.* [microform]. Volume 1[-11]. Philadelphia: Printed by Thomas Dobson, at the stone-house, no. 41, South Second-Street., M.DCC.XCV. [1795] *Mcard 2 no. 28310.* Translation of the first Göttingen edition, 1786. Microopaque. Worcester, Mass.: American Antiquarian Society, 1955–83. Early American Imprints. First series, no. 28310.

Brown, Alice. *Mercy Warren.* New York: Charles Scribner's, 1896.

Brown, Jared. *The Theatre in America during the Revolution.* Cambridge: Cambridge University Press, 1995.

Butterfield, L. H., ed. *Adams Family Correspondence.* 6 vols. Cambridge, Mass.: Belknap Press of Harvard University Press, 1963–1993.

Child, Lydia Maria. *An Appeal in Favor of That Class of Americans Called Africans.* Boston: Allen and Ticknor, 1833.

Coffin, Tristram Potter. *The British Traditional Ballad in North America.* Rev. ed. Austin: University of Texas Press, 1977.

Cooley, Timothy Mather. *Sketches of the Life and Character of the Rev. Lemuel Haynes.* New York: Harper, 1837.

Corry, Mary Jane, Kate Van Winkle Keller, and Robert M. Keller, eds., *The Performing Arts in Colonial American Newsletters, 1690–1783: Text, Database, and Index.* CD. New York: University Music Editions, 1997.

Detsi-Diamanti, Zoe. *Early American Women Dramatists 1775–1860.* New York: Garland Publishing, 1998.

[Dunlap, Jane.] *Poems, Upon Several Sermons Preached by the Rev'd and Renowned GeorgeWhitefield While in Boston.* Boston: Printed and Sold next to the Writing-School, 1771. Early American Imprints. First series, no. 12031.

Earl, Jr. Riggins R. *Dark Symbols, Obscure Signs: God, Self, and Community in the Slave Mind.* Maryknoll, N.Y.: Orbis Books, 1993.

Eccentric Biography, or, Memoirs of remarkable female characters, ancient and modern: including actresses, adventurers, authoresses, fortunetellers, gipsies, dwarfs, swindlers and vagrants: also many others who have distinguished themselves by the chastity, dissipation, intrepidity, learning, abstinence, credulity, &c. &c.: alphabetically arranged: forming a pleasing mirror of reflection to the female mind. Worcester, Mass.: Printed by Isaiah Thomas, 1804. Early American Imprints. Second series, no. 6217.

Fleischner, Jennifer. *Mastering Slavery: Memory, Family, and Identity in Women's Slave Narratives*. New York: New York University Press, 1996.

Foster, Frances Smith. *Written by Herself: Literary Production by African American Women, 1746–1892*. Bloomington: Indiana University Press, 1993.

Fritz, Jean. *Cast for a Revolution: Some American Friends and Enemies 1728–1814*. Boston: Houghton Mifflin, 1972.

Gates, Jr., Henry Louis. "[Phillis Wheatley and the Nature of the Negro]." *Critical Essays on Phillis Wheatley*. Ed. William H. Robinson. Boston: G. K. Hall, 1982: 215–33.

"In Her Own Write." Foreword. *The Collected Works of Phillis Wheatley*. Ed. John C. Shields. New York, Oxford: Oxford University Press, 1988.

Gates, Jr., Henry Louis, and Nellie Y. McKay, eds. *The Norton Anthology of African American Literature*. New York: W. W. Norton, 1997.

Gilroy, Paul. *The Black Atlantic: Modernity and Double Consciousness*. Cambridge, Mass.: Harvard University Press, 1993.

Small Acts: Thoughts on the Politics of Black Cultures. London: Serpent's Tail, 1993.

Gundersen, Joan R. *To Be Useful to the World: Women in Revolutionary America, 1740–1790*. New York: Twayne, 1996.

Harris, Sharon M., ed. *American Women Writers to 1800*. New York: Oxford University Press, 1996.

Hartman, Saidiya V. *Scenes of Subjection: Terror, Slavery, and Self-Making in Nineteenth-Century America*. New York, Oxford: Oxford University Press, 1997.

Holland, J. G. *History of Western Massachusetts*. Springfield, Mass.: S. Bowles and Co., 1855.

Jefferson, Thomas. *Notes on the State of Virginia*. London: J. Stockdale, 1787. Rare Book/Special Collections Reading Room, Library of Congress.

The Writings of Thomas Jefferson. Ed. Andrew A. Lipscomb. Washington, D.C.: Thomas Jefferson Memorial Association, 1903.

Johnson, Odai, and William J. Burling. *The Colonial American Stage, 1665–1774: A Documentary Calendar*. Madison, N.J.: Fairleigh Dickinson University Press, 2001.

Katz, Bernard. "A Second Version of Lucy Terry's Early Ballad." *The Negro History Bulletin*. 29: 8 (Fall 1966): 183–84.

Kern, Jean B. "Mercy Otis Warren: Dramatist of the American Revolution." *Curtain Calls: British and American Women and the Theater, 1660–1820*. Ed. Mary Anne Schofield and Cecilia Macheski. Athens: Ohio University Press, 1991: 247–59.

Latta, Caroline J. Dodge. "The Lady is a Critic." *Women in American Theatre*. Eds. Helen Krich Chinoy and Linda Walsh Jenkins. New York: Theatre Communications Group, 1987: 226–33.

Macaulay, Catharine. *Observations on the Reflections of the Right Hon. Edmund Burke on the French Revolution*. Pamphlet. Boston: I. Thomas and E. T. Andrews, 1791.

Mahard, Martha. "1750–1810." *Theatre in the United States: A Documentary History. Vol. 1: 1750–1915 Theatre in the Colonies and United States.* Ed. Barry Witham. Cambridge: Cambridge University Press, 1996: 7–68.

Montagu, Elizabeth Robinson. *An Essay on the Writings and Genius of Shakespear, Compared with the Greek and French Dramatic Poets. With Some Remarks upon Misrepresentations of Mons. de Voltaire.* London: Printed for J. Dodsley, 1769.

Mugo, Micere M. G. *African Orature and Human Rights.* Lesotho: Institute of Southern African Studies, National University of Lesotho, 1991.

Mulford, Carla, ed. *Only for the Eye of a Friend: The Poems of Annis Boudinot Stockton.* Charlottesville: University Press of Virginia, 1995.

Norton, Mary Beth, *et al. A People and a Nation: A History of the United States.* 2nd ed. Boston: Houghton Mifflin, 1986.

Okpewho, Isidore, Carole Boyce Davies, and Ali A. Mazrui, eds. *The African Diaspora: African Origins and New World Identities.* Bloomington: Indiana University Press, 1999.

Otis, James. *The Rights of the British Colonies Asserted and Proved.* Boston: Edes and Gill, 1764.

Piersen, William D. *Black Yankees: The Development of an Afro-American Subculture in Eighteenth-Century New England.* Amherst: University of Massachusetts Press, 1988.

Proper, David R. *Lucy Terry Prince: Singer of History.* Deerfield, M.A.: Pocumtuck Valley Memorial Association, 1997.

Richards, Jeffrey H. *Mercy Otis Warren.* New York: Twayne, 1995.

Robinson, William H., ed. *Critical Essays on Phillis Wheatley.* Boston: G. K. Hall, 1982.

Schloesser, Pauline. *The Fair Sex: White Women and Racial Patriarchy in the Early American Republic.* New York: New York University Press, 2002.

Seilhamer, George O. *History of the American Theatre During the Revolution and After.* New York: Benjamin Blom, 1968.

Sheldon, George. "Negro Slavery in Old Deerfield," *New England Magazine.* New Series. 8 (March 1893): 790.

　　History of Deerfield, Massachusetts. Vols. 1 and 11. 1895–99. Rpt. Somersworth: New Hampshire Publishing Co., Pocumtuck Valley Memorial Association, Deerfield, 1972.

Shockley, Ann Allen. *Afro-American Women Writers 1746–1933.* Boston: G. K. Hall & Co., 1988.

Smith-Rosenberg, Carroll. "The Female World of Love and Ritual: Relations between Women in Nineteenth-Century America." *Women's America: Refocusing the Past.* Ed. Linda K. Kerber and Jane De Hart Mathews. New York: Oxford University Press, 1982: 156–79.

Thiong'o, Ngugi wa. *Decolonising the Mind: The Politics of Language in African Literature.* Portsmouth, NH: Heinemann, 1986.

Tilley, Terrence W. *The Evils of Theodicy.* Washington, D.C.: Georgetown University Press, 1991.

Warren–Adams Letters, Being chiefly a correspondence among John Adams, Samuel Adams,and James Warren. [Boston]: The Massachusetts Historical Society, 1917–25.

Warren, Charles. "The Federal Constitution in Massachusetts." *Proceedings*, Massachusetts Historical Society, 64 (October 1930–June 1932): 143–64.

[Warren, Mercy Otis], *The Adulateur; A tragedy, as it is now acted in Upper Servia.* Boston: [s.n.] Printed and sold at the new printing office near Concert-Hall, 1773. Early American Imprints. First series, no. 13063.

[   ]"Observations on the New Constitution, and on the Federal and State Conventions by a Columbian Patriot." In Richard Henry Lee. *An Additional Number of Letters from the Federal Farmer to the Republican.* 1st ed. 1788. Chicago: Quadrangle Books, rpt. 1962.

[   ]*Observations on the New Constitution, and on the Federal and State Conventions. By a Columbian Patriot.* Boston printed, New-York reprinted, 1788. Rare Book/Special Collections Reading Room. Library of Congress.

Warren, Mrs. M[ercy Otis]. *Poems, Dramatic and Miscellaneous.* Printed at Boston: I. Thomas and E. T. Andrews, 1790. Rare Book/Special Collections Reading Room. Library of Congress.

Warren, Mrs. Mercy [Otis]. *History of the Rise, Progress and Termination of the American Revolution. Interspersed with Biographical, Political and Moral Observations.* 1805. Rpt. 3 Vols. New York: AMS Press, 1970.

Warren, Mercy Otis. *The Plays and Poems of Mercy Otis Warren.* Ed. Benjamin Franklin V. Rpt. Delmar, N.Y.: Scholars' Facsimiles & Reprints, 1980.

Wheatley, Phillis. *Poems on Various Subjects, Religious and Moral.* London: Printed for A. Bell, bookseller, Aldgate, 1773. Rare Book/Special Collections Reading Room. Library of Congress.

Phillis Wheatley and Her Writings. Ed. William H. Robinson. New York: Garland, 1984.

The Collected Works of Phillis Wheatley. Ed. John C. Shields, NewYork; Oxford: Oxford University Press, 1988.

The Poems of Phillis Wheatley. Ed. Julian D. Mason, Jr. Chapel Hill: University of North Carolina Press, 1989.

Wilmer, S. E. *Theatre, Society and the Nation: Staging American Identities.* Cambridge: Cambridge University Press, 2002.

Witham, Barry, ed. *Theatre in the United States: A Documentary History. Vol. 1: 1750–1915 Theatre in the Colonies and United States.* Cambridge: Cambridge University Press, 1996.

Witzig, Ritchie. "The Medicalization of Race: Scientific Legitimization of a Flawed Social Construct." *Annals of Internal Medicine.* 125 (15 October 1996): 675.

Wolter, Jurgen C. *The Dawning of American Drama: American Dramatic Criticism, 1746–1915.* Westport, Con.: Greenwood Press, 1993.

Wood, Marcus. *Slavery, Empathy, and Pornography.* Oxford: Oxford University Press, 2002.

Zafar, Rafia. *We Wear the Mask: African Americans Write American Literature 1760–1870*. New York: Columbia University Press, 1997.

Zagarri, Rosemarie. *A Woman's Dilemma: Mercy Otis Warren and the American Revolution*. Wheeling, Ill.: Harlan Davidson, 1995.

CHAPTER 3

Republican Women Critics: Performing Christian Activism, American Culture, and Race

I had unusual life and liberty in speaking.

Jarena Lee, *Religious Experience*, 23

Woman was never formed to be the abject slave of man. Nature made us equal with them, and gave us the power to render ourselves superior.

Susanna Rowson, *Slaves in Algiers*, 9

From the 1780s through the 1820s, women critics expanded their access to public debates. Through newly devised host bodies, they demanded positions within the church, established literary societies, published essays and novels in the magazine and book market, took their complaints to court, wrote textbooks for the schools they founded, and staged their plays in newly built theatres. Performance continued to be crucial: they practiced public speaking within female academies, literary salons, and church circles and as they launched careers as actress-playwrights in newly politicized theatres. They strengthened ties with other women through benevolent associations, moral societies, and camp meetings. They preached. They imagined a specifically *American* womanliness, dedicated to life, liberty, and the pursuit of superiority. They articulated this superiority primarily as a standard of religious and moral dominance within Christian activism or as a standard of artistic sophistication and civilization within a specifically American culture. They assumed disparate host bodies as performing critics and as performance critics, shaping race, American-ness, and gender in the new republic, often through religion or American letters. In the midst of a Second Great Awakening, they assumed "Christian activist bodies" to attack racism and class distinctions, and donned "cultured American bodies" either to experiment with moderate attitudes toward race and class or to assert privilege or both. African American critics tended to shield themselves behind Christian activist bodies and European Americans often adopted cultured American bodies, but these hosts were variously occupied. African American women in literary associations, for instance, sought to combat colonization or a forced return to Africa by adopting "cultured American bodies" to distinguish themselves, and white religionists embraced "Christian activist bodies" to wedge their way into the vanguard of liberal religion. Critics could also segue from one body to the other, establishing themselves as religious activists and then as cultured Americans, or they could meld the two shields together, making both a moral and a cultural claim.

In the wake of the political, economic, and social uneasiness caused by the Revolution and the 1803 Louisiana Purchase doubling the land mass of the country, two religious movements erupted: the evangelical Second Great Awakening and the Universalist movement. These movements offered women different ways to perform through the "Christian activist body": as evangelical activists or as "Universalists," members of a new liberal religious denomination that expanded the rationalism of the Revolutionary era. Partly as a result of the Revolution, evangelical and Universalist ministers revised their notions of original sin. The Revolution fostered a belief in free will, a sense that individuals, like nations, chose their own paths. This conviction required a parallel belief that human beings were not, in fact, predisposed toward sin, but rather were capable of choosing moral action. Evangelical conversion, therefore, was recast: instead of helping Christians avoid Hell or redefine Heaven, conversion called Christians to social activism on earth.

European American critics often theorized identity in terms of abstract American citizenship, Constitutional rights, and Protestantism. Many preferred to appear in print rather than in person, through a pseudonym rather than a byline. They tried to benefit economically from their texts, specifically by separating their bodies from their texts. Some embraced a "Christian activist body" as a shield, and a few assumed a "Universalist" host body.[1] Others sought access through a "cultured American body." Through this literate, cultured body they lobbied not only for equality with men but also for superiority over them on the basis of artistic achievement. Shielded thus, white women also appropriated "black" bodies as their own, paradoxically trying to demonstrate their superiority to them even as they entertained the idea of equality. They performed culture as "race," assuming European American literary culture as "whiteness." By adopting feminine as well as male pseudonyms, these women formulated a race-bound, class-bound gender consciousness within their white middle- and upper-class circles. They developed and adapted the notion of "republican motherhood," which justified white women's education by positioning them as the agents for educating citizens for a democracy. A "cultured" woman critic could be a companionate asset in the home, but she might also become a financial asset if others acknowledged her superiority in American letters. Then she could safely disclose her name – and a handful of critics did publish in their own names.

Judith Sargent Murray (1751–1820), an essayist, fiction-writer, poet, and playwright from a wealthy ship-owning family in Gloucester, Massachusetts, felt it unsafe to publish under her own name. Educated alongside her Harvard-bound brother, Judith entered the public arena in her late twenties, shielded by a "Universalist Christian" body. Swayed by James Relly's 1759 Universalist critique of Calvinism, she and her family embraced his disciple, Englishman John Murray, when he arrived in Gloucester in 1774. Married to seafaring captain John Stevens, Judith filled her days by joining Murray's unpopular fledgling congregation in her parents' home. Through these daily gatherings, she helped articulate Universalist theory. Universalists believed in a rational God, a loving, non-gendered "parent deity" that offered salvation to everyone, without conversion or catechism. They advocated universal education and built a conceptual framework – not a practical advocacy – for gradual abolition. Unfortunately, Murray also embraced an Anglo-American federalism that effaced her liberal Universalist ideals. As a federalist, she joined the educated elite in advocating a meritocracy based on class distinctions. And federalists were particularly resistant to the notion of women's direct participation in politics.[2]

By 1780, Judith Sargent's family had built the first Universalist church in the United States, with John Murray as its first minister and Gloucester Dalton, an African American freedman, among the charter members. Two years later, at age twenty-nine, Judith donned a Universalist host body to publish the denomination's first "catechism." That act emboldened her to imagine additional host bodies. In the years that followed, she created a "cultured American" host body which she aligned with racialized whiteness. She individuated that cultured body further as "Constantia," "The Gleaner," and "The Reaper" to publish essays and eventually regular columns in *The Massachusetts Magazine* and the *Federal Orrery*. She published serially and in multiple venues, interlacing her religious, political, and theatrical commentaries with fiction, poetry, and dramatic epilogues. When her sea-captain husband suddenly died – while fleeing to the West Indies to escape debtor's prison – Judith married her minister, John Murray. For years she had been corresponding and even living with him: at the time of her husband's flight, the minister was living in the Sargent home and encouraging her to recite her poetic commentaries at social gatherings.[3] By 1793 the Murrays were moving, with their young daughter, to Boston, where Judith began writing plays for the newly built theatre. She tried to claim the pseudonymous host body of "An American Citizen." Her efforts were in vain: from the moment that money could be made in the American theatre, young male competitors fiercely attacked mature women's efforts to establish them-selves as professionals and citizens. Murray retreated, collecting her work and publishing it in 1798 as *The Gleaner*, by "Constantia."

As Murray discovered, the risk of the cultured host body was that it made women targets of derision if their ambition to become "some body" misfired and their identities were disclosed before their "genius" was established. English-born Susanna Haswell Rowson (1762–1824) avoided most of that derision by signing her own name to her publica-tions from the start and facing the consequences squarely. She first ushered herself into print in England through a particular kind of host arrangement: under the auspices of a patron, the Duchess of Devonshire, she signed her own name to her first novel, *Victoria*, in 1786. The Duchess's patronage, in effect, molded a "cultured English" host body for Haswell, a phenomenon which buoyed up her performances when she later situated herself as an Anglo-American playwright, actress, and headmistress in the United States, her adopted country.

Born in Portsmouth, England, and Episcopal by faith, Susanna Has-well moved at age five with her father to the seaport of Nantasket, Massachusetts. She grew up visiting with her neighbor, James Otis, but that friendship did not save her father and her from being interned as loyalists during the Revolutionary War. In 1778 the Haswells returned to England, broke. Susanna worked as a governess before launching a suc-cessful career as a novelist, actress, playwright, and headmistress. She married William Rowson the same year she published her first novel, and she followed with the wildly popular *Charlotte: A Tale of Truth* in 1791 and a series of other novels, textbooks, poems, songs, and plays. When the Rowsons' hardware business collapsed, they tried their luck as actors during the 1792–93 theatrical season in Edinburgh. Shortly thereafter, they joined Thomas Wignell's new Chestnut Street Theatre in Phila-delphia, where William acted as prompter and Susanna launched her first play, *Slaves in Algiers*, as her benefit performance on 30 June 1794. It was billed as one of two original "American" plays produced that season.

Slaves was restaged in Baltimore and New York, and gained such success that Rowson trimmed it into an afterpiece and began work on other plays.[4] By 1796, the Rowsons had joined her brother in Boston, where they performed at the Federal Street Theatre just months after Judith Murray's second play closed there. Rowson was eleven years Murray's junior. In her five-year stint as an actress, she performed in over a hundred roles. She wrote many song lyrics and a number of original scripts, but the only fully extant script is *Slaves in Algiers*. In 1797 Rowson left the theatre to open her Young Ladies Academy, which quickly became a fashionable school for Boston's elite daughters.

The implicitly Christian "cultured American body" that Rowson, Murray, and others employed to protect themselves was linked to American letters. If a woman achieved superiority within this "cultured body," she could, without major penalties, claim her work in her own name. A "cultured" woman could claim white privilege. Rowson was able to publish in her own name largely because she offered a model of cultured but independent Anglo-ness that elite American women hoped to emulate. Her female characters set agendas and claimed space, though they were also dutiful daughters and wives. Rowson helped upper-class white American women imagine themselves into the public sphere by granting them a notion of an individualized body which not only represented them onstage, but ushered them and their daughters onto the stage as "superior" individuals.

Rowson also experimented with cross-racial and transnational connections among women, though these connections depended upon blanket conversions to Christianity. She posited cross-racial affiliations among characters of different nationalities, until the final scene, when she reinstated the barriers of race, nationality, and religion. Audiences, however, could still recall her earlier images of Christian connectedness. At the turn of the nineteenth century, monogenesis – the idea that all races descended from the same genetic strain and differed from one another only because of the disparate climates in which they lived – was challenged by the pseudo-scientific theory of polygenesis – the idea that the various races descended from separate hereditary strains, with the "European" genetically distinct from the "African." For many European American women critics, this distinction translated into a belief in European superiority; for others, the "romantic racialists," the distinction meant that each race contributed an important set of attributes to the whole of the human race. Responding to competing notions of race, Anglo-American critics like Rowson asked who could claim whiteness.

Rowson experimented in the theatre with race and ethnicity as performative rather than biological categories of identity, linking women through Christian "anti-slavery" activism – but the fictional slaves onstage were *white* Americans, "enslaved" by Africans.

As early as 1807, free black evangelicals Jarena Lee (1783–?) and Zilpha Elaw (*c.* 1790–?) responded to the call of the Second Awakening by occupying the host body of the "Christian activist." By their mid-twenties both women were requesting permission to preach, in the African Methodist Episcopal and Methodist Churches, respectively. Lee was born in Cape May, New Jersey, and "bound out" as a servant at age seven. Converted by Bishop Richard Allen, she married an African Methodist Episcopal preacher in 1811, several years after her formal request to preach was denied. When he died a few years later, leaving her with two children to support, Lee gathered community support and again asked Allen, now the Bishop of the AME, "to be permitted the liberty of holding prayer meetings in my own hired house, and of exhorting as I found liberty."[5] She became the first woman to be licensed to preach in the AME. Hers was an itinerant ministry, like Zilpha Elaw's. Elaw was raised in Pennsylvania and sent to live with Quakers at age eleven, upon her mother's death. She joined the church in 1808, attended her first camp meeting in 1817, and two years later began to exhort. She launched her preaching career without denominational approval or her husband's blessing.[6] When her husband died, she relied upon preaching for support. Entrusting her daughter to friends, she traveled widely from home bases in Philadelphia and Burlington, New Jersey, where for a short time she ran a school. She preached as a free woman through New England, the South (starting in 1823), and in England (1841 to 1846). She spoke in family circles, social gatherings, and in churches. She found, however, "a far less favourable soil" for her evangelism in England, and attributed this fact to a more sophisticated audience and press corps. In England, Elaw followed Wheatley's footsteps, attending services at one of the Countess of Huntingdon's sixty-four Methodist chapels.[7] Nothing is known of Elaw or Lee's lives after they scraped together the money to print their spiritual autobiographies: Lee published the first installment of her autobiography in 1836, the second in 1849; Elaw published her spiritual journal in 1846.

Both traversed thousands of miles, preaching their critiques of American culture before racially mixed as well as segregated congregations in homes, churches, borrowed halls, and camp meetings. They were performing critics helping to launch the independent, politically active black church movement. They linked evangelical rhetoric with natural rights discourse in their anti-racist critiques. They turned to the Bible rather than the Constitution to embody the "word made flesh," but this flesh, they argued, was sanctified and inviolate rather than sinful. Though their views on gender were conservative, their performances of gender were not. They accepted Christian tropes of "blackness" as immorality and "whiteness" as virtue, but refuted the ways many white Christians linked these tropes to notions of race. In their view, all converts performed within a bodiless luminescence, a re-imagined "whiteness" that guarded their material bodies while they engaged in activism. The unconverted of all nations, meanwhile, lived in darkness. Both Jarena Lee and Zilpha Elaw performed religion as race. They helped build the Methodist and African Methodist Episcopal Churches and published popular spiritual autobiographies, making a living through their ministries.[8]

Lee and Elaw appeared in person to launch their critiques, but their Christian activist host bodies helped shield them from danger. Even their auditors' bodies, in their visions, were composed "of resplendant light" rather than flesh and blood (Elaw, *Memoirs*, 66–67). Since they were itinerant, they did not directly threaten established pulpits. They did, however, undermine the nineteenth-century womanly ideal of domesticity that dominated the press and the stage.[9] They linked African American religion and culture, which risked reifying notions of race, but which also fueled political action.[10] They defined "freedom" differently from their Enlightenment predecessors, embedding it in Christian as well as republican discourse. Lee and Elaw were part of a growing free black population. In 1790 free blacks numbered almost 60,000; by 1800 there were over 108,000, almost 11 percent of the black population. Around 1790 one in ten Methodists and one in four Baptists was black.[11] Black ministers were so successful that by 1832 whites passed laws to ban their performances. Custom overrode these laws, and black women discovered other avenues of access, too. A few, like "Belinda of Boston" (fl. 1782) and Elizabeth Freeman (Mumbet) (fl. 1781), sought recompense or freedom in the courts. Others participated in "freedom celebrations," anti-colonization societies, literary and moral associations.[12] Those who participated in literary societies created a "cultured American body": they recited and published, privately and publicly, scores of poems, dialogues, and speeches, thereby linking notions of middle-class literacy to black artistic achievement and critique. A civilized republic required its own literature, and black women critics performed their claim on American-ness by contributing to American culture. They performed literacy not only as individual self-fulfillment and community-building but also as racial advancement. Often black women were performing critics, visible to their audiences, so they developed complex veiling strategies. They occupied host bodies to combat the ways in which whites tried to misname them.

Late eighteenth and early nineteenth-century American women critics expanded their access to public debates through the discourse of Christian activism, through the rhetoric of Universalism, and through the notion of a cultured American womanhood. But their first step toward shaping American culture was to gain an education, which led women critics to a variety of sites. White women particularly valued literary societies, female academies, and theatres as sites of access.

SITES OF ACCESS

Female literary associations gave white women practice in staging their criticism. They fostered public speaking, allowing women to meet informally in one another's homes to discuss a diverse set of readings. Some groups banned novels, to signal their piety. The Anglo-American Boston Gleaning Society, for example, started meeting weekly in 1805, focusing on books "favourable to the improvement of the mind." They read "Divinity, History, Geography, Astronomy, Travels[,] Poetry &c.," but avoided novels (qtd. Kerber, *Republic*, 241). An 1815 pamphlet by Hannah Mather Crocker (1752–1829) offers a glimpse of literary societies such as the Anglo-American Society. It also reveals how members weaseled their way into publications: Crocker opens her pamphlet with a defense of the Freemasons, a secret male society, but quickly digresses to defend another society of "free masons," a Boston female literary society which began meeting in the late 1770s. The women promised "as Masons free, / To think, and speak, and reason." She admits her ruse, then blithely continues her performance. Literary societies served as training grounds for critics eager to perform middle-class white femininity: Crocker published as "a Boston *Lady*." She further cloaked her identity and claimed American-ness for white ladies by publishing, within her pamphlet, a series of fictionalized letters signed "A. P. Americana." She wanted white women to become "associates and friends, not slaves to man."[13]

In her fictional "Story of Margaretta," Judith Murray depicted a similar literary society. It was composed of young white women of varying levels of sophistication, all responding to Murray's story.[14] Like the rubes who proposed marriage to the fictional title character, some were hopelessly lost in romance. Others carefully learned the moral lessons of the story and the non-fiction essays that interrupted its flow: these were the "cultured American" women who could be found in public as well as private schools across the North, training to become spokespersons for white American-ness.

Public and private schools joined literary societies as sites of access for European American women critics. They, too, offered women practice in public speaking. Since education was supposed to serve a democratic function within a republic, some states established free elementary schools after the Revolutionary War. Massachusetts, for example, starting in 1789, required towns to offer a grade school education to all girls as well as boys. Private schools also flourished, with more than 400 female academies established between 1790 and 1830. Southern white girls were typically taught at home, through brothers' tutors, parents, or siblings.[15] School mistresses gradually added grammar, rhetoric, geography, history, and natural science to the standard curriculum of domestic economy and the arts. Historian Mary Kelley estimated that literacy rates for Northern white middle-class women rose from 60 percent to 80 percent between 1780s and 1796 (qtd. Keetley and Pettegrew, *Public*, 60).

This surge toward white women's education as a site of access led Susanna Rowson to open a Young Ladies Academy that flourished for decades.[16] Mothers, encouraged by Rowson's admonitions against romance in *Charlotte Temple* and envious of her pluckiness in the theatre, trusted their daughters to her. Like Sarah Pierce (1767–1852) and others, Rowson published textbooks, including geography and spelling books widely used well into the mid nineteenth century. Her "Sketches of Female Biography" introduced schoolgirls to historical figures from Sappho to the eighteenth-century Russian Empress Catherine. And her dramatic dialogues not only acquainted them with British women writers, but also taught them to engage in literary criticism (Rowson, *Present*, 44).

Rowson's academy and others like it were designed to stage the significance of educating wealthy white girls: in holiday and graduation ceremonies open at first only to families and later to the wider public (for a fee), the girls stood as representatives of their families, performing onstage their submission to their elders, their devotion to the community, and their adoption of the implicitly white "cultured American" body. They modeled obedient, partial citizenship. Training girls in oratory was a particularly American practice. Ellen Donkin, speaking of the English education system of the time, "found no evidence to indicate that young women during this period were trained in declamation or oratory."[17]

Public speaking was at the heart of the American republic, however, and parents enjoyed seeing their daughters onstage, indicators of their familial, cultural, and racializing power.

Wearing "all pure white, a fit emblem of their own innocence," and embracing utter simplicity – not one hair ornament allowed – Rowson's pupils claimed public space and "whiteness" by exhibiting their talents in formal public programs. In mid-October, 1803, for example, they assembled in Boston's Franklin Hall, a major public building bedecked with their writings and maps as well as their drawings and needlework. "With taste and propriety" Miss Warner recited a poem, the "Rights of Woman," and Miss Hutchings spoke about the "Influence of the Female Character on Society in General." Both obstreperously claimed *as rights* the duties typically assigned to women. They demanded the right "to call up all our pride ... to keep invidious flatterers at a distance." Rowson's pupils exalted white womanhood as they stood onstage in a building symbolizing American freedom and industry: "she has a reasoning soul," they argued, "let her improve its powers."[18]

One of the first training grounds for public speakers was the Philadelphia Young Ladies Academy, founded in 1787. This academy published its students' 1793 graduation speeches, providing us with evidence of the teenagers' own debates about the appropriateness of their performances. They voiced anxiety about occupying "cultured" bodies. Student orator Eliza Shrupp voiced her fear of "terrors unfelt before" and Ann Loxley expressed her trepidation about "appearing in public." Loxley, however, also noted the "polite" audience and then hazarded her critique of American culture. Her struggle to authorize her own viewpoint is palpable: "it appears from the little experience I have had, and the best information I can collect, that the female sex, in point of scholastic education, in some measure, have been neglected" (qtd. Keetley and Pettegrew, *Public*, 66–67). Shrupp, having gained confidence through the speech act itself, closed her "Valedictory Oration" with the question, "Shall not our sex be ambitious of gaining the summit?" (67).

Graduate Molly Wallace reassured her audience that she did not want women to "harangue at the head of an Army, in the Senate, or before a popular Assembly," but salutatorian Priscilla Mason countered that position. She deployed the new "middling" oratory, marked by directness and sincerity: "The Church, the Bar, and the Senate are shut against us. Who shut them? *Man*, despotic man, first made us incapable of the duty, and then forbid us the exercise."[19] Mason and her classmates gained a dangerous sense of individual authority through this kind of public performance in their cultured American host bodies. They were, suddenly, authorized to represent themselves as well as their families and communities.

Churches continued to serve as an avenue through which women critics could gain access to debates concerning religion, race, gender, and nation. Judith Sargent Murray became a performance critic through the new Universalist Church. She wrote a religious primer, a dialogue between mother and child, to explain the new denomination to her foster children, and in 1782 fellow congregants urged her to publish it.[20]

Universalists shocked New England by re-imagining God and salvation: they viewed the body as a transient habitation for the invisible, genderless, raceless mind and soul, and they theorized a rational God that consulted with his human family. Identity was tied to a common rationalism rather than to the ecstatic conversion performances of the evangelical Methodists and Baptists, the individualized "inner light" of the Quakers, or the visible "elect" of the Episcopalians and Congregationalists. A rational God did not damn humankind but rather acted as a kind "Parent Deity" to the entire human family, offering salvation and the afterlife to all who believed (Baym, *Gleaner*, vi). No public oath, no conversion performance, no good works were necessary, just a simple affirmation – even if only on one's deathbed. Universalists did not believe in the notion of *visible* signs of grace. They valued the unseeable and unknowable.

Murray believed that religious systems based on a concept of visible difference – including the Congregationalist and Episcopalian systems favoring the visibly "elect" – invited believers to oppress the supposedly "non-elect." They "authoriz[ed] the supposed privilege[d] being to believe, that the eternal difference, which must of necessity forever exist between himself and the greater part of his fellow-mortals, may justify proceedings against them" (*Gleaner*, 152). Difference was inevitable, but was understood as individual difference, and the focus was upon the universal ties that linked human beings across the planet. Universalism seemingly dismantled the binary system that encoded privilege in other denominations. Sargent Murray's theory is fruitfully viewed in light of Walter Benn Michaels's critique of pluralism in twentieth-century constructs of America. Benn Michaels castigates "pluralism's programmatic hostility to universalism – its hostility to the idea that cultural practices be justified by appeals to what seems universally good or true," because by focusing only on local cultural practices (in an effort to avoid using race as an identity marker), pluralists paradoxically reinforce racialized boundaries. Culture becomes a way of reinstating race.[21] Universalists initiated a conversation with subversive potential because it appealed to reasonable notions of what was universally true about humankind. By 1790 Universalists had drafted their own Constitution, which advocated an immediate end to slaveholding among congregants, the gradual abolition of slavery across the colonies, free public education for all races and nationalities, and the condemnation of all warfare. Universalist theory, however, was not effectively linked to politics. Some Universalists worked as abolitionists, but most, like Murray, simply professed a belief in gradual emancipation without developing the individual or institutional initiatives that would implement their belief.

Nonetheless, Universalism opened up a new set of questions and threatened New England religious life so much that John Murray was stoned when he tried to deliver sermons in Boston in 1774 (Murray, *John Murray*, 192). Universalists seemed to be dispensing with religious privilege altogether, which terrified New England clergy and their congregations because religious privilege was the lynchpin of other kinds of privilege. The year before Massachusetts outlawed slavery, Sargent Murray exhorted Universalists to treat all people "as members with them in the same body," because they were "descended from the same stock." This theoretical justification for a monogenetic religious community startled the New England elite. For Universalists, communion bread was, most importantly, a symbol of a rational community: "a gathering together of the many grains constituting one lump in which all distinctions were lost." Detractors jeered that Universalists embraced the "tot'ring drunkard" and "common strumpets."[22] It was dangerous for Judith Murray to redeem the fallen woman and man, minor characters in her "Story of Margaretta:" it signaled her Universalism and linked her host body to that of the prostitute.

Murray meant for her "Universalist body" to shield her as she entered public discourse, but because of her departure from the customary performance of the Christian woman, she risked being accused not only of un-womanliness, but also of heresy. John Murray had already been expelled from area pulpits, and in 1777 he was interrogated by the Gloucester Committee of Safety not only because he was an Englishman (and therefore suspected of being a loyalist), but also because his preaching was read as politics (Murray, *John Murray*, 201). The notion that the abstract American citizen of the Enlightenment was not only Christian but a particular kind of Christian was becoming so strong that by associating herself with Universalism, Sargent Murray risked being seen as a traitor not only to religion but also to America.

Universalists certainly did not answer the question of how to create a sense of American identity without inscribing racial boundaries. In fact, Murray's federalism soon led her to accept the mainstream concept of virtuous subordination and with it, slavery, racism, class discrimination, and certain types of gender bias. Her political conservatism thwarted the radical potential of her early Universalism. The usefulness of her *Catechism* resided in its disentangling the church (and hence, in the public imagination, the state) from a notion of the "visibly elect" or the visibly converted. She advocated a reasonable God that validated all human life equally, independent of one's education, race, gender, nationality, emotional involvement or level of participation in religious services. Through the host body of the "Universalist mother," Murray expanded the late eighteenth-century notion of the "republican mother," who was "a teacher as well as a mother," "an informed and virtuous citizen" and a believer who "observe[d] the political world with a rational eye" and guided her family through it.[23] Republican mothers materialized a patriarchal God's vision of America by educating sons and daughters for the nation. Murray's Universalist mother, in contrast, believed in a non-gendered "parent Deity" and separated maternal functions from the process of giving birth: women could move outside of their nuclear families to teach other youth.

Within her Universalist host body, Sargent Murray developed a sense of herself as an independent thinker: if she could re-invent God, why not re-think womanhood? Self-confidence, she decided, was the key to performing white womanhood in a new way. She began to explore new sites of access, particularly the literary journal. She shielded herself through a cultured American host body, refracting that generalized persona into a proliferating set of individuated pseudonymous hosts. Posing as "Constantia," she published her first essay, on self-confidence, in October 1784. In 1790, she published poems and her expanded essay "On the Equality of the Sexes" in the new *Masssachusetts Magazine*. By 1792 she was contributing two columns to this *Magazine*: as "Constantia" she published short religious and literary reflections in a column titled "The Reaper" – and as the male "Gleaner," she alternated feminist essays, political analysis, and historical commentaries with short chapters of the novella, "The Story of Margaretta."[24] The theatre also proved an inviting site of access in her hometown of Gloucester, Massachusetts. At the request of local townsfolk, she became (like Susanna Rowson) among the first to write for the US stage.

In the 1790s, the theatre emerged as another public venue for white women critics. At a time when many associated the theatre with upper-class

European decadence, prostitution, or youthful rowdiness, Murray and Rowson embraced playwriting as a way to seek financial security, establish white American womanhood, and, in Rowson's case, to experiment with transatlantic connections among women of diverse national, religious, and racial backgrounds. Patriots had banned theatrical activity during the Revolutionary War as an unnecessary expense and as a British provocation, but impromptu performances surfaced among patriots and English soldiers. By the 1790s professional theatres re-emerged, offering plays serious and comic, operas, pantomimes, tightrope acts, sailor songs, hornpipe dances, and Shakespeare. English plays and actors predominated.

Theatres, like literary societies, served as a site of contestation over disputed notions of American-ness, and nowhere was the fight keener than in the North, which was trying to establish itself as the cultural and political center of America. Philadelphia, Boston, and New York competed for cultural precedence, and the elite and artisan classes both tried to claim American culture as their own (Nathans, *Early*). Investors built new theatres: Boston's Federal Street Theatre opened in 1794, and Philadelphia's Chestnut Street Theatre opened two weeks later. By 1796 theatres popped up in Gloucester, Newport, Providence, Hartford, and Portland. New Yorkers, having patronized the American Company since 1794, watched the Park Theatre's construction in 1798. Playwriting was one of the few writing careers which potentially led to a profit. Although the Massachusetts legislature did not license Boston's theatre until 1797 and many Quakers and others in Philadelphia shunned theatre altogether, Murray and Rowson started writing plays as soon as the theatres opened. Unlike most women, Murray and Rowson produced more than one play.[25]

Faye Dudden argues that acting in the 1790s was still in large part an oratorical art: actors' voices, even more than their bodies, absorbed the audience's attention and the theatre was therefore aligned with public speaking, law, and ministry. Indeed, the theatre functioned as a public arena that was ghosted by architectural as well as auditory echoes of the town hall, the courtroom, and the church. But as the Awakening subsided and national imperatives took hold, theatre was uniquely positioned as a medium through which Americans could begin to test ways in which to embody their new nationhood. What behaviors, if any, unified the residents of the "United" States? What made them American? How should the various "types" of citizens, of diverse "original" nationalities, religions, classes, and "races," interact? How should American women perform?

To address the question of how to perform American-ness, theatres very gradually began to promote plays by American authors. Both Murray and Rowson's plays were marketed as American. Newspapers and magazines started offering brief commentaries on the theatre, and gradually a few US theatre magazines appeared, all published by men. Occasionally, however, women appeared as theatre critics. In 1784 an anonymous author argued that women, in fact, made better theatre critics because "their fancies receive lively impressions." Many critics justified theatre-going as a safe way to learn about the "manners of the world."[26] The theatre was a site of access for "cultured" American women critics, but it was also aligned with visions of American masculine power: the proscenium of Boston's Federal Street Theatre, for instance, was framed by a painting depicting the armies of the Massachusetts Commonwealth and the United States, intertwined with the tragic and comic muses and a ribbon that bore the motto "All the world's a stage."[27]

Judith Murray defended the theatre as an arena for patriotism, a place "highly influential in regulating the opinions, manners, and morals of the populace." She first attended the theatre in 1788 in Providence, where she was thrilled by Hannah More's *David and Goliath*. In 1790 she saw Royall Tyler's *The Contrast* and read Warren's published plays. Perhaps she had heard of Susanna Rowson by 1794; by then she had certainly formed a mental image of a successful woman playwright. Dismissing censorship as silly and unenforceable, she squashed the typical objections to the theatre: "*Waste of time – Imprudent expenditures – Encouragement of idleness –* and, *Relaxation of morals.*" To prove that the theatre was not a waste of time, for example, she explained that "rational" theatre-going was preferable to the wastefulness of drinking, card-playing, shopping, and gossiping. In the theatre, a playwright, like a minister, offered rational lessons through hardworking, skillful actors. These actors were refined by the demands of spectators in the boxes, and their refinement, in turn, modeled appropriate behavior for the masses in the pit and gallery. In Murray's estimation, those who shunned the theatre as expensive or superfluous typically wasted money on more costly indulgences. Youth, in particular, benefited from the theatre: they gained a desire for knowledge and learned how "to think, speak, and act, with propriety." Bored, unscholarly girls left the theatre eager to read plays, and, in turn, "history, geography, astronomy." Through the Foucaultian "discipline" of a national theatre, actors would model proper behavior. The result would be a nation of cultured American bodies, and a theatre establishing *"national taste ... by exalting virtue, and adorning religion, rendering vice disgusting, and stigmatizing infidelity."*[28]

While many critics exalted the theatre's ability to teach virtue, inculcate religious values, and promote ethics, few mentioned that it could build the republic by *"stigmatizing infidelity."* Significantly, this infidelity was not confined to men in Murray's work. Nor was it truly stigmatized. Attracted to John Murray long before her husband's death, Judith corresponded with him for years. Often a resident in her home, he continued to live there even after her debt-ridden husband fled to the West Indies. This shocked her contemporaries. In *The Traveller Returned*, Judith forgave herself: when Mr. Montague realizes that his wayward wife is drawn to another man, he sails for England, giving her a chance to come to her senses, setting up the final scene of reunion and forgiveness. True, the wife's flirtation is called a "fatal indiscretion" and nearly causes an incestuous marriage, but Murray nonetheless paints her attraction to another man as a natural, understandable – and forgivable – phenomenon. Murray's women have unruly sexual desires, and the "laws of equity" require their husbands to support and forgive them rather than beat and abandon them (*Gleaner*, 187).

Murray contended that it was crucial "to supply the American stage with American scenes" (*Gleaner*, 763). The "confirmed hatred" of theatrical competitors had to be replaced by collaboration among playwrights as well as cooperation among managers, playwrights, actors, and critics (541). Sympathetic critics should foster a new American drama, so that genius would not be "quenched by *cold neglect*, or extinguished by the *chilling blasts of criticism*" (538). Sympathetic criticism was a scholarly American's duty, because fostering national drama would mold citizens. An "informed, judicious, and well disposed critic" should balance negative comments with positive ones (763).

When the Murrays traveled to Philadelphia, the premiere theatre city in 1790, Judith lobbied for the theatre among progressive Universalists and anti-slavery advocates, but they regarded the stage as "a school for vice" that countenanced "idleness and debauchery."[29] This prejudice crushed Judith, who yearned so much to attend the theatre that friends disguised her in a large black bonnet and scarf so that she could visit the playhouse. There her upper-class federalist bias was clear: she found the production, of Royall Tyler's *The Contrast*, "anti-Federalist," and depicted the working-class men and boys and shady women in the gallery as "horridly clamorous – hissing, hoping [*sic*], stamping most outrageously."[30] Nonetheless, she clearly enjoyed reviewing the production for her parents, and as her trip proceeded, she covered other performances: the public appearance of the Chiefs of the Creek Nation, Linnaeus's display in Peale's Museum, a camp meeting at DuWitt's Grove, a parlor entertainment by free black servants.

By the 1790s, European American women critics began to sense that they could turn to each other for access to the public sphere. They met in benevolent and literary associations together, led prayer services with each other, and wrote for one another in the theatre. Murray imagined professional productions of Warren's plays starring Mrs. Powell, a celebrated actress. She castigated producers for ignoring Warren's work. She envisioned women structuring their workdays to include playwriting, with Hannah Cowley as her prime example.[31] Both Rowson and Murray were connected to Boston's Federal Street Theatre in 1796, but they developed different strategies for appearing in public.

METHODS OF ACCESS

Most late eighteenth-century and early nineteenth-century European American women gained access to the public sphere as performance critics. They appeared within anonymous or pseudonymous host bodies as "*any body, every body, or nobody*" until they felt safe to publish under their own names. But their very invisibility invited their readers – and more particularly their competitors, often young Harvard men forging literary or theatrical careers – to go "*hunting after names* . . . as if . . . a name was replete with information of the most salutary kind."[32] At stake in this fight to "out" European American women critics was the nature of the "body" that would be attached to American letters: could women as well as men write commentaries on American culture? Invisibility protected European American women critics as long as they performed deference and amateurism. As long as a critic was merely "any body" and had no pretensions of becoming "some body," she was safe. Murray, however, refused to defer to male editors and clearly hoped to parlay her pseudonymous performances into fame, so she faced furious opposition.

Murray tried to transform her pseudonyms into useful commodities by assuming multiple bodies: she published her Universalist catechism as a generic "Female"; her short, reflective "Repository" column as "Constantia;" and her longer, more substantive column, published simultaneously, as the male "Gleaner."[33] Each name supported a slightly different fan base. Clearly, she had ambitions as a critic, so her invisibility and multiple pseudonyms threatened the men who chose literature rather than commerce, law, or religion as their chosen profession. As she explained in her epilogue to Cowley's *Who's the Dupe?*, women had signaled that they planned to "soar beyond" the "tribe of *learned fellows*" to gain the "empire" of American culture. Men, she warned, had better arm themselves against the "usurping sex."[34] Murray relied on her various pseudonymous host bodies as a method of access into the theatre, but it was nearly impossible for her to maintain anonymity or pseudonymous status within that public space: playwrights had to negotiate with managers, provide actors with scripts, and respond to reviewers. The process simply involved too many people. Under scrutiny, women's very scripts – handwritten and circulating freely – revealed their identities, especially under the gaze of young competitors.

Susanna Rowson fared somewhat better than Murray. She adopted a different strategy, making herself visible to her audiences on both sides of the Atlantic, right from the start. She did not require the protection afforded by a pseudonym, because she had a more secure shield: the Duchess of Devonshire, to whom she had dedicated her first novel. Rowson turned visibility into an asset by trading on it, parasitically translating name recognition, protected by English peerage, into sales. She was also careful to perform deference early on: in her preface to her wildly popular novel *Charlotte*, for instance, she performed as a "no body," as a woman merely hoping to "save one hapless fair one" through her "trifling performance" that stood "a poor chance for fame" (Rowson, *Charlotte*, 1, 1). Rowson managed to inhabit the "cultured American" host body while retaining her own name. She managed this feat by posing as a deferential professional with playful ambitions. Her strategy worked. She collaborated comfortably with male musician-managers like Alexander Reinagle (*c.* 1750–1809), signing her own name to her plays and even acting in them, accepting end-of-the-year slots and slights. Rowson's deference and tenuous connection with British peerage opened doors for her in America, even after she worked as an actress and playwright. But when she dropped her deference, Rowson, too, was attacked by a jealous male critic. Women playwrights – who dared to make money, claim cultural currency, and stage women's agency – paid the price of visibility. But it was difficult to hurt Rowson, since (unlike Murray, who was trying to establish her success through invisible channels, leading the double life of a minister's wife and a playwright) Rowson was already visible and successful, not only as a novelist and playwright but also as an actress. There was no easy way to use visibility as a weapon against her; in a sense, any publicity was good publicity. Even Rowson, however, could not long sustain a career writing for the theatre. Detractors did not malign her character (as they did Murray's) but they did attack her artistic abilities and her feminism.

Through the theatre, female playwrights and actors tried to surface material bodies through which American women might enter the public sphere. Murray and Rowson were particularly interested in safely ushering the mothers and daughters of Anglo-America into prominence, and the theatre assisted them: first, because women were welcome onstage, and next, because actresses, usually English-born, filtered American characters through their own accents. Dutch, Irish, and German accents were exaggerated onstage, which further naturalized "British English." This custom also normalized the performance of whiteness as Anglo-American-ness.[35] Although this late eighteenth-century theatre was dominated by men, respectable women ventured into the theatre, also freely expressing their views. Women spectators' applause or lack of it, their laughter and audible sighs, helped shape as well as reflect notions of appropriate behavior (Dudden, *Women*). The theatre – more than the privately read or performed novel, poem, or essay – negotiated women's flesh and blood into the public sphere.

Murray and Rowson placed the cultured and Christian bodies of "Female Patriots" center stage, to claim American-ness.[36] They achieved some success – Rowson much more so than Murray – but they were also pilloried for representing women as agents rather than subjects in the new nation. The young men who wrote for the new literary rags, styling themselves the proper vanguard of the new nation of cultured Americans, attacked these middle-aged women for their outrageous temerity. While older, more genteel men defended both Murray and Rowson, their voices did not stem the tide of opprobrium. Rowson escaped fairly unscathed, primarily because she had so little to lose: she was already an actress, making money by displaying her body, not like Murray a minister's wife with relatives in the top ranks of upper-class Boston.

When the press attacked Rowson, she opened a young ladies' academy and taught the daughters of the elite how to perform virtuously onstage: she substituted the daughters of the Republic for herself onstage, and tied her economic well-being to theirs. In contrast, when the press attacked Murray, she lost her public standing as well as easy access to journal publication and stage production. She was cast as an ambitious, sexualized, ridiculous figure. While Bostonians seemed to understand that Rowson, with her profligate husband, did what she did because she required an income, they rejected the idea that an aging minister's wife might need to secure her daughter's upper-class status through the morally ambiguous act of play-writing. They forgave Rowson but not Murray.

Murray's struggle to create a validating "cultured American body" began shortly after she published her Universalist catechism. By appearing as Constantia in 1784, she hoped to remain invisible while creating an individual identity for herself. That effort proved more difficult than Murray anticipated. In January 1790, the well-respected *Massachusetts Magazine* published a number of Constantia's poems as well as her expanded essay "On the Equality of the Sexes." Then, suddenly, the magazine started publishing the work of the wealthy and accomplished Bostonian Sarah Wentworth Apthorp Morton (1759–1846), under the same pseudonym. When the Gloucester-bound provincial Murray asserted her prior claim, the editor added an asterisk to Morton's byline, which simply made Morton seem the better Constantia, the possessor of the star. Some of the members of Boston's elite were beginning to guess who both Constantias were, and being linked in the Boston public's mind with Morton was both flattering and dangerous. A wealthy merchant's daughter, Morton had received one of the finest educations available to any American woman, and she was on her way to becoming a very accomplished poet. In fact, Murray's poetry seemed pedestrian next to Morton's, and Murray's social standing shrank radically in comparison. To complicate matters further, it was rumored in Boston that winter that Morton had published a 1789 novel about her husband's affair with her sister (who had committed suicide as a result of the affair).[37] For Murray, the minister's wife, overlapping her identity, pseudonymous or not, with Sarah Morton, was impolitic.

Murray's unwillingness to share her pseudonym reveals the extent to which she valued it as a commodity. It also reveals the depth of her desire for recognition, monetary reward, and protection, and the difficulty of attaining those goals. Eventually, she hoped, she would be so successful that she could reveal her "true" identity: she, Judith Sargent Murray, was the accomplished Constantia, the virtuous author from Gloucester who had stolen the hearts of Boston! Her pseudonymous persona was not only a valuable commodity but also a revelatory and enabling fiction: she began to sign personal letters to close relatives and friends "Constantia."

Gradually her authorship was becoming visible to a coterie readership. In March 1790 *The Massachusetts Magazine* published an offering that clearly identified Murray as Constantia, at least to friends and family. In the winter of 1790 and 1791, a group in Gloucester had decided to launch a series of benefit performances for the poor. They engaged local boys as actors and asked Murray to provide them with prologues and epilogues, notably for George Farquhar's *The Recruiting Officer*, Richard Cumberland's *The West Indian*, Hannah Cowley's *Who's the Dupe?* She was thrilled by her local fame, "rendered almost giddy, by clapping of hands and various other enraptured expressions."[38]

Protected from censure by the community-based, philanthropic context of the production and by the fact that prominent men had invited her to participate, Murray felt safe. Young boys played the female parts and proceeds went to the poor. She viewed the theatre as "a school of morality" within which she could earn admiration.[39] When her Farquhar epilogue appeared in *The Massachusetts Magazine* under the name "Constantia" and was identified as "Spoken at Gloucester, by Mr. Rogers," it was clear to many readers that Judith Murray and not the sophisticated Sarah Morton had written it. While Murray years later contended that this epilogue was published without her consent, it is tempting to imagine that she published it herself, to resolve the dispute over the ownership of the pseudonym "Constantia." In any case, soon the matter was resolved: Murray retained Constantia, and Morton transitioned from "Constantia*" to "Philenia Constantia" to "Philenia." In the April 1790 *Massachusetts Magazine*, Murray published her "Lines to Philenia," oozing obsequiousness and claiming her prize.[40]

In 1792 Murray, paradoxically, expanded the reach of her invisibility. A year after her daughter Julia's birth, she seemed more determined than ever to make a name for herself while protecting her identity. She launched two regular columns in *The Massachusetts Magazine*, one in February as "The Gleaner," and another in September as Constantia. Constantia shared her spiritual reflections in "The Repository," while the Gleaner published essays on a variety of topics, including women's history and educational needs. The Gleaner also introduced readers to Mr. and Mrs. Vigillius, who narrated the story of educating their adopted daughter, Margaretta, about the ways of the world. Murray clearly enjoyed juggling her twofold invisibility and was particularly pleased with her male disguise. In her third Gleaner entry, she represented the impenetrability of her male mask: her fictional daughter Margaretta reads the *Massachusetts Magazine*, unaware that her own parent is the Gleaner. In like fashion, John Murray read the *Magazine* without recognizing that his wife was the Gleaner. He did not detect his wife's authorship until her thirty-third entry (Murray, *Gleaner*, 804–05).

In the conclusion to *The Gleaner*, published in 1798, Murray justified her male host body. If she could market her work without disclosing her gender – that is, as a white male – she knew that it would be more highly valued, more profitable. She hoped to avoid, at least until she could establish her reputation, "the indifference, not to say contempt, with which female productions are regarded." As the Gleaner, she could use her invisible host body to represent any individual or group, or to disappear entirely, and that made her work more useful. She could satisfy her "ungovernable mania" to write and still hear "the unbiased sentiments of [her] associates." Keenly aware of the widespread acceptance of Rousseau's idea that a male hand guided a woman's literary production, Murray sought to be "considered *independent as a writer*," not only so that she could claim her accomplishments but also so that her "errors" would remain her own. Her pseudonymous body, she reasoned, protected John Murray as well as herself. She knew that her writings could threaten her husband's position, but for quite a while, Murray's strategy worked. It enabled her to range widely across many topics, in any manner she chose, and it forced readers to focus on "the *intrinsic value*" of her writings.[41] Pseudonymous writing initially shielded both Murray and her husband. It was difficult, however, to keep a secret. After the Murrays settled into Sarah Morton's Tontine Crescent neighborhood in Boston – by the summer of 1794, certainly – many knew about Murray's authorship of the Repository and guessed that she was the popular Gleaner.

Suddenly, someone leveled a *"serious accusation"* at Murray, and her Repository and Gleaner columns abruptly disappeared, in July and August 1794, respectively. It is difficult not to imagine a threatened disclosure of Murray's actual identity in the face of some embarrassment. Perhaps the radical Universalism in Murray's Repository had irked an influential Congregationalist. Perhaps her impolitic praise of recognizable private figures had shocked someone's sense of privacy. Or perhaps her editor had accused her of overarching ambition or incompetence: the gulf between Murray's lofty ambitions and inadequate training often led her to attack editors for doing their job, which in turn led them to accuse her of inappropriate defensiveness or just plain stupidity.[42] What is certain is that Murray could no longer sustain, in *The Massachusetts Magazine*, her professionalism and invisibility. She had to start over again, with a new (and less valuable) pseudonym. She began to write as the "Reaper" in Robert Treat Paine, Jr.'s newspaper. She worked privately on *The Gleaner*, publishing it through a 1798 subscription drive.

Although Murray knew that invisibility was necessary and she enjoyed its flexibility, she longed to flesh out her new *Orrery* pseudonym and link it to her other pseudonymous bodies. She wanted to be recognized. She published a Reaper column advocating the "happy medium," thereby surreptitiously announcing her authorship of *The Medium: or, Happy Tea-Party*, an upcoming play "by a Citizen of the United States."[43]

Murray was flirting with fire in other ways. A forty-something woman with three weeks' writing instruction, she lambasted Paine, the newly minted Harvard graduate, for his editorial encroachments on her "Reaper" column. She explained that because of the "unmannerly Pedant" Rousseau, who presumed that there was a man guiding the hand of any female writer, she brooked no man's intervention. She claimed from her Editor "his rectifying assistance – Orthography, capitalizing, punctuation, &c &c &c but the changing or curtailing of sentences, or *even words* should not I think be tolerated."[44]

Paine retaliated by signaling Murray's identity to his readers. He published a sonnet in which "One of the *Gleaners*" praised the *Reaper*. This linked two of Murray's three pseudonyms and gave readers new clues about her authorship. If the Reaper had written the Gleaner columns, there was some sort of gender disguise going on: the Reaper commented on things like children's dance recitals – wasn't the Reaper a woman? If the Reaper was a woman, did that mean the Gleaner was, too? Perhaps the sonneteer who linked the Reaper with the Gleaner detected a similar style in the two columns. Or perhaps Paine wrote the sonnet himself, to enhance the worth of Murray's column even as he jeopardized her cover. It is even possible that Murray was trying to flesh out her own pseudonyms.

One thing was certain: the secret of Murray's invisible authorship was unraveling further, and instead of hiding more adroitly, Murray preened.[45] She thanked her admirer, again exalting a desire for fame. Disgusted by Murray's public posturing and private agitation, Paine scrapped the Reaper column and replaced it with a column by "Thespiad."

He went further. When he heard about the new play, *The Medium: or, Happy Tea-Party*, by "A Citizen of the United States," he immediately realized that Judith Murray was the author. She had virtually announced her authorship in her second Reaper column. In March 1795, two years before the licensing of the Boston theatre, many Bostonians associated the stage with upper-class decadence, class intermingling, loose morals, disease, and prostitution. Associating with those who labored in the theatre ruined a woman's reputation, because to the pious, the theatre was a place of febrile emotions and dangerous imaginings. It was certainly a space forbidden to ministers' wives. And yet, as Paine knew, there was an audacious Boston minister's wife who dared to write for the stage. This was, indeed, news too juicy to withhold. It was also a handy way to achieve revenge against his overbearing contributor Murray, the age of his own mother. Furthermore, the Federal Street Theatre was *his* turf: he had written the prize-winning prologue read at the theatre's dedication ceremony in January 1794, and he was reportedly a budding playwright with three unproduced plays.[46]

Paine simultaneously exposed and dismissed Judith Murray's authorship by announcing that *The Medium: or, Happy Tea-Party*, scheduled to open that evening, 2 March 1795, was "said to be the joint production of Mr. and Mrs. Murray."[47] The effect was electric: it was as if he had suddenly forced all of Judith's pseudonymous bodies to disrobe and hold hands on the Boston Commons with a leading minister. Paine goaded Judith Murray further by suggesting that John Murray was the Rousseau-like "man of letters" who actually did her writing. It was in Paine's interest to make the theatre respectable, however, because he himself hoped to make a living in it, so he published a companion essay defending ministers who exercised their "literary leisure." Boston newspapers lit up with the news of the Murrays' purported authorship. John Murray rejected Paine's statement as "unauthorized and false." A certain "Candour" defended the 2 March production, clearly thinking it the work of Royall Tyler.[48]

As Murray confided to her uncle, *The Medium* was produced "with more *dispatch* than *prudence*."[49] Hers was not the only eighteenth-century play that suffered from insufficient rehearsal, but the savage press she faced reveals a bitter gender dispute. At least one male critic publicly trashed her reputation, and the ferociousness of his attack reveals the magnitude of the gendered fight for control of cultural capital in early America. At stake was the gendering of American literature: would women be able to don a "cultured body" to claim citizenship in the new republic? The young men hoping to make their way as literary lions did not want to compete with self-possessed middle-aged ladies, and the escalating altercation between Paine, Jr., and Murray reveals that the men, even at twenty, held the advantage.

Insulted by Murray's defiant attitude toward his editing and her relative success as an author and playwright, Paine posed as "Ned Gingerly" to publish a scathing, serialized satire of her life in the theatre and at home. It caused a major scandal, punishing her for insulting his editorial work and encroaching upon his theatrical turf. He titled his work "The Tables Turned: or, a bug with a guinea."[50] He dismissed John

Murray as a "bug," an insignificant beetle with pretentions, and referred to Judith Murray as a "guinea," derogatory slang for an African native or the common coin forged for the slave trade. Paine's parody "blackened" the Murrays' reputation: they engaged in casual affairs with morally suspect managers, actors, and actresses and then brutally beat each other in retaliation. Even Paine's fictional "place of publication" signaled his malicious intent: "Wiswal-Den, Cambridge" was legendary among Harvard undergraduates as the dormitory-home once owned by a Mr. Wiswal who flirted with and eventually married his dying wife's nurse, just as John Murray had flirted with and eventually married Judith Murray, the wife of his gracious patron.[51]

In Paine's parody, Mr. Nineholes (John Murray) is slow-witted and self-important; Mrs. Nineholes (Judith Murray) is duplicitous and manipulative. Both are having affairs. When Nineholes accuses his wife of flirting with another man, she defends herself by claiming that, as a widow, she was raising orphans while he was "taking [his] pleasure" in England. He retorts, "Well, and didn't you take your pleasure, too, and don't you take it now? Did I not see Mr. *That's Your Sort* [the leading man] squeeze your hand and Mr. *Cantab* [Charles Powell, the Federal Street Theatre manager] almost kiss you?" Paine is on dangerous turf here, mocking Judith's domesticity, attacking her rumored affair with Murray while she was still married to Stevens, mocking John's subsequent flight to England, depicting Judith as dallying with Powell and his leading man. Powell had been previously accused of improper conduct with Mrs. Abbot, one of his actresses, so fairly or not, the smear seemed plausible (Seilhamer, *History,* III: 229–30). Mrs. Nineholes denies her husband's charges and weeps that he pays too much attention to Mrs. Prettiness, the leading lady (Mrs. Powell). His defense is that she is one of his parishioners and therefore in his care.

Paine explodes Judith's theory of the theatre as a moral schoolroom and represents it as a site of sexual experimentation, where marital rules do not apply and Anglo women turn black. As the scene moves backstage, Mr. and Mrs. Bigamy, both actors, fight over the fact that other actors kiss Mrs. Bigamy onstage. Mrs. Bigamy defends herself by blurting, "It's always my part to be kissed, or bribed, or *done something to.*" In the theatre, Paine suggested, women were sexual objects, and Judith Murray, having placed herself there by proxy, was fair game.

Paine hints that domestic violence attends sexual dalliance in the theatre and in society. Mr. Cantab (Powell, the manager) resolves the Bigamy dispute by suggestively counseling "accommodation *in a narrow pass.*" He adds cheerily, "There Mr. Archer (Mr. That's Your Sort), skip on to the stage with Miss Cherry (Mrs. Bigamy), and to ease this good husband's feelings, don't smack her three times, where twice will do." After associating Murray with a stage that sanctions extramarital sex, Paine links kisses and blows through the word "smack." He ends this scene by mocking Murray's first letter to him, with its over-eager, effusive gratefulness: "Is it possible, *my* charms can have made any impression," Mrs. Nineholes gushes to Mr. Cantab (Powell), as her husband, the "m*[iniste]*r" appears.

In the second installment of his satire, Paine blasts Murray's provincialism, her social and professional ambitions, her selfishness, her secretiveness. He moves actresses into the Nineholes' home: in her drawing room, Mrs. Nineholes insults Mrs. Sly Pleased, an English actress whose social pretensions (like Murray's, perhaps) are undercut by her "provincial accent."[52] Since Americans have no taste, Mrs. Nineholes hints, the applause granted Mrs. Sly Pleased is undeserved. To make his indictment of Murray's own "undeserved" praise clearer, Paine parodies "Candour's" earlier defense of Murray's *Medium*: Cantab (Powell) reveals his passion for Mrs. Nineholes (Judith) in a love letter that echoes and ridicules Candour's "ten categories of Aristotle" as well as the Ten Commandments. Paine depicts the Murrays as ignorant of both theatrical and religious rules. When Mrs. Sly Pleased discloses Mrs. Nineholes' secret infatuation with the theatre manager, Mr. Nineholes starts "beating" his wife, the Judith Murray stand-in, shouting "You faithless b___h! Take that, madam (giving her a dark eye)." Mrs. Sly Pleased, a stand-in for the insulted Paine at this juncture, gloats, "Well, I think I'm pretty well paid now, for my 'profound ignorance.'"

Mrs. Nineholes is left to ask, "Can't one be a little *civil* to a gentleman, and just receive a fan of him, without being so plaguily beaten about Aristotle's ten categories?" Can't Murray be civil to Charles Powell, the manager of the theatre, and receive a production and theatrical "fans" from him, without having to follow the rules of the drama or being accused of breaking the Ten Commandments? Paine's reply was a definitive "No." In the final scene of the satire, Mrs. Nineholes starts "boxing" her husband when he arrives home with Mrs. Prettiness, who purports to have been afraid to walk home alone. As she bashes her husband, Mrs. Nineholes shouts "I'll have MY way!"

Paine doubtless thought that this parody would demolish Murray's desire to be a playwright, but he was mistaken. She had failed in her first effort to make money through her writing, and she had faced a brutal public scandal, but within weeks she was soliciting her uncle's editorial assistance on *The Medium* and trying to convince Ben Franklin's daughter to act as her Philadelphia agent. She corralled her brother into championing her script, hoping that he could encourage managers to develop "a taste for home productions, and open a way to future pecuniary emolument." When she printed the play in 1798, she hid behind multiple pseudonyms, not only as Constantia publishing *The Gleaner*, but also as the abstract citizen herself, as "Philo Americanus." She retitled the play *Virtue Triumphant*. She defended her play fiercely, dismissing Paine as a "coxcomb." Ironically, by 1832 an unnamed historian writing for the *New-England Magazine* was uncertain who wrote *The Medium*, and even in the second edition of William Dunlap's three-volume history of the American theatre, still circulating in 1963, the authorship was connected to "a clergyman" who denied it "as his offspring."[53]

On 16 May 1795, a couple of months after *The Medium* debacle, Murray revealed the extent of her determination. She sent Powell another script, *The Traveler Returned*, confiding "strange as it may seem, my efforts are rather excited than depressed." For protection, she proposed a series of complicated maneuvers. She told Powell that the script should be taken to Newport for copying, with the original returned to her. Rehearsals and the premiere should be staged in Newport, to insure the actors' readiness. The play should open the season, to "preclude every idea of its being mine." The censors should see only the Newport copy of the script, which should *not* be advertised as an "American production." And "every expense ... should be placed to my account."[54] This last stricture suggests that the "serious accusation" that precipitated her exit from *The Massachusetts Magazine* might, in fact, have emerged because someone misconstrued her business dealings with Charles Powell. Did she freely visit the theatre in the summer of 1794 to discuss *The Medium*? Did Powell visit her at home, prompting rumors? For *The Traveler Returned*, she urged a change of practice, asking Mrs. Powell to call upon her with Powell's reply within the week.

Powell agreed to her conditions, but while rehearsing in Newport, he suddenly went bankrupt, and Colonel John Tyler, who was under no obligation to honor Murray's anonymity, succeeded him as manager. Judith finally again confided her secret authorship to her husband, who urged her to ask Sarah Morton (the other "Constantia*") to represent her interests – but Paine prematurely advertised the play and Tyler insisted that withdrawing it would injure receipts.[55]

Billed against Murray's wishes as "An American Production," *The Traveler Returned* premiered at the Federal Street Theatre on 9 March 1796, and was soon linked to the name Murray. It was relatively well received: the *Massachusetts Mercury* praised the comic scenes and the "allusions to WASHINGTON, LIBERTY, &c." which elicited "loud huzzas."[56] It received a second production. Even Paine admitted that "it met with a very favorable reception," and said Judith "possesses a dramatic talent, which is capable of improvement." However, he continued, the play was pedantic and lacked novelty.[57]

It would have been smart to accept Paine's grudging and double-edged compliment. Instead, Judith Murray revealed the extent of her frustration at her predicament: her nagging desire for celebrity despite her lack of a proper education; her increasingly worried search for cash to secure her daughter's future in the face of John Murray's waning income; her anger over losing *The Massachusetts Magazine* column; her fury at twenty-one-year-old Paine's blithe performance of privilege. She pedantically corrected the incredibly detailed plot summary that Paine had fashioned from the live production, launching another war with him, even though he had apologized in advance for any mistakes. Paine ridiculed her in print, in Latin. Judith retaliated by sending John to the home of the *Centinel* editor with a letter from "Fairplay," doubtless penned by Judith herself, further defending the play.[58]

Judith Murray felt certain that Paine knew she had authored *The Traveler*. Two days before its opening, he had visited her fireside, teasing her by pretending to think that John Murray wrote it. She warned him that "if Mr. Murray's congregation were prevailed upon to believe he had written *a play* it would totally ruin his interest among them." Paine, she confided to her uncle, "never supposed Mr. Murray the Author of The TR – I have strong reasons to believe he well knew from whence the production proceeded."[59] Paine clearly was having fun revealing the backstage lives of the stodgy minister's family while protecting his own hopes: Murray tells her uncle that while she has no idea what caused Paine's "rancour," others reported that it was professional jealousy. Paine went so far as to taunt John Murray at his doorstep.

Paine humiliated Judith further: he named John Murray the author of *Traveler*. Then he accused John of posing as "Fairplay" to defend it. He condemned fame-seekers in a lengthy poem castigating a "Scold" whose tongue "flows forever," "like fame." "She who attacks another's honor," warned the irritated editor through the poet, "draws every living thing upon her."[60]

Judith Murray responded with an utter disregard for the power wielded by her young adversary. She tried to perform as Paine did, as a town wit, without realizing that she could not validly occupy that host body. As "Fairplay," she ridiculed Paine's youth, insinuating that wounded feelings prompted his (fairly accurate) criticism of the play. She offered further (and sillier) corrections of his plot summary, ending with a taunt: "Has the *Traveler Returned* met with too much success?" Predictably, Paine published a rejoinder lambasting John Murray and comparing the play with a corpse that even the reverend could not resurrect. Although the *Mercury* published a brief follow-up and the *Centinel* published John Murray's denial of authorship, Judith Murray's reputation was damaged irreparably. She was forced to produce her benefit in honor of orphans and widows and watch Royall Tyler rake in receipts for *The Farm House; or, The Female Duellists* that same month. She had to defend herself from her own brother-in-law. Over two years later she was still defending her actions with regard to the *Traveler* to her estranged friend and Aunt Maria (Mary Turner Sargent 1744–1813).[61]

At this juncture Murray submerged herself once again in the ostensibly safer world of print publication. She worked feverishly to secure subscribers to *The Gleaner*, writing hundreds of notes, sometimes to complete strangers. In each note, she performed a different persona, adjusting her appeals to individual buyers. She enlisted relatives and friends to sell her miscellany across the Atlantic seaboard and in England. And though readers widely recognized that Judith Sargent Murray was the Gleaner and Constantia, Murray retained the fiction of her pseudonymous host body. She published *The Gleaner* as "Constantia," as if to cloak herself in a well-worn garment she could trust. She folded all of her manifold assumed bodies – from Philo Americanus to the various sea captains and romancers, young girls and modest matrons of "The Story of Margaretta" – into one virtuous womanly whole, constant to her self, her desire for recognition, and her daughter's financial security. Through this "cultured body" she continued to stare down accusations that she was selfish: she informed her mother-in-law that far from placing John Murray in debt, she was paying off the mortgage on their Tontine Crescent house through her 1798 publication of *The Gleaner*.[62]

By then her authorial identity was well known, and she encountered further ridicule, especially from young men for whom savaging ladies' literary pretensions had become an eighteenth-century rite of passage. The youth in her own family, subjected to her well-meaning letters and to extended visits in her home, were particularly abusive. Her nephew Fitz

William invited her to compose a poem for his private school's independence day celebration, only to mock her "cruelly" (Skemp, *Judith*,
105). Another nephew – Lucius Manlius Sargent (1786–1867) – also
ridiculed Judith, perhaps prompted by his mother, Murray's beloved but
estranged Aunt Maria, to deride her literary efforts. He launched a series
of attacks on Murray when he graduated from Harvard, assuming the
same pose of superior wit and derision as Paine, Jr., when he graduated a
decade earlier. When a second edition of *The Gleaner* was to appear in
1806, Lucius Manlius criticized Murray's efforts in the *Centinel*, making it
appear that she had published her own "panegyric," signing it with her
new pseudonym, "Honora [Martesia]." He wrote "smut" in the margins
of her book and strewed pieces of it on her porch. He posed as an editor
interested in publishing her work, tricking her into wasting precious
time.[63]

In her next foray into the theatre, Judith Murray adopted more
ingenious and more dangerous methods to protect herself from attacks.
She engaged her thirteen-year-old daughter Julia and her niece of the
same age to fair-copy her script, titled *The African*. She allowed Julia to
act as a courier to deliver the script and to send and receive messages
regarding its status. In a move of astonishing daring, she enlisted her
nemesis, Paine, Jr., as her agent and patron, hoping to throw the curious
off the scent of her authorship. And she tried to establish a pseudonymous host body of "English, or of southern origin" as the author. She
planned to attend the premiere to squash suspicion and she hid her secret
from all but her girls, Paine, and Powell. Again, John Murray knew
nothing. She confided to Paine that if "emboldened by success, I should
consent to throw off the mask." When Paine urged her to reveal her
authorship before the production, she declined.[64]

By the time *The African* opened the 1807 winter season, Murray was
begging the managers of the Boston Theatre to prevent further disclosure
of her authorship. She drafted Paine to write an epilogue to throw people
off her scent. And yet, she did not exactly wish to remain anonymous,
either. She asked that the production be billed as "a Drama found among
the papers of M Marasite," a transposition of "Martesia," part of her
pseudonym. This was a flimsy disguise, and she knew it. She still wanted
desperately to lay claim to the "cultured American body." The play, no
longer extant, was well acted, but it was attacked by a prominent male
critic, laying "prostrate" her theatrical ambitions.[65]

Unlike Judith Murray, Susanna Rowson was not hounded by a desire
for praise or fame. She launched her first staging of *Slaves in Algiers* as a

benefit performance, and she quietly accepted her scheduling in the dog-days at season's end. She billed the benefit in her husband's name as well as her own. She positioned the play as an American production in the *Philadelphia Gazette* and the *General Advertiser*. She incorporated drunken sailor songs into her script. She coupled *Slaves* with a hornpipe dance and a farce, in which she also appeared. But she sanitized her afterpieces, prompting critics to applaud her "delicate taste and sound sense."[66]

The fact that Rowson acted in productions of her original script complicated her performance as a critic. Onstage she occupied a "cultured American" host body to efface her English, loyalist past. Unlike Murray, Rowson stood onstage within that host body, creating individualized characters. Her risk increased with her visibility, but she could adjust to spectators' audible responses, which, together with her fame and earnestness, protected her. As Olivia, the American daughter in *Slaves in Algiers*, Rowson carved out a fiction of womanly, resourceful Americanness, linking it to her lingering English accent. Theatre-goers, of course, could interpret her performance variously: federalists, sympathizing with the English in their war with France, could forgive her loyalist past and enjoy the new voice of America. Democratic Republicans could focus on her interest in (if not her vindication of) Americans who were "held captive" in the new republic: women, immigrants, religious minorities, and, perhaps most tellingly, racial minorities.[67] Typically, Rowson coupled her deferentiality with a playful audaciousness, which enabled her to appeal to diverse segments within her audience.

But sometimes Rowson had to deploy other strategies to gain access to her audience. This became apparent within days after the premiere of *Slaves in Algiers*, when Rowson defiantly published her original prologue to that play in a local newspaper, evidently in retaliation for its last-minute deletion from her premiere. The heretofore lost prologue to *Slaves in Algiers*, reprinted in the present volume, reveals Rowson's complicated strategy for ushering herself and her play into the public arena.[68] On 2 July 1794, the *General Advertiser* published the prologue "written by Mrs. Rowson, and intended to have been spoken by Mr. Wignell" at the *Slaves* premiere. The following day they printed the prologue that was actually performed at Rowson's premiere, the one "written and spoken by Mr. [James] Fennell" (1766–1816). One of Rowson's fellow actors and a sometime playwright, Fennell was a bit of a ne'er-do-well, always in debt, but he exuded manliness and wrote verse dense with classical allusions. He introduced Rowson's play by focusing the audience's attention on its male characters, the "sons of liberty" who *must* be free "*Wher'er* they breathe." He contrasted Achilles' generous freeing of Priam's son Hector with African Muslims' greedy refusal to release the sons of America, at that very moment enchained in Algiers. He appealed to the audience to ransom these men who "help'd to gain / A nation's freedom." Americans must *everywhere* be free: their very souls dictated it. Fennell closed his prologue by identifying the playwright, who "tho a woman" pleaded "the Rights of Man."[69] His prologue clearly framed the play by linking it to Enlightenment tropes of manly freedom and to a specific political agenda, the ransoming of Americans.

Rowson introduced her play very differently. Her prologue is charming, ingratiating, and has nothing to do with the sons of liberty. In fact, it immediately establishes Rowson as "a female bard," the daughter and mother of American culture with a legitimate claim on being "here," on American land. She depicts herself as "trembling with suspense" backstage, having entreated Wignell, the well-respected manager of the playhouse, to "plead her cause to th' utmost of [his] pow'r." Of course, Wignell explains, it would be "unmanly" to refuse. Rowson thus cleverly reminds the audience to be gentlemanly and let her speak. Then she defers to them, judging them just as knowledgeable about theatre as the manager. As to the quality of the play, the manager continues, he has read better plays, but also a few worse. He asks the audience to pardon the flaws of Rowson's play, as a mother ignores a favorite son's faults. Then he justifies Rowson's work as an *American* performing critic: "'Twas here her love of literature grew." Wignell establishes Rowson as an American playwright and actress with a right to speak. Since America had taught her to love literature, she offered her first "brat" to American audiences. If they smiled upon this child, she would "catch a beam of Phoebus' sacred fire" and "offer a future child more worthy" of them. This prologue is a far cry from Fennell's paean of praise for manly liberty and the rights of Americans around the globe. It is a womanly – indeed motherly – claim on Anglo-American-ness. But Rowson did not publish her prologue in the 1794 edition of her play; instead, she printed Fennell's prologue, a sure-fire marketing ploy. This gap between Rowson's intended framing of her play and its actual framing reveals the depth of the challenge faced by both Murray and Rowson: how could they persuade managers and audiences to accept them as arbiters of American culture?

In important ways, the reception of Rowson's and Murray's work overlapped: both women critics triggered a public debate among angry male newcomers eager to establish themselves in American letters and older, more gracious gentlemen willing to defend female playwrights, particularly as amateurs. In Rowson's case, these men were on opposite sides of the political spectrum, so the debate following her play was a vicious fight for political as well as literary turf.

A thirty-one-year-old English immigrant named William Cobbett (1763–1835) launched the attack on Rowson. His true target, however, was the moderate anti-federalist Samuel Harrison Smith (1772–1845), publisher of the *American Monthly Review; or, Literary Journal* (1795). A monarchist, Cobbett viewed Smith as a political enemy as well as a literary competitor. He was furious with Smith for lavishly praising Sarah Morton's poem "Ouabi" in his inaugural January issue, then ridiculing his own diatribe *A Bone to Gnaw, for the Democrats* in February. Instead of attacking the well-placed Morton, Cobbett ridiculed Rowson as a means of mocking Smith. As editor, Smith had called Morton's poem evidence of the United States' "refinement and literary taste." He collapsed the poem, poet, and America together to prove that civilization and liberty marched together. Smith revealed "Philenia's" identity as Mrs. Morton of Boston.[70] Through this move, Smith made Morton visible in a particular way: he made her an emblem of American culture in her own flesh. He linked the poem, the lady poet, the lady scholar, and the cultured American woman to the body politic, the new democratic, cultured America.

In contrast, Smith framed Cobbett as an ineffectual monarchist railing at the popular anti-federalists and the French. He particularly criticized Cobbett's attack on Jacques-Pierre Brissot (de Warville) (1754–93), a French abolitionist who argued that a healthy body politic necessitated the equality of women and blacks. Consumption, which claimed so many women's lives, was, in Brissot's view, caused by women's lack of *"a will or a civil existence."* Apoplectic, Cobbett retorted that anti-federalist women were unfaithful because their husbands tried "to reduce them to a level with their sable 'property,'" and because their men were homosexuals: they engaged in "gander-frolics," "squeezing, and hugging, and kissing one another."[71] He challenged Smith, unmarried and nine years his junior, to ingratiate himself "with the whole tribe of female scribblers and politicians" by reviewing Mrs. Rowson's writings. He described them as "voluminous," critiquing both her body of work and her fleshy body. In a frenzy of anxiety about the gendering and sexualizing of American letters, he mocked an epilogue penned by Rowson's fellow actress, Mrs. Whitlock, who represented genius as "masculine, feminine, and neuter, all at once." Then Cobbett zeroed in on Rowson's contention that women had the "power to render ourselves superior" and demand "universal sway." He associated these sentiments with the dissolution of marriage and the feminization of the House of Representatives. He dismissed Rowson's work as medicine, opium, emetics. Recognizing her as a federalist at heart, he called the Democratic Republicanism of *Slaves in Algiers* sudden and suspect, even as he linked her with the Irish. Rowson fought back, calling him a "loathsome reptile."[72]

Smith may have sided with the women against Cobbett, but it was John Swanwick (1740–98), another Democratic Republican and a poet, who stepped forward to defend Rowson. He had just assumed his post as a representative to the Pennsylvania legislature, and in a courtly manner, he defended Rowson – but only as an amateur. Women's literary refinement, he explained, granted men happiness in civilized society. Rowson's comments about women's superiority were "merely a sally of humor, intended to excite a smile, and not to enforce a conviction." Upper-class gentlemen, he explained, deferred to women, while younger men and lower-class men, both black and white, were threatened by women, so they beat and seduced them. Gentlemen knew that the differences between the sexes were caused by education, not biology. Tellingly, though, Swanwick ends his defense with a threat: he warns Rowson not to respond to Cobbett, and threatens to censure her publicly, at her next benefit, if she does.[73] Rowson, he believed, staged her plays at his pleasure. No matter what methods early European American women playwrights used to enter the public sphere, they faced censure, curtailment, condescension, or a "blackening" of their bodies – but this did not deter them from trying to petition for white privilege.

PERFORMING CRITICISM/PERFORMANCE CRITICISM

During the period from 1789 to 1825, European American women critics often claimed white privilege by romanticizing, domesticating, or appropriating the performance of blackness. In the theatre, however, they could – at least until the final scene – entertain more liberal attitudes toward the tangle of "race," religion, and nation. They could entertain the possibility that "non-white" or non-English residents – including Africans and Jews – could perform whiteness. Rowson took advantage of this fact, experimenting with the permeability of identity categories, imagining them as overlapping performances that one might adopt. She experimented until the final scene, when that permeability is foreclosed and the boundaries (somewhat blurred by her experimentation) are reinstated. If Rowson represented racialized "others" as candidates for – if not yet possessors of – white privilege, Murray represented them as simply subordinate.

Lacking practical experience in the theatre, Murray was less imaginative and more conservative than Rowson in staging race and ethnicity. In *The Traveler Returned*, Murray depicts the Anglo-American family as in full command; they weather even the wife's extramarital flirtation. In contrast, she satirizes the Dutch couple, Mr. and Mrs. Vanisttart, as ineffectual, greedy, and pretentious, incapable of finding happiness. Like Bridget and Patrick, marked as non-white by their status as servants and by the latter's pronounced Irish brogue, the Vanisttarts do not merit even a rehearsal for whiteness. Blacks appear fleetingly in Murray's extant work, through what Toni Morrison, in *Playing in the Dark*, calls "American Africanisms," racialized figurations of African-ness meant to create a notion of American whiteness. Murray paints servants as inferiors who deserve kindness, not as candidates for equality.[74] The child-like Obadiah is confused even by everyday objects such as thermometers (*Gleaner*, 650).

Nonetheless, Murray's staging of American whiteness cannot be dismissed this easily, because when *Traveler* opened in Boston's Federal Street Theatre on 9 and 10 March 1796, audience members probably reacted variously to Obadiah, Patrick, and the Vanisttarts. English actors with English accents played all of these roles, and while some spectators accepted the stage fiction as truthful, others in the audience – immigrants and servants themselves, perhaps a few slave attendants, and maybe a few early European American abolitionists – surely saw through the minstrelsy. For them, the English actor playing Obadiah was clearly a counterfeit Brit blacking up and speaking a ridiculously fabricated dialect, the performer playing Patrick a sober Englishman posing as an inebriated Irish stock type. For them, the performance of whiteness onstage was obviously a sham, perhaps a cause for anger or merriment.

Murray's script of *The African* is not extant, but the remaining evidence suggests that it deployed American Africanisms, using the title character Zulima, the African woman, as an exotic but subservient figure that heightened white American-ness through contrast. The cast of characters included a father and son, a mother and son (from another family), plus three unmarried female characters, one of them Zulima. Selico, named for a seaport in Bolivia, appears to have been an ethnic comic servant: Murray suggested that Mr. Wilson, an actor who could play comic or serious roles, could play Selico or the (more serious role of the) Quaker Turgood, probably an abolitionist. She viewed the actor playing one of the sons, Henry Warrington, as possessing "sufficient spirit" for that role, suggesting, perhaps, a romantic lead.[75] Perhaps Warrington "warred" for a romance with Zulima, just as Henry in Rowson's *Slaves* served as a potential if not an actual suitor for Zoriana. But by 1807, when Murray's *African* premiered, it is quite possible that Zulima, unlike Zoriana, was shaped by the polygenetic notion that Africans were more docile and emotional than Europeans.

The presence of an African woman, a "spirited" white man, and a Quaker, as well as the timing of the production, suggest that the managers, at least, viewed *The African* as an anti-slavery (which is not to say an anti-racist) play. After letting the script languish for several years, they suddenly scheduled it to open just after the British House of Commons passed a hotly debated 1807 bill to abolish slavery. Mr. Dickenson, the actor playing Harcourt, tried to derail the production by denouncing it in the Green Room, and it is tempting to imagine that his objections were political.[76]

However, despite the liberalism of Murray's *Deductions*, with its monogenetic reading of race, and despite her part in shaping the Universalists' constitutional indictment of slavery, Judith Murray's *African* probably echoed George Coleman the Younger's wildly successful British comic opera *Inkle and Yarico* (1787). In fact, Murray's fervent hope was that Mrs. Powell, who had "repeatedly performed Yarico," would play Zulima. Murray's linking Zulima with the Yarico "type" reveals the limits of her political critique. The Barbadian story of Yarico (popular enough, in 1999, to prompt the publication of a "reader" and a musical staging at the Edinburgh Festival) tells of a "native" maiden who saves an English castaway, Inkle, off the shores of her island. She follows him to England to marry him, only to witness his change of heart: he sells her and their unborn child into slavery and renews his profitable engagement with an English girl.[77] In his opera, Coleman reveals the embarrassments triggered by Inkle's lack of a moral compass. Perhaps Murray depicted a similar story in *The African*, with a gentle Zulima romantically linked to Warrington until Act v, when he married Charlotte despite Quaker Turgod's remonstrance.

The theatre often showcased the fluidity of identity categories for audiences at the turn of the century, as playwrights and actors experimented provisionally with interracial liaisons and with the performance of "race" itself. In Rowson's production of *Slaves in Algiers*, for instance, a white-skinned English actress, in tawny makeup, played Zoriana, a

Muslim Moor who converted to Christianity and performed all the requisite acts of Christian activism and cultured republican womanhood. Zoriana proved thereby her claim on American freedom and white privilege. Until the final scene, Mrs. Warrell, portraying Zoriana, demonstrated the plausibility of this claim. The key to Zoriana's performance of whiteness was her conversion to Christianity: she performed Christianity as race. Cloaked in her performance of Christianity, Zoriana is poised to flee to America. In the final act of *Slaves*, however, Rowson ended her experiment with the performativity of race, religion, and nation in the transatlantic world of capitalism.[78] Zoriana decides to stay in Africa to teach her father, the Dey, the benefits of freedom – so that he can Christianize Africa. All the world is claimed for a white Christian American freedom, which may be shared by reasonable former Muslims, but only at a distance.

Slaves in Algiers was inspired by an actual event: in 1793 Algierian pirates captured over a hundred American sailors off the North African coast and enslaved them for ransom. Rowson investigated this reversal of republican cultural practice: how could *Africans* hold *Americans* hostage? "White" Americans, by their very "nature," were supposed to be incapable of remaining in captivity: they would, by definition, break free, from the Africans as from the British. That was the logic of polygenesis and chattel slavery. But the European American sailors in Algiers had not, in fact, broken free, so Rowson staged their successful revolt against the Algerine captors, to relieve American audiences and to test the performance of whiteness. In *Slaves*, an Anglo-American family and their friends free themselves and convert their African-Muslim and British-Jewish captors to Christianity and to a free Algiers. The play is, certainly, an attack on the North African practice of kidnapping Americans for ransom in the 1790s. It is also a republican tract validating the Revolution against British "enslavement" of American colonists. It is furthermore a negotiation concerning the status of American immigrants and non-Christians: should they, also, be freed and ushered into American whiteness? Finally, the play is a proto-white-feminist manifesto and, through its linkage of Muslim harems with Southern plantations, a protest against American slavery and the Southern male practice of taking slaves as forced sexual partners.[79]

Rowson wrote the play "hastily" but with a keen awareness of her positionality as a British-born body living in a newly minted American republic. She announced that her play contained nothing "prejudicial, to the moral or political principles of the government under which I live."[80]

She herself played Olivia, the self-sacrificing, confident Anglo-American daughter of the Constants, whose foresight saves all the captives. The Constants, an English-born husband and American-born wife, are separated by the Revolutionary War and then captured separately, and without each other's knowledge, by Barbary pirates along the northern coast of Africa. An African Muslim leader or "Dey," always searching for slaves and wives for his harem, holds Mr. Constant and his daughter Olivia hostage, while a sly diasporic (German-English-African) Jew-turned-Muslim named Ben Hassan holds the mother Rebecca and her son for ransom. The Dey jails the father and seeks to convert Olivia to Islam, so that he can marry her. His attempt fails, but Olivia successfully converts his daughter Zoriana to Christianity. Meanwhile Ben Hassan, the Jewish "master," demands double ransom for the mother and sells her young son on the auction block. Hassan is the abject outsider who has bartered his daughter, English-born Fetnah, to the Dey, though Rebecca Constant has taught Fetnah to embrace Christian American liberty.

Rowson constructed Christian American femininity, then, as a performance of whiteness, linked to the pursuit of liberty and individual happiness. As a performance, it could be learned by women of other races, nations, and religions. Rowson imagined at least the possibility of a diversely inhabited citizenship. In the final scenes, however, she rejected the notion that Africans and Jews could perform white American Christianity on American ground: though they wish to immigrate to the United States, Zoriana and Fetnah remain with their fathers in Africa, to educate them about building a free Algiers. Rowson thereby short-circuits her exploration of race as performance and instead stages American religious and racial imperialism. This is not a simple nod to the necessities of pleasing the theatre audience, but a rooted sense of privilege hemmed in by the boundaries of religion, race, and nation. Enlightenment notions of freedom foreclose all other considerations: Olivia echoes the imperialist newspapers of the day: "may Freedom spread her benign influence thro' every nation, till the bright Eagle, united with the dove and olive-branch, waves high, the acknowledged standard of the world" (Rowson, *Slaves*, 75). But once Rowson staged the performativity of this notion of "freedom" and its relationship to slavery, her audiences could not fully ignore it.

Setting her play in a Muslim harem, Rowson compared upper- and middle-class white American marriages of convenience to harem-bound slavery. She simultaneously suggested that Southern plantations were, in effect, harems, run by husbands who supported multiple sexual partners in a setting of luxury and moral decadence. The play opens as Fetnah, the plucky English Jew-turned-African Muslim, explains her new American Christian viewpoint to Selima, a docile African Muslim harem-mate. The two women chatting in their harem might easily be interpreted as two well-married European American women in their beautifully appointed homes, reacting in different ways to their marital confinement. Fetnah, the Dey's "favorite," finds her new home lovely but seeks "liberty." Rowson invited the upper-class Anglo-American women in the audience to critique their marriages, but she simultaneously encouraged them to feel superior to Southern and Muslim women, subjected to worse treatment. Northern upper-class women, her patrons, at least had the power to choose their "masters." Rowson also ridiculed men's sexual advances and revealed women's power to thwart them, staging Fetnah's demonstration of how she shouted "I can't love you" at the Dey when "he laid his hand upon his scymetar."[81]

Rowson's theatrical critique of the Dey's and Hassan's practice of holding slaves and taking several wives is implicitly an attack on American slavery as well as marital "bondage," so the play is also an exercise in regionalism: the New England states had already begun to dismantle slavery, while Southern plantation owners continued to take slave mistresses and hold slaves hostage. Rowson creates a separate North and South as she indirectly probes the "peculiar" institution of slavery. She also represents the ways in which slaves might refuse their masters' power over them: the Jewish master Hassan, like the Muslim Dey, is frustrated by the fact that "masters may not do what they please with their slaves." Hassan's power is further circumscribed. In Hassan, in fact, Rowson conflates the stock figures of the Jew, the German immigrant, the black, and the woman. Represented as a greedy petty criminal who "cheated the Gentiles" in England before fleeing to Africa, Hassan readily converts from Judaism to Islam in order to ingratiate himself with the Dey, but the stock attributes of "Jewishness" remain: he speaks through an ersatz German Yiddish accent ("v" for "w"). Furthermore, his accent links him to black stereotypes: his speech reveals touches of what passed for slave dialect ("d" for "th"). Finally, when he dons a dress to escape the Dey's presumptive displeasure, he is represented as a woman onstage – an obscenely ugly, old woman. Frederic argues that "if any one deserves slavery," it is Hassan.[82] He is the ultimate scapegoat upon whom the entire representation of liberty rests. But since Hassan is still associated with a thwarted desire to own slaves, Frederic's indictment that Hassan deserves slavery is simultaneously an attack on American slaveholders.

In fact, Rebecca Constant, the mother figure, may be read at moments as an anti-slavery advocate: she pleads, "let us not throw on another's neck, the chains we scorn to wear." There is a limit to her advocacy: her blush upon speaking about slaves links Christian freedom to her "white European body." However, the Jewish and African women in the play also voice anti-slavery sentiments. Furthermore, there is no outcry against the cross-racial liaisons of the women: Fetnah (the British Jew turned African Muslim turned almost-American Christian) appears to be headed toward becoming a wife to Frederic, Olivia's fiancé's American friend (who thinks Fetnah is a Moor). Similarly, Zoriana (the African Muslim turned Christian) pursues Henry, Olivia's European American fiancé. The women are represented as connecting with each another as well, across the boundaries of "race" and nationality. Of course, the English actresses portraying them all spoke with British accents, effectively translating them all, orally, into Anglo-Americans. Curiously, Zoriana's love for Henry brings her closer to Olivia. In fact, Schueller reads the moment when Olivia and Zoriana pledge their love for Henry as their displaced love for one another.[83] When Olivia faces death, she asks Zoriana to replace her as daughter and wife, and no one objects. Henry treats Zoriana as he would any respectable woman, and in return, Zoriana performs her "Christian duty" by releasing him to Olivia and helping them escape.

The differences among female characters in the play, variously marked in terms of race, religion, and nationality, at times seem inconsequential: as Frederic, the hapless suitor puts it, "Moor or Christian, slave or free woman, 'tis no matter" (Rowson, *Slaves*, 23). They all perform acts of womanly self-sacrifice and bravery, claiming "whiteness" through intelligence and self-abnegation. Zoriana and Rebecca both offer ransom for the "white slaves." When the slaves escape, however, it is Olivia who competes the most successfully as a self-sacrificing woman: she remains behind to appease the Dey in case their escape is thwarted. When the slaves' plan is, in fact, discovered, she prevents the Dey from executing them by agreeing to marry him, while secretly plotting suicide. Rebecca Constant enters at that very moment, reuniting her family and announcing that she and her daughter Olivia "will die together" to avoid living as slaves (Rowson, *Slaves*, 68). Their deaths are forestalled by a general uprising of all the captives in the city, who storm the palace so forcefully that the Dey frees all his slaves. He asks Hassan and Fetnah to stay in Africa, while the American, British, and Spanish-born freed slaves plan their return to America and freedom. This image of the slaves returning to their "native land" evokes images of colonization as well as the freeing of African Americans from slavery.

In the end, Rowson, like Murray, helped build not only what Schloesser calls "racial patriarchy" but also a religious patriarchy which linked notions of Christian American-ness with "freedom." But audiences could not altogether forget her cross-cultural experimentation with interracial romance and gender solidarity. As Olivia, Rowson offered a final imperialist blessing: "may Freedom spread her benign influence thro' every nation," then retreated backstage. Moments later, the Prompter (played by her husband William Rowson, the actual prompter) demanded "COME – Mrs. Rowson! Come!" and Rowson emerged as "herself," though she was still protected by Olivia's costume. She thereby encouraged the audience to transfer their image of the virtuous, virginal character onto their image of the more equivocal but charming married playwright-actress, so sweetly pretending to be obedient to her husband and frightened of the audience's disapproval, while simultaneously claiming "superiority" for all the women in the auditorium. Shielded within her cultured American host body, "Mrs. Rowson" asked the audience to "overlook [her] errors," then directly addressed the "Ladies."[84]

Realizing the power of a female fan base, Rowson made the women in the audience visible and audible to themselves by asking them, saucily, "how d'ye like my play?" Then she answered for them, sharing an unspeakable truth as a joke the men could easily dismiss: "She says that we should have supreme dominion, / And in good truth, we're all of her opinion." In this moment, Rowson created a host body for all the women in the house: she claimed gender superiority for each and every woman, whatever her racial or national affiliation – even as she signaled through her central position onstage the particular claim of Anglo-American women on whiteness. She linked that claim to a feeling body: "You must feel it yourself, and make others feel too," she had advised a fellow actress. Then she invited the audience to view her play as a meditation against slavery in any form: she asked them to imagine the destitution of "many a Christian, shut from light and day, / In bondage, languishing their lives away" and then picture their "rapt'rous joy" at being freed.[85] That image lingered after the curtain fell. Through the Christian body she linked Anglo-American captives in Algiers, Christianized slaves in America, immigrant converts to Christianity, and Christian, Muslim, and Jewish women.

Rowson's rehearsal for change subsumed all bodies within Christian American culture, even as she celebrated all women's "genius." As more women critics emerged in the aftermath of the Revolutionary War, it became difficult simply to dismiss them as "geniuses" or as curiosities. It was even riskier to label them all brilliant. The best way to minimize their intelligence was to follow Rousseau's lead and contend, as Murray reported with considerable derision, "that although a female may *ostensibly* wield the pen, yet it is certain some man of letters sits behind the curtain to guide its movements." When that strategy failed, American culture represented white women critics as nicely competent. Murray knew that once her gender was disclosed, her writing would no longer be viewed as exemplary, but would be characterized as full of "*effeminacy* and *tinsel glitter.*"[86]

Murray and Rowson, atypically, did refer to their own "genius." Murray did so anxiously, behind the mask of "Modestus Mildmay." In the "Story of Margaretta," Mildmay demanded pensions for writers "of *real genius*, whether it be found in the male or female world." Rowson's references to her genius were more playful than Murray's, probably because she had no pseudonym to protect her. In the preface to *Mentoria, or the Young Lady's Friend* (1794), Rowson bemoaned the fact that she could not easily claim "genius" because she had to follow the convention of apologizing in advance for her flaws. This was counterintuitive, since it prepossessed readers against the work and forced her to "acknowledge myself an idiot, for suffering it to meet the public eye, in such an imperfect state."[87] It was difficult to exercise self-confidence under such circumstances, but that was precisely the goal of the new American individual, especially the republican mother.

Linda Kerber, Mary Beth Norton, Nina Baym, and others have theorized that European American women shaped American-ness by becoming "republican mothers" dedicated to raising sons and daughters for the nation through virtuous subordination. Baym explains that "in eighteenth-century political thought *virtue* referred to the supposedly highest state of individual development, in which moral rectitude combined with civic responsibility; *subordination*, to the supposedly highest condition of social development, in which respect for others functioned within a hierarchy that ranked individuals by such measures as class, property, occupation, age, and gender" (intro. Murray, *Gleaner*, iii). Rowson and Murray may indeed be viewed as republican mothers, educating children in American notions of virtue and subordination. However, they also believed fervently in "self-approbation," which often undermined their federalist investments in a class system that marked them as subordinates. This was the contradiction within Rowson's work that infuriated William Cobbett: she wrote for a largely federalist theatre, but the rhetoric in her *Slaves in Algiers* was anti-federalist. Rowson and Murray performed contradictory notions of American-ness, touting "liberty" but propelled by self-interest to advocate an America involving subordination for anyone but them.

Murray viewed American equality as impractical, but, like Rowson, she simultaneously claimed it for white women in the arts, where they would not perform subordination but rather demonstrate their genius and forge a peculiarly American culture. She envisioned a republic with secure class and racial boundaries, permeable through individual industry and virtue, and softened by philanthropy as well as a liberal war debt policy. She compared a well-run America to a well-regulated home at harvest time. Anti-federalism, in her view, would be like a hurricane, "inmingling the various classes of mankind" and destroying their various, harmonious contributions to the nation. This passage, unlike her early Universalist catechism, relies on a polygenetic concept of America. Influenced by the excesses of the French Revolution, Murray insisted on hierarchies to guard a fragile democracy.[88]

Both Rowson and Murray chafed at hierarchies in their artistic endeavors, however. They argued that women required a sense of intellectual and spiritual self-worth to build the nation. Murray championed "a reverence of self." Like Rowson, who playfully suggested that women had the power to make themselves superior, Murray told women "that every thing in the compass of mortality, was placed within their grasp."[89]

Both women critics hoped, through their individual genius, to become part of the cultured body and voice of the nation. In fact, one of the challenges of creating an idea of American-ness was forging a specifically American speech out of the myriad dialects and languages spoken across the new republic, and both labored to stage "American" speech. For Murray, northern Anglo-American speech provided the standard. Rowson helped create this "common American tongue" by speaking American sentiments with an Anglo-American accent onstage and by compiling a popular dictionary. She merged middle-class Boston speech with a fading English accent, granting Northern white America a dominant voice. Reviewers perceived Rowson as contributing to "a well regulated" and "American stage," which would serve as a "school for virtue, patriotism, and morality."[90]

Partly as a result of European American women's engagement in the Revolutionary War, gender codes shifted. Having proven their worth during the war, women no longer had to apologize as they expressed their political views. Both Murray and Rowson published their apprehensions about the French Revolution. They constructed white womanhood in terms of middle-class respectability within a family circle, with virtuous young girls who educated themselves to become moral mothers for the republic. While they viewed marriage as elective, their ideal woman was clearly a self-possessed, well-educated white mother. The Gleaner described her as "a sensible and informed woman – companionable and serious – possessing also a facility of temper, and united to a congenial mind – blest with competency – and rearing to maturity a promising family of children." Both sensed that America offered Anglo-American women extraordinary opportunities. As the Gleaner explained, "'the Rights of Women' begin to be understood; we seem, at length, determined to do justice to THE SEX."[91] Rowson, having been interned as a loyalist during the War, was somewhat more sanguine in her assessment of the situation, but she repeatedly positioned white women as potentially equal to if not superior to men.

This optimism emboldened Anglo-American readers and spectators to imagine gendered equality. In *The Gleaner*, Murray insists that women are (like Rowson's characters) equally "capable of enduring hardships," "equally ingenious, and fruitful in resources," as capable of "fortitude and heroism," "equally brave," "as patriotic," "as influential," "as energetic, and as eloquent," "as faithful," "as capable of supporting, with honour, the toils of government," and "equally susceptible of every literary acquirement." To prove her case, she points to her British contemporaries, women like Hannah Cowley, Fanny Burney, and Mary Wollenstonecraft. Among Americans, she lists only Mercy Otis Warren by name, adding "a Philenia, an Antonia, a Euphelia, &c. &c."[92] The presence of so many feminine pseudonyms signals American women critics' difficulty claiming and fully authorizing their own productions – their continuing need for host bodies – but the "&c. &c." also foregrounds their ubiquity, their expanded access to the public sphere. Rowson focused on women's achievements in many of her school dialogues and textbooks, as well as her "Sketches of Female Biography."

New gender codes for educated white women prepared them to look skeptically upon romance, suitors, and marriage in general. *The Gleaner* lists the requisites of marriage as "mutual esteem, mutual friendship, mutual confidence, *begirt about by mutual forbearance.*" "If minds are not congenial," Murray contended, "celibacy" is preferable. A happy alternative to marriage was a "holy friendship" of the sort that Murray experienced in the early years of her relationship with her Aunt Maria: eighteenth-century women moved across a spectrum of sexualities, including various versions of same-sex attraction and love.[93] In fact, European American women's practice of masking themselves behind pseudonyms, even in private letters to one another, enabled them to explore various types of romantic identification.

In "The Story of Margaretta," Murray represents several unsuitable male partners for Margaretta, not only through the primary plot line with Courtland, but also through fictional readers of Margaretta's story. Several "readers" – from sea captains to earnest young orphans – ask the Gleaner for Margaretta's hand. Their letters read like performance pieces in dialect, with stock characters such as the profligate male ingenue, Bellamour, and the stingy old bachelor, Timothy Plodder. All are represented as inappropriate husbands. When Margaretta visits Mrs. Worthington and her daughter Amelia in New Haven, she meets Mr. Sinisterus Courtland, the evil love interest and another bad marital choice. Margaretta's ever-vigilant parents know that Courtland is incapable of mutual esteem, but they allow Margaretta herself to discover the error of her ways. She finds that a "Frances Wellwood" has born three out-of-wedlock sons with Courtland. The Vigilliuses adopt Frances, secure Courtland's release from debtors' prison, set him up in business, and restore him to his family circle, so that Murray can expand her reworking of gender codes: Murray thus demonstrates that fallen women and men may be redeemed in a rational Universalist society (Murray, *Gleaner*, 106). Edward, having fallen prey to gambling during Margaretta's flirtation with Courtland, is also redeemed, not only through a companionate marriage to Margaretta but also through his willingness to live frugally to repay his debts. Margaretta's birth father soon saves the day, miraculously appearing to grant Margaretta a fortune.

During the late eighteenth and early nineteenth centuries, European American women critics often shielded themselves by adopting cultured American host bodies, disseminating their criticism in print and in performance. They also found avenues of access in new liberal religions, such as the Universalist movement. Their work as critics, however, particularly in the fleshly zone of the theatre, was hemmed in by attempts to discredit them. The young men who hoped to make their way in American letters were not giving up without a fight.

SITES OF ACCESS

African American critics identified many of the same sites of access that Murray and Rowson located: they gained entrance into public conversations through benevolent associations and courtrooms as well as literary societies and schools. They also participated in African American freedom celebrations and Election Day ceremonies. And, as Jarena Lee and Zilpha Elaw demonstrate, by 1807 they exhorted and by 1815 they preached to diverse audiences in parlors, sanctuaries, and town squares as well as in the charged camp meetings of the Second Great Awakening. Their early preaching – preceding by two decades the work of black female anti-slavery activists – is especially important, because it evinces a claim on the African American church, increasingly the site of political activity.

As individual slaves were manumitted and as the free black population grew after the Revolutionary War, African Americans established benevolent associations. Through these associations, critics provided each other with disability assistance, burial aid, schooling, and sisterhood. It is no surprise that the groups were popular. Orbour Collins, the President of a Rhode Island society, was delighted at how many women joined her group. Societal rules fostered respectability as well as sisterhood. In Salem, for instance, the members of the Colored Female Religious and Moral Society vowed "not to ridicule or divulge the supposed or apparent infirmities of any fellow member."[94] Black critics found safety and a friendly audience through the new benevolent and educational societies. From 1808 until 1842, for example, the African Female Benevolent Society of Newport served as a social safety net and helped maintain "a free school, for any person of colour in this town." Free Northerners had easier access to formal schooling, but in cities, even in the South, many African American children attended school.[95] Philadelphia had authorized a white-run school for African Americans in the 1740s, and by 1760 there were two schools in operation. By 1789, black literacy was so strong in Philadelphia that a new association tried to quell white anxiety by calling itself the "Society for the Free Instruction of Orderly Blacks and People of Color."[96] Implicit in this *orderly* cultured body is a notion of class within the African American community: critics who assumed a cultured American body to protect themselves were claiming a certain privilege within their intra-racial communities. Mutual aid societies, like schools, provided these women critics with access to literacy. The women who spoke at the gatherings of these societies and who led discussions in these schools often shielded themselves from censure by adopting a "cultured American" host body melded with a "Christian activist" body.

In addition to establishing benevolent associations and schools, African American women initiated literary societies, granting women access to the public sphere by redefining private homes as public arenas. Literary associations addressed educated women's desire for further study, but as Elizabeth McHenry has demonstrated, they also offered women with limited print literacy an opportunity to practice engaging in formal discussion and debate. These societies were often segregated by race. The Colored Female Religious and Moral Society of Salem, organized in 1818, was typical. At each meeting the women read passages from "'some profitable book'" and engaged in a Bible discussion.[97] By displaying their talents to each other and sharing their own literary and theological understandings, they formed not just a sense of community but also a sense of spiritual and political agency. Through their performances, they claimed a "cultured body" aligned with American-ness as well as literate African American-ness.

Women critics provided leadership in this movement for black literacy, especially within the church. They spearheaded informal and then more formalized Sunday schools in northern communities, alongside prayer groups. As Jarena Lee gathered converts in western New York, she encouraged them to find a teacher and then become teachers themselves. She inspired converts in Toronto to establish a new school. Among religious groups, the Quakers, especially in Pennsylvania and New York, educated all girls, fostering the belief that women had the duty to follow their inner light and speak in public assemblies.[98]

Another avenue through which women could enter civic conversations was through what Geneviève Fabre calls "freedom celebrations." At these festive public celebrations, women critics adopted "Christian activist bodies" to mark important events in African American history, events such as the ending of the foreign slave trade. Building upon Election Day and Pinkster, freedom celebrations were characterized by a will to create "an African-American memory – one which often ran counter to the national memory." They fostered "an unfinished revolution." The cele-brations helped forge disparate African and American colonial experiences into African American as well as American culture. Men customarily delivered the addresses at these celebrations, but black churches and neighborhoods hosted them, and female exhorters offered prayers and short commentaries. Fourth of July celebrations typically acknowledged American independence while also staging anti-slavery. Leaders read national documents such as the Declaration of Independence and the Bill of Rights and delivered activist speeches. Nat Turner and others launched revolts on the anniversaries of the freedom celebrations. From 1808, one of the most widely observed dates was the annual New Year's Day observance of the end of the African slave trade. Particularly in

Philadelphia and New York, these observances opened with group songs and prayers, moved to a sermon and a formal oration, and concluded with a public parade.[99] Women celebrants joined the processions, which featured special costumes and banners sewn and painted for the occasion. Crucially, Thanksgiving celebrations took place in public squares rather than the church, and military elements gradually entered the festivities, with emblems, bands, and gun salutes. These celebrations, then, figured a collective African American body with activist access to political and paramilitary power and a claim on American-ness. The members of black women's associations and the participants of freedom celebrations set the stage for black women's emergence, later in the century, as reform-minded, cultured activists in the abolitionist, health reform, woman's rights, temperance, and lyceum movements.

From the late eighteenth to the mid nineteenth century, black women used itinerant preaching to claim public space and to re-imagine Christian American-ness. They became Christian activists or "doers of the Word."[100] They performed the radical anti-racist faith they hoped to instill in all Americans. Both Jarena Lee, arguably the most prominent African American critic in the decade from 1815–1825, and her fellow Christian Zilpha Elaw, initiated their speaking careers within the new Methodist Church. Their path to this church was circuitous: Elaw lived with Quakers and Lee first worshiped with Presbyterians and Episcopalians. Faced with Quaker silence and an English minister with a largely white congregation, however, both embraced Methodism. Lee concluded that the African Methodist Episcopal Church housed "the people to which my heart unites," while Elaw exhorted in a variety of Methodist settings.[101]

Joining the AME church meant both claiming and creating an African American people. Twenty-seven-year-old Richard Allen had established his Bethel Church in Philadelphia, in 1787, to escape the racism of mainstream Methodists. Gradually branches sprang up in central and southern New Jersey, where Lee and Elaw both lived, and in nearby Baltimore and Wilmington, Delaware. It was not until 1816 that these churches forged the AME denomination and elected Richard Allen their first Bishop, so Lee and Elaw seized a rare opportunity, launching their ministries right at the outset of the movement, before it had solidified its institutional structures. Lee was especially aggressive in securing her right to speak. Sometimes in the sanctuary, she "forgot" that she was licensed only to exhort or intensify the preacher's message. She began to preach for herself. For example, one morning when Richard Allen was visiting the

Bethel Church where she worshiped and where Reverend Richard Williams suddenly "lost the spirit," Lee "sprang, as by altogether supernatural impulse, to [her] feet" and preached on the passage Williams had just introduced. Allen conceded that she "was called to that work, as [much as] any of the preachers present."[102] Lee, in a very real sense, performed her criticism of the limits of the emerging AME denomination.

Partly because they were not allowed to occupy a settled pulpit, and partly because their outspokenness caused friction, both Lee and Elaw acted as itinerant performing critics. Lee, slightly older than Elaw, started preaching (as opposed to exhorting or leading prayer groups) around 1817, two years before her colleague. She justified her preaching through logic and scriptural citations, opening her spiritual narrative with an apology that was simultaneously an "assertion of special authority." Arguing that Christ died for women as well as men, she asked why it should be considered "impossible, heterodox, or improper for a woman to preach." Citing Mary as the first preacher, she quoted the Biblical prediction that "your sons and your *daughters* shall prophecy."[103]

Lee's licensed prayer meetings, in effect, became church services, eventually installing her as a de facto settled preacher in her own home. As a prayer leader, she re-imagined domesticity as holy activism. Preaching was "a consciously political act, directly defying conventions of female self-effacement and modesty" (Foster, *Written*, 74). Lee initially exercised caution, however: when she felt moved to speak the week after Allen's visit, she waited until after the service and gathered a group together in the nearby home of a female friend. She carefully rotated from home to home thereafter, building a following and justifying her eventual move into itinerant preaching. By 1819, after her husband's death and with two children to support, Lee was formally licensed to exhort outside of her home, in AME church meetings.

Within months of launching her career as a performing critic, Lee was speaking at county court houses, town meeting halls, churches, and private homes throughout Pennsylvania and New Jersey. In an early four-year period, she traveled sixteen hundred miles, walking over two hundred miles. In one year, she delivered 178 sermons within 2,325 miles. Itinerant preachers traveled in overlapping circles, and Lee and Elaw even shared the pulpit at a later point, in 1839. Lee reports that "sister preached and I gave an exhortation and closed, in which there was a great shout for victory." By that time, however, the AME church had become more interested in an educated ministry, and Lee was limited to preaching on

Thursday night in Philadelphia's AME churches, with Sundays given over to the men.[104]

In 1836 Lee published a twenty-page booklet, the first of two installments of her spiritual autobiography. The second text, printed in 1849, lengthened the narrative considerably by including an itinerary of her ministerial travels up until 1842. The frontispiece portrait in Lee's autobiography echoes Wheatley's, with both women in a dark dress with a white shawl collar and cap, both looking upward with book, pen, and paper in hand, but Lee is turned more toward the reader, and has twice as many books, pens, and papers. And Lee's portrait specifically marks the progress made by women critics by announcing the title she claimed: "Preacher of the AME Church."[105] The AME church required that itinerant preachers secure formal approval from the Book Concern committee before publishing their work, but Lee independently printed a thousand copies of her narrative to sell at camp meetings and church gatherings. Within three years her book went into a second printing of a thousand copies. Despite this success, when Lee asked the book committee to sponsor an expanded version of her spiritual autobiography in 1844, the group responded with "strong resistance and biting criticism." They argued that the manuscript was "'written in such a manner that it is impossible to decipher much of the meaning contained in it.'" By this time, black leaders such as Daniel Alexander Payne (1811–93) had begun to advocate an educated ministry, which made Lee's work unwelcome and in some ways incomprehensible. In defiance of denominational rules, Lee published her book anyway in 1849, and Bishop Allen's widow bought a copy that very day. Lee justified her rebellion: "I preached and sold my books, and paid my own way."[106] In doing so as an itinerant, she claimed huge tracts of the American land mass as her "territory," traveling unaccompanied when it was risky to do so.

A younger Zilpha Elaw followed in Lee's path. She justified her call through her visions and through Biblical references to women leaders such as Deborah and Huldah as well as evangelists like Phebe. Any curbing of her speech led to depression and illness, she explained, because it was a stifling of God's power to speak through her body: to have a healthy Christian body was, of necessity, to become a performing critic. It was God, Elaw contended, that forced her to go to the home of the richest white man in her hometown and reduce him, his family, and their guests to tears by acquainting them with their manifold sins. It was God who helped her weather the jealousy of her fellow congregants. In 1846 Elaw independently published a record of her life and work. She established a path for other women critics. Four years later, African American women at an annual AME church conference formally petitioned to be licensed to preach, and though male delegates defeated their resolution, they continued to preach and petition.[107]

During this period, African American women gained greater access to each others' work, through their interaction in mutual aid societies, benevolent, burial, moral, and literary societies, as well as through various freedom celebrations, church gatherings, and camp meetings. At camp meetings, in fact, they could create what Schloesser calls a "heterophonous base for community," in which all voices could be heard simultaneously.[108] These religious gatherings were a crucial site of access for African American women critics.

Both black and white women attended religious camp meetings at the turn of the nineteenth century, engaging in a crucial joint performance of Christian citizenship. At a particularly famous camp meeting on 6 August 1801, in Cane Ridge, Kentucky, 20,000 worshipers gathered for a week-long revival, creating a noise like the "roar of Niagara."[109] While accommodations and tangential activities were typically separate even before 1825, both black and white preachers addressed the mixed gatherings of men and women. The camp meetings offered diverse celebrants a way to acknowledge their sameness and negotiate their differences. They also solidified African Americans' claim on American Christianity as a pathway to Constitutional rights, even as they offered a counter-space, a celebratory site of transfiguration. Peterson describes campsites as liminal spaces, in Victor Turner's sense of that term: she notes the dangers of separating women from their homes and exposing their bodies to view in these gatherings, but she also demonstrates that through them the "social hierarchies of race, class, and gender are overturned and deconstructed as the congregants merge in varying degrees of religious ecstasy with the Godhead" (Peterson, *Doers*, 18–19). Lee and Elaw, protected by their host bodies, had much to gain from camp meetings.

Elaw offered a detailed description of an early nineteenth-century camp meeting: families left their work, set up individual tents in a large clearing in the country or at the beach, erected a large stage (often more than one) at one end of the clearing, and participated in prayer and worship services three times a day for as long as seven days in a row. Two or three thousand people at a time gathered for camp meetings. Most were middle- or lower-class Methodists and Baptists, but well-to-do politicians often attended, to build their constituencies. Specific models of class behavior circulated, with converts abjuring the theatres and ballrooms associated in their minds with the upper and unconverted middle classes, even as they incorporated theatre, dance, and music into their own camp meetings.

While most of the gatherings were "promiscuous," with black, white, and mixed-race male and female congregants, black leaders sometimes called separate meetings for African Americans. Lee reported that these all-black meetings, such as those held on the eastern shore of the slave state of Maryland, were "much persecuted" because of the perceived threat they posed to local authority. It is significant that Second Awakening revivals no longer took place in the hometowns of the celebrants, but rather in the more liminal space of the woods or meadows far from town, where a liberal concept of God could edge out local biases. In fact, Lee reported that when local rowdies disrupted a meeting near Albany, New York, "the Elder gave a very appropriate address to the gentlemen of the State of Massachusetts, showing how our rights were invaded, after which the gentlemen took it on themselves to guard the camp ground, and we had good order."[110]

At her first camp meeting, Elaw participated in the "falling exercise," which helped her gain access to the opportunity to preach. This performance echoed the conversion experiences and African spirit possessions of the First Great Awakening. In it, "the individual felt the constriction of the large blood vessels, a shortness of breath, an acceleration of breathing, and dropped prostrate. The hands and feet were cold. He lay from one to twenty-four hours ... often he rejoiced that his sins were forgiven and immediately began to exhort others." This performance, like "the jerks," "the barking exercise," and the "holy laugh," was a virtuoso one, handed down from African and eighteenth-century evangelical practices through various sites of memory. These performances afforded practitioners access to a larger "body," that of Christian American believers. Elaw acknowledged her host body: she reported that she did not know "whether [she] was in the body, or whether [she] was out of the body, on that auspicious day," but her spirit ascended as she looked down to see thousands of "bodies of resplendent light." This phrase is telling: her auditors were composed not of flesh but of luminescence, unmarked by race. At that moment, she heard a voice calling her to preach. Her sense of being disengaged as well as fully immersed at the moment of conversion may reveal the psychological efficacy of black Christianity and the Christian activist host body for her: she could engage the world without being named by it.[111] This strategy enabled a rearguard political move through religion.

In the Second Great Awakening, then, women again combined African and Scots-Irish evangelical performance practices. Before converting to Christianity, some Southern slaves tied white bands around their heads or cut their hair, to enter the state of mourning associated with the initiation rites of African spirit possession. Often free blacks reincorporated the African ring shout into conversion performances, introducing it to white congregants in the process. At camp meetings some whites joined in this circular dance, with its rhythmic, clapping accompaniment, or found that it "visibly affected" their "religious manners," while others tried to ban the practice. John Watson, a revivalist in the Philadelphia conference in 1819, was among the latter. He described the complicated African songs, with their emphasis on "call and response, polyrhythms, syncopation, ornamentation, slides from one note to another, and repetition," as "short scraps of disjointed affirmations, pledges, or prayers, lengthened out with long repetitious choruses." He was shocked that over fifty evangelists crowded into a single tent and "there continue[d] the whole night, singing tune after tune . . . scarce one of which were in our hymn books."[112] As African Americans authorized their own staging of the spirit, whites both borrowed and attacked their practices.

During the "love feasts" which often closed camp meetings, tents were struck and preachers marched in a procession around the entire camp-ground, with the worshipers falling in behind them, singing until a circle resembling the ring was completed. The preachers, black and white, then stood still and shook hands with participants as they filed out, still singing, in a direct echo of the African "breaking exercise" practiced in eighteenth-century Southern churches (Dick, "Religious", 113). At the camp meetings where Lee and Elaw preached, black and white religious practices overlapped in hybrid forms as they discovered new methods of access.

METHODS OF ACCESS

Before the mid 1820s, African American women critics typically acted as performing critics, appearing in person to critique American culture. Itinerant preachers spoke before religious assemblies long before publishing spiritual autobiographies. If critics did appear in print, they usually identified themselves by name or race, to claim their literacy. Before the anti-slavery movement, they seldom assumed pseudonyms, though they might be listed only through their first names on court petitions. African American women critics' visibility – mediated by an itinerant "Christian activist body" – was often intentional. Becoming visible was a way to claim space and status as a respectable, free Christian resident of the United States. This strategy of adopting a host body differs from both of the performance strategies that Peterson identifies: deliberately calling attention to the black body, and deliberately disembodying the voice.[113] It marks a route in between these two options and grants the critic additional room to maneuver.

Like Lucy Terry who sang her ballad in person but did not directly refer to her race or gender in her lyrics, Lee and Elaw appeared before congregants but did not always call direct attention to their race or gender. They used Biblical allusions to lobby indirectly for their rights. Elaw sought to throw the focus upon "a representation, not, indeed, of the features of my outward person, drawn and coloured by the skill of the pencilling artist, but of the lineaments of my *inward man*, as inscribed by the Holy Ghost." She faced many practical challenges, not the least of which was the generic "man." There were customs regarding seating in the church sanctuary, for instance, that she could not easily alter: for a typical appearance in Mount Tabor, Maryland, the sponsoring church seated slaves and free blacks in the gallery, and masters, along with poor whites, downstairs. Before Elaw began preaching, the host minister asked the congregation "to restrain the expression of their feelings." After she preached, however, "the coloured people in the gallery wept aloud and raised vehement cries to heaven; the people below were also unable to restrain their emotions."[114] Elaw had managed to offer gallery congregants an invisible shield so that they could voice their "cries to heaven," which were also demands issued to the whites. Some whites suddenly became aware of their status as "the people below," hellishly sinful because they performed "whiteness" as privilege rather than as piety.

Elaw, in particular, tested notions of visible identity. By the 1820s internal slave traders were moving slaves from the North to the South, so Elaw's decision to travel to the South at that time seriously jeopardized her safety. As a performing critic, she was clearly visible to her audiences and could be misidentified as a slave. She carried her free papers, but they did not necessarily protect her. While she preached in a small town "in one of the slave states," she noticed that her novel ministry "had produced an immense excitement": "people were collecting from every quarter, to gaze at the unexampled prodigy of a coloured female preacher." At that moment, she considered "the prospect of an immediate arrest and consignment by sale to some slave owner." Even in the North, as Lee reveals, magistrates and relatives sometimes had to rescue female preachers from racist attacks.[115] In 1840 the Virginia Supreme Court of Appeals ruled custom into law, stating that "'in the case of a person visibly appearing to be a negro, the presumption is that he is a slave,' and the burden of proof otherwise lay with the accused."[116] This meant that through her very visible presence, an articulate female preacher contested congregants' views regarding the "nature" and legal status of black bodies.

Elaw's vision of her own (in)visible identity was quite distinct: in three separate visions she saw herself as "standing on a very elevated place in the midst of tens of thousands, who were all seated around, clothed in white; my own complexion and raiment were also white, and I was employed in addressing this immense concourse; it was such a scene as had never before entered into my conceptions" (Elaw, *Memoirs*, 135). By imagining herself swathed in a Christ-like whiteness – a whiteness that critiqued mainstream cultural notions of both Christianity and race-based white- ness – she redefined "white"as a radical anti-racist Christian oneness, and tried to hold her audiences to her revised definition. She performed whiteness as Christian piety rather than social privilege. She took her visions as a sign she should return to her itinerant ministry, so in 1835, laden with donations from her Christian "sisters," she left home for a full fifteen months. In a very real way, she represented these women on the dais.

Female preachers developed complex strategies that, paradoxically, retained their invisibility even as they exhorted. Elaw's vision of herself as Christ enabled her to wear what Paul Laurence Dunbar called a mask, "a synonym for the performance of an identity fit for white consumption," or what Du Bois referred to as a veil, "the nearly palpable screen drawn down between white and black Americans, the cloud that, paradoxically, lends a second sight to those of African descent." Rafia Zafar sees this veil as "doubled, imposed from within and without." Whites imposed a "veil" on black women preachers, refusing to see their full humanity, but the preachers, in turn, relied upon the Christian idea of God as a second veil. Thus God "covered" them, protecting them from harm and muting their private lives as they created for themselves the host body of a Christian activist. They were Christian soldiers fighting to save the racialized, ersatz Christian world. By means of their double veil, black critics could refuse to disclose details of their own lives, while aiming the spotlight on the flaws embedded within the lives of their white listeners.[117] If she had not worn the host body of a Christian activist when she visited

the home of the richest man in town to show him and his white family
their sinful natures, Elaw would have been arrested. Through this veil, she
generalized her body and linked it to her listeners' bodies. She performed
visible sameness through her adoptive Christian body, while protecting
her invisible private life and cultural difference. She articulated common
ground with liberal whites as well as blacks within the discourse of the
Christian activist.

Lee and Elaw's descriptions of the moment they first spoke out as
women critics are telling, because they reveal how they chose to don the
second veil. Both exorcised the ghost of the sexualized black body to clear
the way for their revelations. They spoke through bodies "set at glorious
liberty." Three Sundays after joining the AME church, in 1804, Lee
experienced conversion, intercepting Reverend Allen when he had "barely
pronounced" the opening Biblical passage:

That instant, it appeared to me as if a garment, which had entirely enveloped my
whole person, even to my fingers' ends, split at the crown of my head, and was
stripped away from me, passing like a shadow from my sight – when the glory of
God seemed to cover me in its stead ... Great was the ecstacy [sic] of my mind.[118]

As Houchins suggests, this passage borders on the erotic (*Spiritual*, xxxvii).
Its impact, however, is to evoke that sensual awareness of embodiment in
order to transfer it to the service of a God that breaks through customary,
constricting notions of African American womanhood to replace them
with a new concept of "the word made flesh."

Conversion recast and revalued the convert's body. As Nelle Morton
explains, the woman's body "had to be dealt with before she would be
allowed to preach or before the word could be heard from her as Word."
By appearing within the Christian activist body, Lee gained the power to
speak the gospel over ordained male authority figures. Normally exhortation followed the sermon, but when Lee felt God's "glory" cover her
like a garment, she reported that "the minister was silent, until my soul
felt its duty had been performed." When she underwent her "sanctification" experience, Lee compared it to Paul's ecstacy upon hearing
unlawful words. As if to diminish her culpability, she described her "Call
to Preach the Gospel" as an "utter surprise." Likewise, Elaw preached
"involuntarily, or from an internal prompting."[119]

Claiming the invisible shield of Christianity, these critics published
spiritual narratives which reveal how they used Biblical parables to slip
hidden messages into their sermons in the early decades of the nineteenth
century. Their American spiritual autobiographies, like slave narratives,

opened with "I was born," but instead of recounting freedom from slavery, these free black women critics recounted a journey toward spiritual and geographic "life and liberty." As preachers, they were performing critics; as autobiographers, they became performance critics. Their autobiographies are a virtual compendium of Biblical citations, chapter and verse, revealing the nature of their criticism of American culture.

PERFORMING CRITICISM/PERFORMANCE CRITICISM

The fluidity of earlier racial labels – terms such as "swarthy," "dusky," and "dark" earlier used to describe the Spanish and the French as well as the Africans, African Americans, and evangelicals – had all but disappeared by the 1780s. Country-of-origin labels also began to fade as markers of American identity. The Revolutionary War had forced a coalition of the European-born with European Americans of various classes under the rubric of whiteness. Poll taxes replaced property requirements for voting in states from Connecticut to South Carolina, enabling European working-class immigrants to stake a claim on whiteness, just as propertied Anglo-Americans had. The binary of whiteness and blackness joined the dichotomy of free and slave, as race very gradually replaced slavery as the primary means of curtailing economic and legal equity in the new republic.

From 1790 to 1810, the United States Census categorized Americans as "free white," "other free," and "slave." Only "free whites" with two years' residency could be naturalized as citizens, but the vague label "other free" linked free European immigrants with free blacks in the cultural imaginary. By 1820, however, this diverse category of "other free" was replaced with the designation "free colored." European immigrants auditioned as "whites," while "free coloreds" constituted a separate socioeconomic group for the purposes of the Census.

To combat these developments, religious exhorters tried to reveal that "race" as it functioned in dominant American discourse was antithetical to Christianity as well as natural rights. At countless junctures in her spiritual narrative, Jarena Lee declared, "I had life and liberty to speak," echoing natural rights catchwords but within the context of Christian worship.[120] By appropriating these catchphrases, she pressed listeners and readers to revise their ideas of race as well as their concepts of Christianity and American-ness. She created a "Christian upper-class" whose superior status depended upon a heightened piety and rational activism rather than dominant notions of class or race.

Through their black feminist vision of Christianity, Lee and Elaw critiqued ordinary concepts of whiteness and substituted their own definitions. Elaw wrote: "the pride of white skin is a bauble of great value with many in some parts of the United States, who readily sacrifice their intelligence to their prejudices, and possess more knowledge than wisdom." She cautioned, "the Almighty accounts not the black races of man either in the order of nature or spiritual capacity as inferior to the white; for He bestows his Holy Spirit on, and dwells in them as readily as in persons of *whiter* complexion" (Elaw, *Memoirs*, 85, italics mine). By damning whites for their prideful behavior, she discounted their claim on Christianity. By using the word "whiter" rather than "white," Elaw refused the dichotomy of "black" and "white" central to the workings of race as class exclusion. She placed race on a bogus continuum, thereby critiquing census categories. She established one of the strategies that black women critics expanded later in the century: she used an activist notion of God to combat pseudo-scientific notions of the "order of nature."

Elaw leveled her critique of whiteness at live audiences as well as readers. When she traveled to Alexandria, Virginia, she became "a topic of lively interest" among wealthy slaveholders, who were curious about the woman who sought to teach them about God. They found it strange, Elaw reported, that she was able to show them their sins, inextricably interwoven with their performance of whiteness. She stood in front of them and

drew the portraits of their characters, made manifest the secrets of their hearts, and told them all things that ever they did. This was a paradox to them indeed: for they were not deficient of pastors and reverend divines, who possessed all the advantages of talents, learning, respectability and worldly influence, to aid their religious efforts; and yet the power of truth and of God was never so manifest in any of their agencies, as with the dark coloured female stranger, who had come from afar to minister amongst them. But God hath chosen the weak things of the world to confound the mighty. (Elaw, *Memoirs*, 92)

She revealed their perverted performance of "white" respectability and modeled an alternative. As she met with European Americans in their homes and churches, at teas or camp meetings, she castigated those who "reprobate the morals of their sable brethren, without an adequate occasion," trying to cast themselves as more respectable and therefore more Christian than their black counterparts. She loathed the unfairness of requiring those in "widely different" circumstances to conduct themselves within the same performance codes (Elaw, *Memoirs*, 117).

More importantly, Elaw deconstructed the intricate moral system of mainstream whites as a destructive appendage "superadded to the Christian precept." This fake "whited exterior" was encrusted with the kind of "covetousness and worldly pride" that prevented whites from finding God: "no principles are more vicious, no practices more immoral and debasing." Blacks' failings were all too obvious when they occurred, she felt, and easily corrected through their individual churches. Whites' moral failings, in contrast, flowed "in a deep and mighty under current," making it nearly impossible to make them visible, much less to correct them. If churches began to discipline all the whites guilty of vice, all the Christian denominations would crumble.[121] Elaw counterposed a redeemed "Christian whiteness" against mainstream racist notions of white supremacy. Within her Christian activist host body, Elaw disseminated a knowledge about the performativity of race and nation that European Americans could not easily grasp.

Both Lee and Elaw developed a strategy to force listeners and readers to acknowledge their intelligence and base of knowledge. Like the exhorters of the First Great Awakening, who championed lived experience over schoolroom learning, they claimed intelligence of the most important kind. They claimed knowledge of the Bible and of God, the lynchpin of the American Constitution, the Creator who promised true rather than sham equality. In this sense, their work was highly political. Both used their supposed inferiority to highlight the miraculous nature of their work and thereby establish themselves as superior to their audiences (Foster, *Written*, 57). It was "the dark coloured stranger," Elaw argued, who could see southern slaveholders for who they were. "He who would be a master in Israel should possess such an experimental knowledge of the Christian religion," Elaw intoned, "as an university cannot bestow, but which is the exclusive endowment of the Holy Ghost." A knowledge of Christianity and life experience provided believers with a politically useful, true intelligence. She cautioned ministers not to preach with "college lore, nor with orations such as are emitted by divines not yet out of their teens," and she exalted her sermons by calling attention to the fact that she had earned her own way through the world (Elaw, *Memoirs*, 115). Her word came from above: God's genius was revealed through her.

African American women critics had to choose very carefully when to display and when not to display their genius, not only to avoid reprisals but also to avoid being trapped by authenticating mechanisms organized by whites. When Elaw published her work in 1846, she noted that it was "Written by Herself," reminding her readers of her print literacy, but in her sermon performances in the early decades of the nineteenth century, her emphasis was on her mastery of oral literacy, the ability to sway a crowd inured to the ministrations of the educated elite. Genius was earnest industry and intelligence in the service of the Lord. Jarena Lee's first edition of her spiritual narrative did not contain the phrase "Written by Herself," and its addition in the 1849 edition speaks volumes about her claim to print as well as oral literacy. As Zafar explains, spiritual autobiographers used "another culture's means without a corresponding espousal of that society's ends," a process that sociologists call "antagonistic acculturation" (Zafar, *We*, 69). Lee and Elaw adopted and redirected print literacy while also building upon the oral tradition of Christian and African spirit possession and Christian exhortation. They built upon the unrecorded voices of eighteenth-century black women converts. The cadences and repetitions, the conversational road maps, the secret shorthand of disruptive Biblical references in their works, all stem from but also honor their oral as well as their print tradition. It is a performative black Christian tradition which qualifies as "antagonistic acculturation," because it redefines Christian goals for the building of a democratic United States.

The United States was a nation "under God," populated by individuals endowed by their "Creator" with "certain inalienable rights." African American critics seized on this rhetoric to create what Elaw called "a *regenerated constitution*." This constitution linked "comeliness with blackness ... riches with poverty, and power in weakness" (Elaw, *Memoirs*, 51, italics mine). Through their "unusual life and liberty" (Lee, *Religious*, 23), black women preachers contested dominant ideas of American-ness. They foregrounded "true" religion as a direct link to the Enlightenment ideas of freedom and equality, but provided new connections between those abstractions and the politics of race, gender, and class.

African Americans were increasingly bound together not only by republican discourse but also by their own sites of memory. As Pierre Nora explains, "*lieux de mémoire* originate with the sense that there is no spontaneous memory, that we must deliberately create archives, maintain anniversaries, organize celebrations, pronounce eulogies, and notarize bills because such activities no longer occur naturally" and "without commemorative vigilance, history would sweep them away." Threatened with being subsumed into the new American nation without a place in its recorded history, blacks performed their African American-ness. Jarena Lee's book is African American literature because it reveals certain performative sites of memory. The danger of this growing sense of nationhood within the African American community, however, was that whites might feel threatened enough by it to retaliate. And, in fact, that is just what happened with the colonization or back to Africa movement: if free blacks took it upon themselves to form a nation within a nation, the logic went, let them move that nation back to Africa. Many white religionists approached black preachers to do missionary work in Africa, but Elaw, like many others, refused, associating such overtures with a desire to silence the growing and politicized African American church movement in the United States.[122]

Like their male counterparts, many black women critics during this period theorized African American-ness across the lines of class, across the divide of freedom and slavery. Because of the colonization movement and the threat of being shipped to Africa, there was a new urgency among free blacks to form alliances. Although many traveled to Africa and some embraced the idea of settling in Africa, most wanted to remain in the United States, in a radically reformed republic.[123] Blacks organized anticolonization associations, and though there is no extant evidence that women spoke at these meetings, they were certainly engaged in the debates.

As if to combat the movement to send free blacks to Africa, Lee and Elaw began to traverse more and more of the United States to claim it as their own. From very early on in their ministries, they traveled, often covering thousands of miles a year. Starting in 1811 they exhorted at camp meetings and in their churches, and starting in 1817 they traveled around the country to preach. As they did, they referred over and over again to their "life and liberty" to speak. They claimed American republican rhetoric for a Christian nation in which blacks were on equal footing with whites. In a typical passage, Lee reports that in the mid 1820s in eastern Maryland she preached "to an immense congregation of both the slaves and the holders, and felt great liberty in word and doctrine; the power of God seemed without intermission" (Lee, *Religious*, 37).

The Christian unity that Wheatley articulated in the 1770s to bridge "African" and "American" no longer functioned in the same way by the 1780s. In 1773 Northern black Christians had worshiped in white-run churches and sat in the back pews or the galleries, but by 1784 the Methodist Episcopal Church had banned slave practices within the church, and by 1816 blacks had formed the independent African Methodist Episcopal Church. Wheatley may, for whites, have served as evidence of the Wheatley family's virtuous stewardship of the "servant for life" in their home, but by 1811 Lee and Elaw, free blacks working within the new black church denominations, served up evidence of their independence from an ersatz Christian nation.

By choosing her Bible verses carefully, Lee critiqued mainstream American culture and outlined a more democratic nation. For instance, when she preached at a camp meeting of blacks and whites just outside of Philadelphia in 1822, she spoke from Psalm 137: "For there those who carried us away captive asked of us a song, and those who plundered us requested mirth, saying, 'Sing us one of the songs of Zion!' " Faced with these requests, the psalmist asks, "How shall we sing the Lord's song in a foreign land?" and vows "If I forget you O Jerusalem, let my right hand forget its skill!" (137: 3–5). In the new republic, as in Biblical times, kidnappers "carried away" captives and plundered their communities, demanding that their slaves sing and provide mirth for them. The oppressed in the Bible and among Lee's listeners found ways to resist the oppressors and yet not reject their own spirituality. They found ways to connect to Jerusalem, but also to Africa and America. Jerusalem is part of the Black Atlantic world. In her performances, in person and in print, Lee drew upon the intensely individual Puritan spiritual narratives but also the intentionally collective African praise song, a declaration of group identity and historical connection. Scholars such as Joyce A. Joyce have argued that many early Christian performance traditions are African in origin, suggesting that Western spiritual practices such as evangelical preaching may depend more on African customs such as praise songs than is widely recognized.[124]

When Lee used the phrase "life and liberty," she evoked the parallel phrase "life, liberty, and the pursuit of happiness," linking Christian preaching with Constitutional imperatives (Lee, *Religious*, 23). Perhaps her vision of her role in fostering a Christian America comes into focus most clearly in particular vignettes, such as her account of trying to convert a white slaveholder at a gathering in her uncle's home near Cape May, New Jersey. Through her exhortation, Lee convinced an elderly slaveholder that "coloured people had souls," at which point he "became greatly altered" and abandoned his cruel ways (Lee, *Religious*, 19). Black preachers taught whites that blacks, indeed, had souls, and that whites might be able to salvage theirs if they listened very carefully. This critical strategy eventually was transformed into a valorization of African Americans as especially, even "essentially," spiritual or soulful, as critical Christianity was translated into "romantic racialism." But by then, black women critics had devised new strategies to subvert American nationalist narratives.

African American critics who worked as preachers subverted gender codes through their performances if not through their rhetoric. They acted independently from their roles as wives and mothers, even as they championed marriage and motherhood. This ambivalence – a refusal to play the role of wife and mother in a traditional way and yet a strong defense of the institutions of marriage and the family – was under-standable at a time when many black women were denied access to domesticity because of poverty or enslavement. Female itinerant preachers tried to re-imagine notions of a wife's responsibilities. They decided that women could "defy men – for God." Elaw did not bother to tell her husband that she had begun to preach, and when he discovered what she was doing and objected, she responded that she "was very sorry to see him so much grieved about it; but my heavenly Father had informed me that he had a great work for me to do; I could not therefore descend down to the counsel of flesh and blood." Jarena Lee was equally unwilling to succumb to male directives. During her travels, Lee encountered many ministers, black as well as white, who were out-raged by her preaching. When she preached in Salem, New Jersey, for example, a male elder protested, and she retorted with an apt Biblical defense: "maybe a speaking woman is like an ass – but I can tell you one thing, the [Biblical] ass seen the angel when Balaam didn't."[125]

Lee recounted this gender-based "prejudice" in her narratives, usually with a report of a punishment later visited upon the guilty. In Reading, Pennsylvania, for instance, a black preacher who refused to let her speak in his pulpit was very quickly turned out of it himself. She could be very witty in her condemnation: in 1835 after she encountered "some false brethren" while speaking at Bethel Church, she warned "may the Lord pardon their errors, and make them be careful how they handle edged tools."[126]

Like Julia A. J. Foote (1823–1900), another spiritual autobiographer, Elaw linked herself to the "Ethiopic eunuch" baptised by Phillip in the Bible, and thereby diverted attention from distorted nineteenth-century notions of the gendered and hyper-sexualized black female body (Elaw, *Memoirs*, 57). Elaw's readers and listeners probably had heard of the baptism of this Ethiopian, who guarded the treasures of Candace, queen of the Ethiopians (Acts 8: 27). Through this story, Elaw evoked the image of a black queen with independent authority and economic power; the image of an African woman and man working together independent of whites; the image of black Christians who pose no sexual threat to out-siders and who graciously invite a white interlocutor to step *up* into a theological discussion. Like the disciples who used parables to hide their most radical messages, Elaw used Biblical stories to issue new ideas about the relationship between gender, race, and Christian witness, and her stories had political implications.

During this period African American and European American women were interpolated into different performances of gender, codes supported and maintained by the system of slavery and the racism that underlay them. To justify their sexual advances against black women, white men constructed a notion of black women as sexual predators, and many white women preferred that concept of black womanhood to an idea of white men as predators. This gendered construction of the sexualized black woman

also perpetuated an enormous division between black people and white people on the 'scale of humanity': carnality as opposed to intellect and/or spirit; savagery as opposed to civilization; deviance as opposed to normality; promiscuity as opposed to purity; passion as opposed to passionlessness. The black woman came to symbolize, according to Sander Gilman, an "icon for black sexuality in general."[127]

This image of sexualized black womanhood justified violence against black men as well as women, so it was a primary target of women critics. Lee and Elaw combated this construction primarily through their stories, silence, and spirituality. Sometimes, as with the story of Candace and the Eunuch, they told stories to refigure black sexuality. But more often, they excised black women's sexuality from their public considerations. Darlene Clark Hine calls this practice a "culture of dissemblance," designed to silence stereotypes and protect black women's privacy.[128] They did not, as Murray and Rowson did, represent male and female romantic interchanges onstage; they did not, as many newspaper poets did, focus on the predicament of the fallen woman. Elaw was even quiet about her relationship with her husband.

The alternative to the sexualized idea of African American womanhood in mainstream white culture was a concept of her as a worker: the black woman as man. Lee faced this stereotype in a slightly different context: in New Hope, New Jersey, she preached about brotherly love to an audience with "some very ill-behaved persons, who talked roughly, and said among other things, 'I was not a woman, but a man dressed in female clothes.'"[129] These congregants could not resolve the gender confusion they encountered while listening to an African American woman preach. They jeered at Lee's supposed masculinity to side-step their discomfort with her obvious intelligence and power.

To combat the stereotype of the sexualized or masculinized black female body, Lee and Elaw studiously avoided discussions of sexual matters and instead situated black women's bodies as spiritual repositories of womanliness. They often espoused a gendered performance striking in its traditionalism. Elaw, for example, called young women's rebellion against their parents or husbands "indecent and impious," arguing that it showed "a wanton disrespect to the regulations of Scripture." Arguing a gender subordination that outstrips many white women's prescriptions, Elaw argued "that woman is dependant on and subject to man, is the dictate of nature; that the man is not created for the woman, but the woman for the man, is that of Scripture. These principles lie at the foundation of the family and social systems; and their violation is a very immoral and guilty act" (Elaw, *Memoirs*, 61–62). Subordination was at the heart of their theorizing about gender, and yet, Elaw did not even consult her husband before launching her ministerial work, and felt no compunctions about ignoring his negative response to her work. Nor did she shy from castigating black and white men for their various short-comings. Black female exhorters did not accept the routine performance of their gender – nor did they simply try to adopt white women's required code of domestic respectability, though Elaw's disquisition on female obedience seems to suggest just that.

Instead, they created a gendered performance in which the responsi-bilities of being a wife, and more particularly a mother, were distributed across a wider community. In addition to granting them the authority to speak their truths, Lee and Elaw's preaching enabled them to theorize what might be called the "Christian mother." Unlike the white critic's concepts of the republican or Universalist mothers educating their own children or those of their community for democracy, the "Christian mother" had to acknowledge her responsibility to an even wider com-munity of "God's children." Sometimes, to reach this wider circle of "children" with her teachings, the Christian mother had to temporarily share the responsibility of caring for her own nuclear family. Lee often relied on friends or her mother to care for her son, but she reported that during her travels, her worries about him were "hidden" from her, so that she could do God's work (Lee, *Religious*, 18–19). This meant not only that Lee escaped the daily responsibilities of raising children, but also that she strengthened the bond between herself and those additional Christian mothers, all the while giving her son an extended family, greater eco-nomic security, and a new reason to be proud of his mother. As Foster explains, the "church family often replaced the biological family in

providing a sense of security, a sense of purpose, and a model for living"
for black women preachers (Foster, *Written*, 70).

Claiming gender was, for black women, an act with radical as well as
conservative effects. When preachers advocated Christian motherhood,
they claimed for slave women the respect attached to being a wife and
mother. They fought against the separation of husbands from wives and
children from mothers, even as they created new models of how to
perform mothering. Early church and moral societies encouraged African
American women to claim for themselves the title of "woman" or the
more elevated title of "lady," labels jealously guarded by white culture.
Lee claimed the mantle "Coloured Lady" in the title of her 1836 autobiography, which foregrounds her pride of "colour" and her determination to be accorded equal rank. Tellingly, the 1849 edition of her
autobiography does not contain this phrase; instead, it advertises Lee's
work as simply "Written by Herself," which links her work to newly
popular slave narratives and reduces the threat posed by Lee's critique.
Zilpha Elaw also claimed gender equality. She signed her narrative with
the prefix "Mrs.," which signified her status as a married woman and also,
in an age without reliable birth control, her status as a potential mother, a
respectable Christian mother. Lee and Elaw constructed a gender performance that validated them as Christian ladies, conferred respect, and
granted them freedom of movement.

"BODIES" OF CRITICISM

Three of the four women critics who provide the main focus of this
chapter forged a living disseminating their cultural critiques: Lee, Elaw,
and Rowson depended upon the income they generated. Murray paid the
mortgage on her Boston home through the profit from her major publication. This was an important departure from the early Revolutionary
War years, because it meant that women could imagine speaking independently. In effect, they became professional critics of American culture,
receiving remuneration and building the institutions of the academy and
the church through their work. In various sites, they possessed "the power
to render [them]selves superior" (Rowson, *Slaves*, 9) to man, and they
frequently circumvented male directives even as they espoused subordination. They fashioned an education through literary societies and
prayer groups as well as private academies and free schools, justifying
their learning through Christian, Universalist, or republican motherhood

and practicing their oratorical skills in public. At camp meetings and in parlors, women gained access to each others' work.

Black and white critics' methods of access often differed during this period. African American women frequently found access to civic space as performing critics, appearing in person before their listeners, but they also issued non-fiction texts based on their life experiences and knowledge of the Bible. They often had to couch their criticism as fiction or as revelation. They faced the dangers of appearing in a "marked" fashion, visibly present to their listeners or represented to their readers through portrait engravings, but they invented various ways to thwart biased attempts to misread their bodies. They turned visibility into an asset as Christian activists and cultured Americans.

Anglo-American women often acted as performance critics, publishing anonymously or pseudonymously in print, within whatever genre best fit their needs. Rowson, the Englishwoman who adopted America, provided one of the exceptions to this custom, publishing in her own name to trade on her early success in London under the patronage of an English duchess. Masculine pseudonyms such as Murray's "Gleaner" kept alive the performance tradition launched by Timothy's "Mr. Editor" or Warren's "Columbian Patriot," allowing individual white women to speak out, but it was increasingly difficult for them to obscure their authorship, particularly within the highly charged theatres. Feminine pseudonyms such as Murray's "Constantia" and "Honora-Martesia" exploded on the literary scene, adding "a Philenia, an Antonia, a Euphelia, &c. &c." to the roster of women critics in the 1780s (Murray, *Gleaner*, 727). This phenomenon created a class-conscious performance of implicitly white womanhood.

By the late eighteenth century, American women critics discovered new host bodies to shield themselves from censure. By separating their material bodies from their cultural critiques and donning abstract rhetorical bodies, they tried to insure their financial and social security. Lee and Elaw adopted itinerant Christian activist bodies to claim America for a radical anti-racist and African American Christianity; Murray initially deployed a "Universalist body" to broaden notions of individual rights, though her federalism effaced her Universalism. She joined Rowson in creating the "cultured body" of the individualized Anglo-American woman, performing culture as race. Behind this bodily shield, Rowson experimented with various kinds of cultural crossings over racial, religious, national, and gender lines.

African American women critics lobbied for a regenerated Constitution during the early Republican period by adopting Christian activist bodies and redefining Biblical whiteness as anti-racist life and liberty. European American critics, in contrast, reinforced the racism embedded within the Constitution by donning cultured American bodies and redefining whiteness as virtuous Christian Anglo-American-ness. One white critic, Rowson, opened up a thorny but potentially fruitful path of inquiry by focusing, fleetingly, on whiteness as a performative process. She took advantage of the fact that in the theatre, multiple host bodies surfaced through patrons, characters, and prompters. In the theatre, critics could simultaneously call attention to the materiality of the bodies claiming American-ness and to the host bodies shielding them. Early American women critics during this era professionalized their efforts in the theatre, the church, the schoolroom, and their homes. They performed their critiques of American religion, race, politics, and culture, shaping the highly contested public conversations of their time.

NOTES

1   This chapter focuses primarily on African American women's exhortations, but many European American women also preached during the Second Great Awakening; they also signed their own names to their work. See Brekus, *Strangers* for a full analysis of women as early nineteenth-century preachers: between 1790 and 1845, fifty women preached itinerantly and voted within the Baptist and Christian Church denominations (Brekus, *Strangers* 135). See Westerkamp, *Triumph* and *Women* for studies of the Scots-Irish religious movement and women's religious involvement in the seventeenth and eighteenth centuries.
2   Norton, *People*, 156; Kerber, *Republic*, 279.
3   [Stevens], *Some Deductions*. Judith initiated the correspondence with Murray, suggesting they "with the strictest propriety, mingle souls upon paper." Judith Stevens to John Murray, 14 November 1774, Gloucester, Judith Sargent Murray Papers, Microform, Reel 1, Letterbook 1, Letter 14, Jackson, Miss.: Mississippi Dept. of Archives and History, 1989. This microform reproduces Judith Murray's twenty newly discovered letterbooks on seven reels. Subsequent citations to the same source will be abbreviated, with all available information: JSMP, R1, L1, let.14. Murray's first essay, "Desultory Thoughts," was published under the pseudonym Constantia. Perhaps she hoped to make money even then; by 1784 wartime trade restrictions had ruined John Stevens's business. But her essays did not generate cash. The year after her marriage to Murray, Judith gave birth to a son, George, who was stillborn. She sent his eulogy to *The Massachusetts Magazine, or Monthly Museum of Knowledge and Rational Entertainment*, which then became the primary venue for her work ("Lines Occasioned by the Death of an Infant," *The Massachusetts Magazine*, 2 January 1790: 57).

Constantia's "On the Equality of the Sexes" appeared in *The Massachusetts Magazine, or Monthly Museum of Knowledge and Rational Entertainment* 2.3–4 (March–April 1790): 132–35, 223–26.

4 On "American," see Pollock, *Philadelphia*, 58; on "afterpiece," see Parker, *Susanna*, 72.

5 Lee, *Religious*, 15. This and subsequent Lee citations are to the widely available (expanded 1849) edition reprinted in Houchins, *Spiritual*. Page numbers are noted in parentheses in the text.

6 In addition to Lee and Elaw, at least six other early nineteenth-century African American women preached without formal approval: "Old Elizabeth" (1765?–1866), Juliann Jane Tilmann, Sojourner Truth (1797–1883), Julia A. J. Foote (1823–1900), Julia Pell, and Rebecca Jackson (1795–1871). Rachel Evans was a licensed preacher (Brekus, *Strangers*, 134).

7 Elaw, *Memoirs*, 144, 140, 243 n. 39. These and subsequent Elaw citations are to the Andrews, *Sisters* edition. Page numbers are noted in parentheses in the text.

8 Lee and Elaw trod a well-worn path, from sin to repentance, through depression and suicidal thoughts, to redemption, salvation, and sanctification. Both viewed their early speaking engagements, the subject of this chapter, as "preaching," though church officials regarded them as merely exhortation. Exhorters did not interpret scripture; they were licensed to intensify the preacher's call to salvation (Andrews, *Sisters*, 239). Church services curtailed black unrest as well as offered opportunities for subversion. Indeed, in the South plantation owners rewarded obedient Christians. Nonetheless, the sanctuary was the one performance site where whites were forced to hear blacks' "vehement cries." And slave narratives are full of instances of moral pressure subtly brought to bear against slaveholders through the church as well as examples of bigots using the Bible to defend slavery.

9 This made it difficult for them to construct narratives about their lives (Grammer, *Some*).

10 Paul Gilroy and Kwame Anthony Appiah, among others, have written eloquently about the dangers of linking identity to culture and nationhood, implicitly reifying "race." See Gilroy's *Against Race* and *Black Atlantic* and Appiah's *Ethics*.

11 Raboteau, *Fire*, 44–45 and *Slave*, 137, 131; Norton, *People*, 161. By 1810 there were fifteen African American churches in ten far-flung cities (Sawyer, "Sources," 59).

12 Freeman's case set a precedent for freeing slaves in Massachusetts. Vermont started dismantling slavery in 1777, Pennsylvania in 1780, Rhode Island and Connecticut in 1784, New York in 1799, and New Jersey in 1804. Virginia, Delaware, and Maryland eased laws preventing masters from freeing slaves. Geneviève Fabre coins the term "freedom celebrations" to describe public African American commemorations: Fifth of July celebrations, New Year's Day celebrations marking the abolition of the foreign slave trade, state-by-state Emancipation Celebrations, Pinkster and Election Day observances (Fabre, "African-American," 72).

13 [Crocker], *Series*, 8–10.
14 [Murray] *Gleaner*, 346–47. All *Gleaner* citations are to *The Gleaner: A miscellaneous Production/In three volumes/By Constantia* (Boston: I. Thomas and E. T. Andrews, 1798), Early American Imprints. First Series, no. 34162. See also [Murray, Judith Sargent], *The Gleaner: A Miscellaneous Production in Three Volumes by Constantia* (Boston: I. Thomas and E. T. Andrews, 1798), Rare Book/Special Collections Reading Room, Library of Congress. Murray even presented scenes in which her characters read the "Gleaner" column and responded to it. For instance, by reading the Gleaner, the title character's father discovered that his daughter was still alive.
15 Norton, *People*, 158; Schloesser, *Fair*, 45; Norton, *Liberty's*, 260.
16 Rowson may have left the theatre because of its financial difficulties, or because some viewed her as an anti-federalist in a "federalist" theatre. However, federalists and Democratic Republicans served on the Boards of both Boston theatres (Nathans, *Early*, 106–10). See Durham, *American*, on Boston and Philadelphia theatres.
17 Donkin, *Getting*, 9.
18 Anonymous, "Mrs. Rowson's," 2.
19 Qtd. Keetley, *Public*, 69. On middling oratory, see McConachie, "American," 134.
20 The foster children were John Stevens's orphaned relatives. Harris, *Selected*, xix.
21 Thus, although the move from racial identity to cultural identity appears to replace essentialist criteria of identity (who we are) with performative criteria (what we do), the commitment to pluralism requires in fact that the question of who we are continue to be understood as prior to questions about what we do. Since, in pluralism, what we do can be justified only by reference to who we are, we must, in pluralism, begin by affirming who we are; it is only once we know who we are that we will be able to tell what we should do; it is only when we know which race we are that we can tell which culture is ours (Michaels, *Our*, 14–15).
22 On members, descended, and gathering, see Murray, *Gleaner*, 25, 20, 38. On drunkard, see Anonymous, "Universalism," 283.
23 Kerber, *Republic*, 235. See Rowson, *Present*, 84, 99, on republican motherhood.
24 The editorial placement of her essays in this journal often extended her critical edge: her essay "On the Equality of the Sexes," for instance, followed an article about the rights of citizens to review and reform their constitution.
25 Most women managed to publish only one play in the 1790s: Mrs. Marriott of the Old American Company, for example, wrote *The Chimera: or Effusions of Fancy: A Farce in Two Acts* in 1795, and Madame Gardie followed with a 1796 pantomime (Schofield, "Quitting," 268, 271). Margaretta Bleecker Faugeres (1771–1801) published her patriotic blank-verse tragedy, *Belisarius*, in 1795. In 1807 Sara Pogson published *The Female Enthusiast* "by a Lady" and in 1819 Frances Wright (1795–1852) authored

Altorf under a pseudonym. On new theatres built in 1796, see Schofield, "Quitting," 261.

Rowson's theatrical legacy is partially obscured because her only fully extant script is *Slaves in Algiers*. *The Female Patriot; or Nature's Rights* was performed at the Chestnut Street Theatre in Philadelphia during the 1794–95 season, but no known copy exists. *Female Patriot* was an adaptation of Philip Massinger's *The Bondman* (1623), the story of a slave insurrection in Syracuse, Greece. In it, Timeon warns that "he that would govern others, first should be the master of himself," signaling Rowson's critique of American masculinity (Act 1, scene 3). Rowson's musical *The Volunteers* (1795) satirized a 1794 Pennsylvania protest against a federal tax on whiskey. It was published, in part, as *The volunteers, a musical entertainment, as performed at the New Theatre*. Philadelphia. Printed for the author and sold at the music shops [1795]. *The American Tar, or the Press Gang Defeated*, by Rowson, was performed in Philadelphia on 17 June 1796, but was evidently not published. The Federal Street Theatre in Boston produced Rowson's *Americans in England, or Lessons for Daughters* on 19 April 1797. This comedy drew on her knowledge of British customs, but no known copy survives. *Hearts of Oak* (Boston, n. p., 1810–11) is another Rowson piece; this is the title of the regimental song of the Worcester, England, regiment responsible for the Boston Massacre. In 1788 Rowson published a spoof of Drury Lane and Covent Garden actors and playwrights, titled *A Trip to Parnassus*; see Weil, *Defense*, 11 for a discussion of this dramatic poem.

26 See Banham, *Cambridge*, 251. Mott, *History*, 165–67, 173. Anon., "Sketches," 199; Anon., "Defence [*sic*]."

27 Qtd. Henderson, "Scenography," 391. Boston and Philadelphia's theatres had separate entrances to the pit, box, and gallery (Henderson, "Scenography," 391–92). Men outnumbered women, but audiences were increasingly diverse in the mid 1790s: wealthy men seated wives and daughters in boxes; working-class women and rowdy "sailors, apprentices, servants" sat in the gallery; and "the pit held working-class men and boys, artisans, and some professionals"; "by the 1800s, most theatres were reserving the top tier of boxes for prostitutes, but they could be found throughout the playhouse" (McConachie, "American," 131–32). On theatre as an oral art, see Dudden, *Women*, 16.

28 Murray, *Gleaner*, 184–89, 197; JS to Anna ____, 7 November 1788, Gloucester, JSMP, R2, L3 no let. no. Foucault, *Discipline*.

29 Judith Murray "To My Sister," 14 June 1790, Philadelphia, JSMP, R2, L4, let. 751.

30 Judith Murray "To My Father and Mother," 10 July 1790, Philadelphia, JSMP, R2, L4, let. 768. In Tyler's play, a foppish British officer provided the "contrast" to a manly Yankee patriot; Tyler's production was followed by a farce, a Chinese shadow display, and a pantomime.

31 Murray, *Gleaner*, 764–65.

32 On *"any body"* see Murray, *Gleaner*, 48; on *"hunting"* see Murray, *Gleaner*, 105.

33 Murray published her final poems as Honora-Martesia and Honora. When John Murray suffered a stroke in 1809, Judith arranged his letters and, later, his posthumous autobiography. Rowson published her 1822 religious primer under a male pseudonym. Hannah Mather Crocker (1752–1829) published under male and female pseudonyms. Sometimes pseudonyms were ambiguously gendered: Maria Brooks (1794–1845), for instance, published as "a Lover of the Fine Arts." Anonymity was quite customary: Tabitha (Gilman) Tenney (1762–1837), Lydia Howard (Huntley) Sigourney (1791–1865), and Hannah Webster Foster (1758–1840) published anonymously. Margaretta V. Faugeres published her essays and poems as an addendum to the posthumously printed work of her mother, Ann Eliza Bleecker (1793). See Donkin, *Getting*, 89 and Gallagher, *Nobody's*, xix on pseudonyms as commodities.

34 JSMP, R6, p. 346.

35 Joseph Roach explains that "whether the eccentric character is foreign or native born, whether its fate is to be assimilated or excluded, eccentric business draws the constantly redrawn line between 'us' and 'them'" (Roach, "Emergence," 344). Eccentric accents also draw this racialized line.

36 Susanna Rowson, *The Female Patriot; or, Nature's Rights*. Philadelphia: n. p., 1794. No copy extant.

37 In fact, the seduction novel in question, *The Power of Sympathy*, was written by William Hill Brown, a neighbor.

38 JS to Mrs. Sargent, 19 January 1790, Gloucester, JSMP, R2, L4, let. 728.

39 JS to Madam Walker, 19 January 1790, Gloucester, JSMP, R2, L4, let. 729.

40 *The Massachusetts Magazine; or, Monthly Museum*, March 1790; 2, 3; American Periodicals Series Online (subsequently abbreviated as APSO), p. 186; *The Massachusetts Magazine; or, Monthly Museum*, April 1790; 2, 4; APSO, p. 248.

41 Murray, *Gleaner*, 804, 15, 805, 805, 105.

42 On *"serious accusation"* see Murray, *Gleaner*, 806; on Universalist propaganda, see Field, *Constantia*, 70. On private matters: in December 1795, when *The Massachusetts Magazine* resumed publication after a short hiatus, the new editor mentions having finally received "the strictures of *Impartialis*," who has criticized Murray for her August 1794 *Gleaner* column on "Fraternicus," a generous brother who supports his sister's family. *The Massachusetts Magazine; or, Monthly Museum*, December 1795; 7, 9; APSO, p. 512. Cf. Field, *Constantia*, 32. Perhaps Murray was accused of incompetence: when Robert Treat Paine, Jr. (1773–1811), a twenty-one-year-old Harvard graduate poised to launch his *Federal Orrery* in October 1794, sent her a flattering invitation to write for his journal, she replied effusively that he rescued her from the path to which she had been "condemned." JSM to Mr. Paine, Editor of the *Federal Orrery*, 15 October 1794, Boston, Franklin Place, JSMP, R2, L8, let. 496. Although she refused

to acknowledge to Paine that she was, as he suspected, the "Gleaner," she leapt to embrace his flattery.

43 "The Reaper – No. 11," *Federal Orrery*, 27 October 1794: 1,3: 2; JSM to my Brother, 23 April 1796, Boston, Franklin Place, JSMP, R3, L9, let. 176.

44 JSM to Mr. Paine, 11 November 1794, Boston, Franklin Place, JSMP, R2, L8, let. 498.

45 "Sonnet, addressed to a writer in the Orrery, under the signature of 'The Reaper,'" *Federal Orrery*, 17 November 1794:1,9: 4. In her fifth column, Murray publicly accepted the sonneteer's praise and celebrated, once again, the stimulating effect of fame: "The Reaper – No. v," *Federal Orrery*, 27 November 1794:1,12: 1.

46 "Prize Prologue," *The Massachusetts Magazine*, January 1794; 6, 1; APSO, p. 49. Paine may have initially approached Murray because as the Gleaner she praised him for winning this contest: The Gleaner, No. xxi, *The Massachusetts Magazine*, February 1794; 6, 2; APSO, p. 100. See Field, *Constantia*, 42 on Paine's plays.

47 *Federal Orrery*, 2 March 1795:1,39:2. For ads, see *Federal Orrery*, 26 February 1795: 1,38: 3; *The Mercury*, 24 February 1795: v, 17: 3; *Boston Gazette & Republican Weekly Journal*, 2 March 1795, with cast list. Doors opened at 5pm, and the curtain rose at 6pm, with the following ticket prices: "Boxes 6/. Pit 3/ 9. Slip 3/. Gallery 1/6."

48 Murray, *Federal Orrery*, 5 March 1795: 1,40: 3; Candour, *Columbian Centinel*, 11 March 1795: xxiii, 1145: 2. Murray thought that Joseph Dennie (1768–1812) had written this letter (Field, *Constantia*, 42), but his irreverent style makes him an unlikely ally. Seilhamer attributed *The Medium* to Tyler (*History*, iii: 248).

49 JSM to Mr. S[argent], 4 May 1795, Boston, Franklin Place, JSMP, R2, L8, let. 519.

50 "For the Federal Orrery," by "Ned Gingerly, Wiswal-Den, Cambridge," "Extracts from a new play, called, 'The tables turned: or, a bug with a guinea,'" *Federal Orrery* 26 March 1795: 1, 46: 2.

51 Hall, *Collection*, n.p.

52 "Ninehole's Drawing Room," *Federal Orrery*, 30 March 1795: 1,47: 1.

53 JSM to Mr. S[argent], 4 May 1795, Boston, Franklin Place, JSMP, R2, L8, let. 519. JSM to Mrs. B[ache] of Philadelphia, 19 June 1795, Boston, Franklin Place, JSMP, R2, L8, let. 526. JSM to my Brother, 30 November 1795, Gloucester, JSMP, R3, L9, let. 163. See also 7 March 1795, Boston, JSMP, R3, L9, let. 172. "Coxcomb" in Murray, *Gleaner*, 544–55. "Dramatic Reminiscences, no. v," *New-England Magazine* (1831–35); July 1832; APSO, p. 33. Dunlap, *History*, 270.

54 JSM to Mr. Powell, Manager of the Boston Theatre, 16 May 1795, Boston, Franklin Place, JSMP, R2, L8, let. 521.

55 JSM to Mr. S[argent], 9 January 1796, Boston, JSMP, R3, L10, let. 555. It is tempting to read John Tyler's treatment of Murray in the context of his brother, Royall Tyler's, ongoing ambitions as a playwright: his *The Contrast*,

one of the earliest professional productions of an original American play, had premiered at the John Street Theater, New York City, on 16 April 1787. Nathaniel Hawthorne reportedly modeled Judge Pyncheon in *The House of Seven Gables* on Royall Tyler, who, rumor has it, fathered several illegitimate children before romancing two sets of mothers and daughters: Abigail and "Nabby" Adams, then Mary Palmer and her daughter Mary. He seduced Mary Palmer and upon her suicide married her identically named daughter, Mary Palmer Tyler (1775–1866). See Thomas St. John, "Nathaniel Hawthorne: Studies in the House of Seven Gables," 8 January 2005, *http:// www.geocities.com/seekingthephoenix/t/judgeroyalltyler.htm.* Hawthorne's mother-in-law, Elizabeth Palmer, disclosed the "seducer" behind this "polished man of literary eminence" in "Art III. Seduction," *Christian Examiner and General Review* (1829–44); November 1833; 15, 2; APSO, p.163.

56 11 March 1796: vii, 21: 3.

57 "Theatrical," *Federal Orrery*, 14 March 1796; 1,42: 2.

58 "A Card" and "Nil de mortuis," *Federal Orrery*, 17 March 1796; 1,43,3. "Fairplay," *Columbian Centinel*, 19 March 1796: xxv, 4: 3.

59 JSM to Mr. S[argent], 2 April 1796, Boston, Franklin Place, JSMP, R3, L10, let. 564.

60 "Theatrical," "The Pedler," and "The Scold and the Parrot," *Federal Orrery*, 21 March 1796; III, 44: 2–4.

61 "To the Editor of the Orrery. Mr. Paine," *Columbian Centinel*, 23 March 1796: xxv, 5: 3. *Federal Orrery*, 24 March 1796: 3,45: 3. *Massachusetts Mercury*, 25 March 1796:v11,25: 2. *Columbian Centinel*, 26 March 1796: xxv,6: 3. JSM to "My Dear Sister," 22 April 1796, Boston, JSMP, R3, L10, let. 640. JSM to Maria, 8 October 1798, Boston, JSMP, R3, L10, let. 779; JSM to Maria, 23 December 1790, Gloucester, JSMP, R2, L5, let. 396.

62 JSM to the Mother of Mr. Murray, 10 August 1797, Boston, JSMP, R3, L10, let. 647. Murray sold 759 subscriptions, printed 859 multi-volume sets, and grossed $2,475 (Smith, *From Gloucester*, 46). As Nathans has explained in *Early*, the Boston Tontine Association was an influential mix of state representatives, lawyers, merchants, and former army officers who pooled their finances to claim American cultural and economic capital: they built the Tontine Crescent, a new urban neighborhood, complete with a theatre, the Federal Street Theatre. The Murrays could barely sustain their place in the neighborhood, economically and socially.

63 See *Columbian Centinel*, 27 August, 6 and 13 September 1806; *Repertory*, 19 August and 19 September 1806. JSM to Lucius Manlius Sargent, August 1806, qtd. Smith, *From Gloucester*, 55; JSM to Centinel, 29 August 1806, qtd. Smith, *From Gloucester*, 55. See also JSM to "Sir" [Lucius Manlius], n.d., JSMP, R4, L14, no let. no., pp. 4–5. See Sheppard, *Reminiscences*.

64 On messages regarding the status of the script, see JSM to [Robert Treat Paine, Jr.], 23 October 1804, Boston, Franklin Place, JSMP, R3, L12, no let. no. On "origin," see JSM to "Sir" [Robert Treat Paine, Jr.], 6 September

1804, Gloucester, JSMP, R3, L12, no let. no., and 6 October 1804, Boston, Franklin Place, JSMP, R3, L12, no let. no. On remaining in the background, see JSM to "Sir" [Robert Treat Paine, Jr.], 6 October 1804, Boston, Franklin Place, JSMP, R3, L12, no let. no. On declining, see JSM to "Sir" [Robert Treat Paine, Jr.], n.d. [December 1804?], JSMP, R3, L12, no let. no.

65 On drafting Paine, see JSM to [], n.d. [February 1807], Boston, Franklin Place, JSMP, R4, L14, no let. no. On her "prostrate" ambitions, see JSM to "Respected Sir" [Alexis Eusteaphieve], 21 December 1816, Boston, Franklin Place, JSMP, R5, L20, no let. no.

66 On "American" production, see "Theatre," *The Philadelphia Gazette and Universal Daily Advertiser*, 28 June 1794, XI, no. 177 6: 3; and *General Advertiser*, 30 June 1794, no. IIII: 3. See Meserve, *Emerging*, 127–28, for a discussion of English managers' biases. For a listing of the afterpieces, see "New Theatre," *The Philadelphia Gazette and Universal Daily Advertiser*, 30 June 1794, XI, no. 1777: 2. On "delicate taste," see "The citizens of Philadelphia," *The Philadelphia Gazette and Universal Daily Advertiser*, 1 July 1794, XI, no. 1778: 3.

67 This balancing act, however, was harder to sustain in Boston than in Philadelphia. In Boston, relations between federalists and Democratic Republicans were so acrimonious that Judith Murray feared a civil war. There were theatrical riots in Boston in the spring of 1796, to protest the Federal Street Theatre's slate of purportedly "anti-French" plays and the British immigrant actors' improvised jokes against the French. Both Colonel Tyler and his managerial replacement John Williamson were seen as federalists who took the English side in the war between England and France (Parker, *Susanna*, 17). Rowson occupied the Federal Street stage just as this turf battle erupted. JSM to my Brother, 23 April 1796, Boston, JSMP, R3, L9, let. 177; "Dramatic Reminiscences, no. v," *New-England Magazine* (1831–35); July 1832; APSO, p. 33.

68   PROLOGUE
            To the new Comedy of Slaves in Algiers, as written by
         Mrs. Rowson, and intended to have been spoken by Mr. Wignell.
                  A female bard this night invites you here,
              Who, trembling with suspense and pale with fear,
                    Just now intreated I would step before
              And plead her cause to th' utmost of my pow'r—
                      And when a Woman for a favor sues
                   Sure it would be unmanly to refuse.
               So here I am – but what to say or do
                 Upon my soul I know no more than you!
            As to the play, your judgments I'll not fetter,
               Between ourselves I have read many better;
                   Yet, let me be entirely understood,
            I've seen some *few* that were not quite so good;
             And then the [hustling?] of an elder brother,
               As such a mighty fav'rite with the mother:

Tho' conscious it has faults, she'd gladly hide'em,
For her sake then, don't *too severely* chide'em.
'Twas here,* she says, in youth's delightful hours
She first aspir'd to pluck Parnassian flow'rs;
Here pleasure with interest was combin'd,
Here knowledge first dawn'd on her infant mind,
'Twas here her love of literature grew,
And here she gladly dedicates to you
The first dramatic offspring of her muse
And trusts you will its many faults excuse.
Such as it is let it not be rejected,
If by your fost'ring hands it is protected.
If by your smiles the little brat's befriended,
Mark but its errors and they'll be amended,
While the fond mother shall with joy aspire
To catch a beam of Phoebus' sacred fire,
And, urged by gratitude's impelling laws,
Offer a future child more worthy your applause.

*Mrs. R. was educated in America. [The prologue that was spoken, and some account of the play in our next.] *General Advertizer* 2 July 1794: 1113.3.

69 "Prologue" *General Advertizer* 3 July 1794: 1114.2.

70 Anon., "Art. x. Ouabi," 61, 63, 66.

71 Anon., "Art. xxii, A Bone," 191. Qtd. Anon., "Art xxii, A Bone," 194–95.

72 "Peter," *Kick*, 20, 22, 23, 24, 27–28. Rowson, qtd. Halsey, *Charlotte*, xxv.

73 Anon., *Rub*, 18, 25, 26.

74 One of her letters bemoans the mistreatment of African Americans, but she accepted slavery, as is evident in her letters to her brother Winthrop, a slaveowner and Southern governor (Schloesser, *Fair*, 173).

75 JSM to [Robert Treat Paine, Jr.], 23 October 1804, Boston, Franklin Place, JSMP, R3, L12, no let. no.

76 JSM to Mrs. Powell, 15 September 1806, Boston, Franklin Place, JSMP, R4, L14, no let. no. The bill passed on 23 February 1807, and was endorsed by Royal Assent on 25 March; the legal British slave trade ended as of 1 May.

77 On Mrs. Powell as Zulima, see JSM to "Sir" [Robert Treat Paine, Jr.], 6 September 1804, Gloucester, JSMP, R3, L12, no let. no. see Felsenstein, *English*, for the Inkle and Yarico reader.

78 See Dillon, "*Slaves*," for an examination of the ways in which Rowson's play shows how early notions of nation are imbedded in global concerns that are both racialized and economically driven.

79 In linking protests against Algierian slavery to those against American slavery, Rowson joined writers like Benjamin Franklin, who published a series of satirical letters, posing as Algierian Muslims and justifying the incarceration of Americans in Algiers through the language of US pro-slavery advocates. Bostonians encountered his letters in Paine's *Federal Orrery* (see, for example, 24 November 1794; 1, 11: 2). Northern indictments of "lazy" Southern plantation owners were also common as New Englanders

forged the industrious Yankee type: see, for example, the anonymous "Satirical Character of the Virginians," originally written in 1686 but published in *The Massachusetts Magazine; or, Monthly Museum*; April 1792; 4, 4; APSO p. 242. This essay immediately precedes Murray's "Gleaner" entry no. 111, which through contrast applauds the performance of white middle-class industry. Ten months after Rowson's play production, "the United States signed a treaty with the Dey of Algiers agreeing to pay tribute to halt the attacks" (Davis, "Plays," 246).

80 Rowson, *Slaves*, ii. Citations from the 1952 Readex edition listed in Works cited.

81 *Ibid.*, 5, 8.

82 *Ibid.*, 14, 70.

83 *Ibid.*, 70. On Rebecca's blush, see Margulis and Poremski, *Slaves*, xxi. Schueller, *U.S.*, 66.

84 Schloesser, *Fair*, 14. Rowson, *Slaves*, 75–77.

85 Rowson, *Slaves*, 77–78. On feeling body, see Rowson, *Trip*, 18, qtd. Parker, *Susanna*, 64.

86 Murray, *Gleaner*, 805, 804.

87 *Ibid.*, 15; 45–46. Rowson, *Mentoria*, ii.

88 Murray, *Gleaner*, 218, 254–55.

89 [Murray] Constantia, "Desultory," 253.

90 *General Advertiser*, 30 June 1794, no. IIII: 3.

91 On French Revolution, see [Murray], "Sketch of the Present Situation of America, 1794," *Gleaner* 1: 26–27; Rowson, *Present*, 32–36; 48. Claghorn lists three-hundred pages' worth of citations for women who "performed a public service" during the revolution (*Women*). Murray, *Gleaner*, 705, 703.

92 Murray, *Gleaner*, 711, 727.

93 *Ibid.*, 111, 322, 148. Smith-Rosenberg, "Female," 171.

94 Qtd. Sterling, *We*, 107–09.

95 Qtd. Porter, *Early*, 79. In Charleston, the Brown Fellowship Society and in New York the African Marine Fund (1810) established schools for free blacks and the poor (Sterling, *We*, 108).

96 Porter, *Early*, 79.

97 Qtd. Foster, *Written*, 45.

98 On Toronto, see Lee, *Religious* 69–70. On Quakers, see Gundersen, *To Be*, 84. By 1688 Quakers in Pennsylvania pronounced slavery unlawful, and a century later, they barred slaveholders from their fellowship. By 1770 Philadelphia Quakers had opened an African School, where Grace Bustill Douglass (1782–1842), later an officer in the Philadelphia Female Anti-Slavery Society, studied.

99 Fabre, "African-American," 72, 79; Porter, *Early*, 310–12; 335–401.

100 Carla Peterson's book of this title contextualizes Jarena Lee's preaching in terms of later nineteenth-century black women's speaking and writing, using Foucaultian discourse theory to highlight the relationship between idea and action (Peterson, *Doers*, 5). Lee and Elaw's sermons are not extant,

but scholars can glimpse their early activist practices through their spiritual autobiographies.

101 Elaw, *Memoirs*, 55; Lee, *Religious*, 4–5. After working as an itinerant preacher from 1780 to 1785, Richard Allen, an ex-slave and eventually a licensed Methodist minister, founded the Bethel African Methodist Episcopal Church in Philadelphia in 1794. He did so to protest the racism of St. George's Church. Black Methodists were the first to establish independent denominational control of their own church budgets and governing structures.

102 Lee, *Religious*, 17.

103 On "assertion," see Foster, *Written*, 60; Lee, *Religious*, 11, 3, her italics.

104 On 178 sermons and preaching with Elaw, see Lee, *Religious*, 36, 51, 88. On Thursday night, see Wills, "Womanhood," 138.

105 Despite Lee's claim, women were not formally ordained in the AME Church until 1948. The first woman ordained in an African American denomination was Mary J. Small of the AME Zion Church in 1898 (Lincoln and Mamiya, "Black," 367). The first black female AME. Bishop, Vashti Murphy McKenzie, was elected in July 2000 (*Washington Post* 1 August 2000:C1).

106 On an educated ministry, see Peterson, *Doers*, 75. On independent printing, see Andrews, *Sisters*, 6. On "strong resistance," see Foster, *Written*, 57. "Impossible to decipher" qtd. in Andrews, *Sisters*, 6. "I preached" in Lee, *Religious*, 79. Lee's legacy was still fighting for admission as late as the 1992 "Conference on Psychoanalysis in African American Contexts: Feminist Reconfigurations," held at the University of California at Santa Cruz. A Saturday afternoon session on "Spirituality/Psychoanalysis: Cultural Encounters" triggered an especially lively exchange between black and white critics. Akasha [Gloria] Hull delivered a paper which "foregrounded spirituality," and

what made her paper so provocative was that she asked the question, 'Where in the current theorizing about poetic form and politics is there space to situate such matters?' What ignited the audience was that Hull introduced a different subject of intellectual inquiry into an academic conference about race and psychoanalysis. This affirmation of African American women's spirituality signaled the return of the repressed. (Abel *et al.*, *Female*, 4)

107 Elaw, *Memoirs*, 73, 147, 131; 83, 87, 68–70, 6–7.

108 Schloesser, *Fair*, 107.

109 James Finley, quoted in Buckley, "Paratheatricals," 442. As Buckley notes, "men and women, whites and black slaves" as well as free blacks "appeared to be blended in a promiscuous mix of enthusiastic dancing, vocalizing, and prayer" ("Paratheatricals," 442).

110 Lee, *Religious*, 39, 93.

111 Dick, "Religious," 117–18; Elaw, *Memoirs*, 66–67; Earl, *Dark*, 163.

112 On white bands, see Raboteau, *Slave*, 73. As late as 1878 Bishop Payne was trying unsuccessfully to squash the ring shout. Raboteau, *Slave*, 68, 74; Watson, qtd. Raboteau, *Slave*, 67.

113 Peterson is discussing the strategies that Sojourner Truth (1797/1800?–1883) and Frances Ellen Watkins Harper (1825–1911), respectively, deployed when audience members (accustomed to masculinized images of black women as workers) literally perceived them as men; Lee, too, faced this phenomenon (*Doers*, 21–22).

114 On "inward man," see Elaw, *Memoirs*, 51, italics mine. On restraint, see Elaw, *Memoirs*, 101.

115 *Ibid.*, 91. Lee, *Religious*, 36, 60.

116 Elaw, *Memoirs*, 241 n. 19.

117 Zafar, *We*, 152, 155, 154.

118 Lee, *Religious*, 5. Lee's vision and its disruptive timing are echoed in later narratives like Julia A. J. Foote's *A Brand Plucked from the Fire* (Cleveland: W. F. Schneider, 1879). On "set at . . . liberty," see Elaw, *Memoirs*, 57.

119 Morton, qtd. in Houchins, *Spiritual*, xxxviii; Lee, *Religious*, 5, 10. Elaw, *Memoirs*, 82.

120 Lee, *Religious*, 19, 21, 23, 36, 37, 43, 55, 56, 59, 60, 70, 91, 92, etc.

121 Elaw, *Memoirs*, 117–18.

122 Nora, "Between," 289. On "*African American* literature," see Foster, *Written*, 59. On Elaw's refusal, see Elaw, *Memoirs*, 96.

123 A few early colonization initiatives were spearheaded by free blacks like well-to-do businessman Paul Cuffee and the members of the Free African Societies in Rhode Island and Philadelphia, who discussed the possibility of joint action as early as 1789. In 1811 Cuffee hoped to settle a colony of free blacks in Sierra Leone. Within five years, however, whites dominated the colonization movement, fueled by fears of free black independence. They established the American Colonization Society in 1816 and funded a settlement in Monrovia in 1822. See Quarles, *Black* and Mullane, *Crossing*, 67.

124 Foster, *Written*, 64; Joyce, *Warriors*, 4.

125 On defying men, see Foster, *Written*, 70. Elaw, *Memoirs*, 84. Lee, *Religious*, 23.

126 Lee, *Religious*, 44, 77.

127 Higginbotham, "African-American," 263.

128 Qtd. *ibid.*, 266.

129 Lee, *Religious*, 23.

WORKS CITED

Abel, Elizabeth, Barbara Christian, and Helene Moglen, eds. *Female Subjects in Black and White: Race, Psychoanalysis, Feminism.* Berkeley: University of California Press, 1997.

Andrews, William L., ed. *Sisters of the Spirit: Three Black Women's Autobiographies of the Nineteenth Century.* Bloomington: Indiana University Press, 1986.

Anonymous [Samuel Harrison Smith]. "Art. x. Ouabi: Or the Virtues of Nature. An Indian Tale; in four Cantos. By Philenia, a Lady of Boston." *The American Monthly Review; or, Literary Journal* (1795–95); January 1795; 1, American Periodicals Series Online: 61–66.

Anonymous [Samuel Harrison Smith]. "Art. xxii. A Bone To Gnaw for the Democrats; or, Observations on a Pamphlet, entitled, 'The Political Progress of Britain.'" *The American Monthly Review; or, Literary Journal* (1795–95); February 1795; 1, 000002; American Periodicals Series Online: 191–95.

Anonymous. "A Defence [sic] of the Stage." *The Thespian Oracle; or, Monthly Mirror.* January 1798, 1. 1; American Periodicals Series Online: 1.

Anonymous. "Mrs. Rowson's Academy." *The Boston Weekly Magazine, Devoted to Morality, Literature, Biography, History . . . .* 30 October 1803; 1,1; American Periodicals Series Online: 2.

Anonymous. "New Theatre." *The Thespian Monitor, and Dramatick Miscellany.* 25 November 1809, 1, 1, American Periodicals Series Online: 3.

Anonymous [John Swanwick]. *A Rub from Snub; or a Cursory Analytical Epistle: Addressed to Peter Porcupine, Author of the Bone to Gnaw, Kick for a Bite, &c. &c., Containing Glad Tidings for the Democrats, and a Word of Comfort to Mrs. S. Rowson, Wherein the Said Porcupine's Moral, Political, Critical and Literary Character is Fully Illustrated.* Philadelphia: Printed for the Purchaser, 1795.

Anonymous. "Sketches in favour of the Ladies, from the comparative view of the Sexes." *The Gentleman and Lady's Town and Country Magazine.* September 1784. American Periodicals Series Online: 199.

Anonymous."Universalism Indeed!" *The New-Haven Gazette, and the Connecticut Magazine.* 25 October 1787, 2, 36, American Periodicals Series Online: 283.

Appiah, Kwame Anthony. *The Ethics of Identity.* Princeton: Princeton University Press, 2005.

Banham, Martin, ed. *The Cambridge Guide to Theatre.* Cambridge: Cambridge University Press, 1992.

Buckley, Peter G. "Paratheatricals and Popular Stage Entertainment." *The Cambridge History of American Theatre.* Vol. 1. Eds. Don B. Wilmeth and Christopher Bigsby. Cambridge; New York: Cambridge University Press, 1998: 424–82.

Claghorn, Charles E. *Women Patriots of the American Revolution: A Biographical Dictionary.* Metuchen, N.J.: Scarecrow Press, 1991.

[Crocker, Hannah Mather]. *A Series of Letters on Free Masonry, by a Lady of Boston.* Boston: John Eliot, 1815.

Davis, Peter A. "Plays and Playwrights to 1800." *The Cambridge History of American Theatre.* Vol. 1. Eds. Don B. Wilmeth and Christopher Bigsby. Cambridge; New York: Cambridge University Press, 1998: 216–302.

Dick, Everett. "Religious Democracy." *The Social Fabric: American Life from 1607 to 1877.* Eds. John H. Cary and Julius Weinberg. Vol. 1, 6th ed. New York: Harper Collins, 1991.

Dillon, Elizabeth Maddock. "Slaves in Algiers: Race, Republican Genealogies, and the Global Stage." *American Literary History*. 16.3 (2004): 407–36.

Donkin, Ellen. *Getting into the Act: Women Playwrights in London, 1776–1829*. New York: Routledge, 1995.

Dudden, Faye E. *Women in the American Theatre: Actresses & Audiences 1790–1870*. New Haven: Yale University Press, 1994.

Dunlap, William. *History of the American Theatre*. 2nd ed. New York: Burt Franklin, 1963.

Durham, Weldon B., ed. *American Theatre Companies, 1749–1887*. New York: Greenwood Press, 1986.

Earl, Riggins R., Jr. *Dark Symbols, Obscure Signs: God, Self and Community in the Slave Mind*. Maryknoll, N.Y.: Orbis, 1994.

Elaw, Zilpha. *Memoirs of the Life, Religious Experience, Ministerial Travels and Labours of Mrs. Zilpha Elaw, An American Female of Colour; Together with Some Account of the Great Religious Revivals in America [Written by Herself]*. London: Published by the Authoress. 1846. Rpt. in *Sisters of the Spirit: Three Black Women's Autobiographies of the Nineteenth Century*. Ed. William L. Andrews. Bloomington: Indiana University Press, 1986.

Fabre, Geneviève. "African-American Commemorative Celebrations in the Nineteenth Century." *History and Memory in African-American Culture*. Ed. Geneviève Fabre and Robert O'Meally. New York: Oxford University Press, 1994: 72–91.

Felsenstein, Frank, ed.. *English Trader, Indian Maid: Representing Gender, Race, and Slavery in the New World. An Inkle and Yarico Reader*. Baltimore: Johns Hopkins University Press, 1999.

Field, Vena Bernadette. *Constantia: A Study of the Life and Works of Judith Sargent Murray*. Orono, Me.: Printed at the University Press, 1931.

Foucault, Michel. *Discipline and Punish: The Birth of the Prison*. Trans. Alan Sheridan. New York: Vintage, 1979.

Gilroy, Paul. *The Black Atlantic: Modernity and Double Consciousness*. Cambridge, Mass.: Harvard University Press, 1993.

Against Race: Imagining Political Culture Beyond the Color Line. Cambridge, Mass.: Belknap Press of Harvard University Press, 2000.

Grammer, Elizabeth Elkin. *Some Wild Visions: Autobiographies by Female Itinerant Evangelists in Nineteenth-Century America*. Oxford: Oxford University Press, 2002.

Gundersen, Joan R. *To Be Useful to the World: Women in Revolutionary America, 1740–1790*. New York: Twayne, 1996.

Hall, Benjamin Homer. *A Collection of College Words and Customs*. Part 4. Prod. Rick Niles, John Hagerson, Tony Browne. 3 January 2005. n.p. *http://www.fullbooks.com/A-Collection-of-College-Words-and-Customs4.html*.

Halsey, Frances W. Introduction. *Charlotte Temple, a Tale of Truth; reprinted from the rare first American edition (1794)*. 1905. By Susanna Haswell Rowson. Electronic Text Center. Early American Fiction. University of Virginia Library. 1 October 2004. *http://etext.lib.virginia.edu/eaf/authors/shr.htm*.

Harris, Sharon M., ed. *Selected Writings of Judith Sargent Murray*. New York: Oxford University Press, 1995.

Henderson, Mary C. "Scenography, Stagecraft, and Architecture in the American Theatre, Beginnings to 1870." *The Cambridge History of American Theatre*. Vol. 1. Eds. Don B. Wilmeth and Christopher Bigsby. Cambridge; New York: Cambridge University Press, 1998: 373–423.

Higginbotham, Evelyn Brooks. "African-American Women's History and the Metalanguage of Race." *Signs: Journal of Women in Culture and Society*. 17.2 (Winter 1992): 251–74.

Houchins, Sue E., ed. *Spiritual Narratives*. New York: Oxford University Press, 1988.

Joyce, Joyce A. *Warriors, Conjurers and Priests: Defining African-centered Literary Criticism*. Chicago: Third World Press, 1994.

Keetley, Dawn, and John Pettegrew. *Public Women, Public Words: A Documentary History of American Feminism. Vol. 1: Beginnings to 1900*. Madison, Wis.: Madison House, 1997.

Kerber, Linda. *Women of the Republic: Intellect and Ideology in Revolutionary America*. Chapel Hill: University of North Carolina Press, 1980.

Lee, Jarena. *The Life and Religious Experience of Jarena Lee, a Coloured Lady, giving an account of her call to preach the gospel* (Philadelphia, Published for the Author, 1836), Rare Book/Special Collections Reading Room, Library of Congress; Rpt. in *The Female Autograph*. Ed. Domna Stanton. New York: New York Literary Forum, 1984.

Religious Experience and Journal of Mrs. Jarena Lee, Giving an Account of Her Call to Preach the Gospel, Revised and corrected from the Original Manuscript, written by herself. Philadelphia: Printed and Published for the Author, 1849. Rpt. in *Spiritual Narratives*. Ed. Sue E. Houchins. New York: Oxford University Press, 1988.

Lincoln, C. Eric and Lawrence H. Mamiya. "The Black Denominations and the Ordination of Women." *Down by the Riverside: Readings in African American Religion*. Ed. Larry G. Murphy. New York: New York University Press, 2000: 367–80.

MacLain, Paul. "Unitarian and Universalist Denominational and Individual Involvement in the Anti-Slavery Movement Prior to the U. S. Civil War." Starr King School for the Ministry. 20 June 2003. *http://online.sksm.edu/1/papers/frmset_pres.htm*.

Margulis, Jennifer, and Karen Poremski, eds. *Slaves in Algiers or, A Struggle for Freedom*. Acton, Mass.: Copley, 2000.

McConachie, Bruce. "American Theatre in Context, from the Beginnings to 1870." *The Cambridge History of American Theatre*. Vol. 1. Eds. Don B. Wilmeth and Christopher Bigsby. Cambridge; New York: Cambridge University Press, 1998: 111–81.

Meserve, Walter. *An Emerging Entertainment: The Drama of the American People to 1828*. Bloomington: Indiana University Press, 1977.

Michaels, Walter Benn. *Our America: Nativism, Modernism, and Pluralism.* Durham, N.C. and London: Duke University Press, 1995.

Mott, Frank Luther. *A History of American Magazines Volume 1: 1741–1850.* Cambridge, Mass.: Harvard University Press, 1938.

Mullane, Deirdre, ed. *Crossing the Danger Water: Three Hundred Years of African-American Writing.* New York: Doubleday, 1993.

Murray, John. RECORDS *of the* LIFE OF THE REV. JOHN MURRAY; *Late Minister of the Reconciliation and Senior Pastor of the Universalists, Congregated in Boston.* Written by Himself. The Records Contain Anecdotes of the Writer's Infancy, and Are Extended to Some Years After the Commencement of His Public Labours in America, To Which Is Added, *A BRIEF CONTINUATION.* To the Closing Scene by a Friend [Judith Sargent Murray]. Boston: Munroe and Franch [sic], 1816.

[Murray, Judith Sargent.] Constantia. "Desultory Thoughts upon the Utility of Encouraging a Degree of Self-complacency, Especially in Female Bosoms." *The Gentleman and Lady's Town and Country Magazine; or, Repository of Instruction and Entertainment* 6 (October 1784): 251–53.

Constantia. *The Gleaner.* 1798. Ed. Nina Baym. Schenectady, N.Y.: Union College Press, 1992.

Nathans, Heather. *Early American Theatre from the Revolution to Thomas Jefferson: Into the Hands of the People.* Cambridge: Cambridge University Press, 2003.

Nora, Pierre. "Between Memory and History: *Les Lieux de Memoire.*" *History and Memory in African-American Culture.* Ed. Geneviève Fabre and Robert O'Meally. Oxford: Oxford University Press, 1994: 284–300.

Norton, Mary Beth. *Liberty's Daughters: The Revolutionary Experience of American Women, 1750–1800.* Boston: Little, Brown, 1980.

A People and a Nation. 2nd ed. Boston: Houghton Mifflin, 1986.

Parker, Patricia L. *Susanna Rowson.* Boston: Twayne, 1986.

"Peter Porcupine" [William Cobbett]. *A Kick for a Bite; or, Review upon Review; with a Critical Essay, on the Works of Mrs. S. Rowson, in a Letter to the Editor, or Editors, of the American Monthly Review.* Philadelphia: Thomas Bradford, 1795.

Peterson, Carla. *Doers of the Word: African-American Women Speakers and Writers in the North (1830–1880).* New York, Oxford: Oxford University Press, 1995.

Pollock, Thomas Clark. *The Philadelphia Theatre in the Eighteenth Century.* New York: Greenwood Press, 1968.

Porter, Dorothy. *Early Negro Writing 1760–1837.* Boston: Beacon Press, 1971.

Quarles, Benjamin. *Black Abolitionists.* London: Oxford University Press, 1969.

Raboteau, Albert J. *Slave Religion: The "Invisible Institution" in the Antebellum South.* New York: Oxford University Press, 1978.

Roach, Joseph. "The Emergence of the American Actor." *The Cambridge History of American Theatre.* Vol. 1. Eds. Don B. Wilmeth and Christopher Bigsby. Cambridge, New York: Cambridge University Press, 1998: 338–72.

Rowson, Mrs. [Susanna Haswell]. *Charlotte: A Tale of Truth*. Philadelphia: D. Humphreys for M. Carey, 1794. 2 Vols. Rare Book/Special Collections Reading Room, Library of Congress.

MENTORIA; *or the Young Lady's Friend*. Vol. 1. Philadelphia: Robert Campbell, 1794. Early American Imprints. First Series. Microcard 2. No. 27654. Micropaque. Worcester, Mass.: American Antiquarian Society, 1955–83.

Rowson, Susanna [Haswell]. PRESENT *for Young Ladies; Containing Poems, Dialogues, Addresses, &c. &c. &c. As Recited by the Pupils of Mrs. Rowson's Academy, at the Annual Exhibitions*. Boston: John West, 1811. Early American Imprints. Second Series. Microcard 3. No. 23840. Micropaque. New York: Readex, 1972.

SLAVES in ALGIERS; *or, a Struggle for Freedom: A Play, Interspersed with Songs, in Three Acts*. Philadelphia: Wrigley and Berriman, 1794. Microcard 11. American, 1714–1830. Micropaque. New York: Readex, 1952.

[Rowson, Susanna Haswell]. *A Trip to Parnassus; or, the Judgment of Apollo on Dramatic Authors and Performers*. London: John Abraham, 1789.

Sawyer, Mary R. "Sources of Black Denominationalism." *Down by the Riverside: Readings in African American Religion*. Ed. Larry G. Murphy. New York: New York University Press, 2000: 59–67.

Schofield, Mary Anne. "'Quitting the Loom and Distaff': Eighteenth-Century American Women Dramatists." In *Curtain Calls: British and American Women and the Theater, 1660–1820*. Ed. Mary Anne Schofield and Cecilia Macheski. Athens: Ohio University Press, 1991.

Schueller, Malini Johar. *U.S. Orientalisms: Race, Nation, and Gender in Literature, 1790–1890*. Ann Arbor: University of Michigan Press, 1998.

Seilhamer, George O. *History of the American Theatre* [1774–1797]. 3 vols. Philadelphia: Globe Printing, 1888–91.

Sheppard, J. H. *Reminiscences of Lucius Manlius Sargent: with an Appendix Containing a Genealogy of His Family*. Boston: D. Clapp, 1871.

Skemp, Sheila L. *Judith Sargent Murray: A Brief Biography with Documents*. Boston: Bedford, 1998.

Smith, Bonnie Hurd, ed. *From Gloucester to Philadelphia in 1790. Observations, Anecdotes, and Thoughts from the 18th-century Letters of Judith Sargent Murray with a Biographical Introduction*. Cambridge: Judith Sargent Murray Society, 1998.

Smith-Rosenberg, Carroll. "The Female World of Love and Ritual: Relations between Women in Nineteenth-Century America." *Women's America: Refocusing the Past*. Ed. Linda K. Kerber and Jane De Hart Mathews. New York: Oxford University Press, 1982: 156–79.

Sterling, Dorothy, ed. *We Are Your Sisters: Black Women in the Nineteenth Century*. New York: W. W. Norton & Company, 1984.

[Stevens, Judith Sargent]. *Some Deductions from the System Promulgated in the Page of Divine Revelation: Ranged in the Order and Form of a Catechism: Intended as an Assistant to the Christian Parent or Teacher*. Norwich: Trumbull, 1782;

Microform Card 2 no. 17729, Early American Imprints, 1639–1800. Ed. Clifford K. Shipton. Readex Microprint. Evans numbers. Worcester, Mass.: American Antiquarian Society.

Weil, Dorothy. *In Defense of Women: Susanna Rowson (1762–1824)*. University Park: Pennsylvania State University Press, 1976.

Wills, David W. "Womanhood and Domesticity in the A. M. E. Tradition: The Influence of Daniel Alexander Payne." *Black Apostles at Home and Abroad: Afro-Americans and the Christian Mission from the Revolution to Reconstruction*. Eds. David W. Wills and Richard Newman. Boston: G. K. Hall & Co., 1982: 133–46.

Index